A CALENDAR OF
THE REGISTERS OF APPRENTICES
OF
THE CITY OF GLOUCESTER
1700–1834

Edited by Jill Barlow, M.A.

The Bristol and Gloucestershire Archaeological Society

2011

The Bristol and Gloucestershire Archaeological Society
Gloucestershire Record Series

© The Bristol and Gloucestershire Archaeological Society

ISBN 978 0 900197 77 2

British Library Cataloguing in Publication Data
A catalogue entry for this book is available from the British Library

The title page illustration of a pinmaker's workshop is adapted from Diderot's Encyclopedia.

Printed in Great Britain by 4word Ltd, Bristol

CONTENTS

ACKNOWLEDGEMENTS

My thanks are due to David Smith for persuading me to complete the calendar of Gloucester apprenticeship registers begun in Gloucestershire Record Series volume 14, for offering constant helpful advice and for spending many painstaking hours checking the text. I am grateful that Professor Christopher Elrington found time during his last illness to advise me on the structure of the volume, and that his successor as General Editor, Dr James Hodsdon, has continued to give help and guidance. Thanks too to James's daughter Alice Hodsdon for her eagle-eyed proofreading, to Paul Evans, Vicky Thorpe and the search room staff at Gloucestershire Archives, and to my family for tolerating my 'toy boys' for so many years.

I also thank the Bristol & Gloucestershire Archaeological Society for providing me with a microfilm of the Inland Revenue records held at the National Archives and the City of Gloucester for permission to print copyright material in its possession.

The Diderot engraving of the pinmaker on the title page was kindly supplied by the Gloucester Folk Museum from their excellent exhibition on pinmaking in the city.

12 April 2011   Jill Barlow

BIBLIOGRAPHY

Jill Barlow (ed.), *A Calendar of the Registers of Apprentices of the City of Gloucester* (BGAS, Gloucestershire Record Series, vol. 14, 2001)

Richard Burn, *The Justice of the Peace and Parish Officer*, 29th edition (1845)

Daniel Defoe, *The Complete English Tradesman, in familiar letters [etc.]* (1726)

O. J. Dunlop, *Apprenticeship and Child Labour* (1912)

Nicholas Herbert (ed.), *The Victoria History of the Counties of England: Gloucestershire, vol. IV, The City of Gloucester* (1988)

John Juřica (ed.), *A Calendar of the Registers of the Freemen of the City of Gloucester 1641–1838* (BGAS, Gloucestershire Record Series, vol. 4, 1991)

Joan Lane, *Apprenticeship in England 1600–1914* (1996)

Peter Ripley, *The Economy of the City of Gloucester, 1660–1740* (BGAS, *Transactions,* vol. 98, 1980)

David Welander, *The History, Art and Architecture of Gloucester Cathedral* (1991)

Irene Wyatt, *Calendar of Summary Convictions at Petty Sessions 1787–1837* (BGAS, Gloucestershire Record Series, vol. 22, 2008)

ABBREVIATIONS

BGAS   Bristol and Gloucestershire Archaeological Society
GA   Gloucestershire Archives, Gloucester
TNA   The National Archives, Kew

A representative page (p. 424) of GBR C10/3; calendared at p. 6 below.

INTRODUCTION

A first calendar of the registers of Gloucester apprentices appeared in 2001 as vol. 14 in this series, covering the years 1595–1700. This volume continues the calendar to 1834, when the registers stop. Although there is an unexplained gap from 1742 to 1765 in the registers held in the Gloucestershire Archives,[1] information on Gloucester apprentices for this period has been supplied from the Stamp Duty records held at the National Archives[2] and is included here as an appendix. The names of boys who were to be bound apprentice with money from charities administered by the municipal authority have been collected from Gloucester's Common Council minute books[3] and are included here as footnotes.

The Gloucester apprenticeship registers were maintained by the Common Council to verify that men claiming the freedom of the city by apprenticeship were entitled to do so. Freemen enjoyed trading rights but these privileges ran counter to the growing national belief during this period that every man should be free to practise his trade. As a result successive statutes reduced and eventually abolished restrictive practices. The number of apprentices registered in Gloucester declined steadily throughout the 18th century. There were fewer advantages to be gained by serving an apprenticeship and the introduction of a tax on apprenticeship premiums in 1709 discouraged people from going to the trouble and expense of arranging formal indentures. The mayor's impatience with paperwork (see below, p. xiv) may have contributed to the fall in Gloucester registrations, but by the end of the century when the political parties wished to create large numbers of new freemen in order to give them the right to vote in municipal elections, they made very little use of the apprenticeship register.

The apprentices appearing in these pages were not paupers. Even though many were bound with charity money most were the sons of freemen who were being taught a trade and were placed by their fathers, not the overseers of the poor. The parish apprentices employed in great numbers in large workshops were placed there to stop them becoming a

---

[1] Between the end of GA GBR C10/3 and the start of GBR C10/4.
[2] TNA IR 1/50–55.
[3] GA GBR B3/7–14.

burden on the parish. They were not expected to learn anything nor were their masters expected to teach them.

The trades learned by the apprentices changed over the course of the 18th century. At the beginning they were trades which would have been recognised by the medieval guilds who began the system – blacksmiths, cordwainers, tailors, butchers and bakers. By the end we have perukemakers, confectioners, booksellers and bankers, all free of the regulations imposed by the guilds and catering to an increasingly sophisticated public.

Apprenticeship in the 18th century[1]

An apprenticeship agreement was binding on both parties. An apprentice was not a servant: he received no wages and his time was his master's. A master could not rid himself of an apprentice who was ill but had more authority over him than over a common servant and could legally correct him for negligence or other misbehaviour. 'Where a master in correcting his apprentice happens to occasion his death, it shall be termed homicide by misadventure'.[2] Only if the punishment was 'so barbarous as to exceed all bounds of moderation' or resulted in the death of the apprentice was the master likely to face legal punishment.

If an apprentice ran away, a warrant would be issued for his arrest and even if he escaped from the county he could be caught and returned.[3] The Gloucestershire apprentices who absconded from their masters and appeared before magistrates in Gloucester during the period were all sentenced to a month's hard labour in a house of correction.[4] The Seven Years' War (1756–63) encouraged many to run away to enlist but this provided only a temporary escape. The length of time an apprentice had been missing from his master's service was added to the original term.[5] Conversely, in 1785 a watchmaker who brought an action against the father of an apprentice who had absconded, lost the case because he 'was not in a condition to perform his part of the covenant, i.e. to teach the apprentice' – he was in prison.[6]

Originally the only money which changed hands in an apprenticeship agreement was a small sum given to the apprentice at the end of his term. By the end of the 17th century the practice of paying a premium to the

---

[1] A discussion of the origins of the system of apprenticeship and its recording in Gloucester appears in Barlow, pp. xi–xxxi.
[2] Burn, vol. I, p. 194.
[3] 24 Geo. II c.55.
[4] Wyatt, pp. 88, 312–313.
[5] 6 Geo. III c.25.
[6] Ilberry v. Godfrey: *The Times* Law Report, 26 Feb. 1785.

master had become widespread. According to Daniel Defoe[1] it began as a small present given to the master's wife to encourage her to 'take motherly care' of the boy, but the size of the premiums increased and masters in the wealthier trades were able to charge hundreds of pounds. Apprentices whose families had paid large premiums were reluctant to observe the restrictions imposed by their covenant and were not prepared to carry out menial tasks. The behaviour of some apprentices, particularly in London, became so unruly that acts of parliament were found necessary to ban them from hunting[2] and to forbid them to play cards, dice, shuffle-board, mississippi or billiards, tables, skittles or ninepins in public houses.[3]

In 1709 the government recognised that apprenticeship premiums could be a useful source of revenue. The Stamp Act[4] introduced a tax of 6d. in the pound for premiums of less than £50 and 1s. in the pound for premiums over £50 plus 6d. stamp duty. It was to be paid by the master for every clerk, apprentice or servant within two months of the date of the indenture. The indenture, stating the amount of the premium, was to be produced to the collector and the receipt would be endorsed on the indenture. The original intention was for the tax to last for five years but it proved so lucrative that in 1710[5] it was made perpetual. No tax was payable on premiums given by a charity to bind apprentices. Inevitably people tried to avoid paying the tax. One master who was paid four guineas to take a boy apprentice was not willing to pay the tax nor the expense of the indentures and instead came to an agreement whereby the boy was paid a wage and given time off on Sundays. The court found that the boy was not an apprentice and therefore not qualified to become a freeman.[6]

Traditional apprenticeships were originally arrangements between equals – master craftsmen training the sons of fellow craftsmen – but the 1563 Statute of Artificers,[7] by giving local justices the right to bind the offspring of paupers and vagrants, introduced a new form of apprenticeship. The 1601 Poor Law,[8] which allowed churchwardens and overseers to bind the children of families who seemed likely to become a burden on the parish, extended the use of apprenticeship as a means of curing the problem of poverty.

---

[1] Defoe, p. 147.
[2] 4 & 5 Wm. & Mary c.23.
[3] 30 Geo. II c.24.
[4] 8 Anne c.5.
[5] 9 Anne c.21.
[6] The King against the Parish of Heynham: *The Times* Law Report, 8 Sept. 1785.
[7] 5 Eliz. c.4.
[8] 43 Eliz. c.2.

However:

> 'In the establishment of parish apprentices the legislature does not appear even to have had in view the instruction of youth or to fit them for any trade or useful occupation; it is a misapplication of terms to call the parties bound an "apprentice"; there is not even a direction to or covenant by the master to afford the party bound any instruction.'[1]

As craftsmen working alone and providing individual training to their indentured apprentices were replaced by bigger workshops and eventually by factories, large numbers of pauper apprentices were employed as cheap labour. They could be taken on by masters for the sake of the premium paid with them and then passed on to another employer. Their working conditions were in some cases so bad that a number of laws were passed to protect them from exploitation. The Health and Morals of Apprentices Act of 1802[2] was intended to regulate the conditions of children where three or more apprentices were employed. It restricted their working day to 12 hours and stipulated that they should be taught reading, writing and arithmetic.

Several of the 18th century acts governing the treatment of apprentices applied only to those with whom a specified level of premium had been paid. Since this was very low at first it affected few other than parish apprentices, but the level was gradually raised to give more rights to more apprentices. By an act of 1747[3] an apprentice whose premium had been less than £5 could complain to two local justices of cruelty or ill treatment. If this was proved the child was discharged from service but the master kept the premium and received no punishment. From 1793[4] apprentices with premiums of less than £10 could complain of ill usage and if found guilty the master could be fined up to £2. This was either given to the apprentice as compensation or contributed to the poor relief of the parish. In 1823[5] the level of premium was raised to £25 and the master could be compelled to return the premium. So complicated did apprenticeship legislation become that it eventually required the passing of An Act to Explain the Acts for the Better Regulation of Certain Apprentices.[6]

---

[1] Burn, vol. I, p. 212.
[2] 42 Geo. III c.73.
[3] 20 Geo. II c.19.
[4] 33 Geo. III c.55.
[5] 4 Geo. IV c.29.
[6] 5 Vic. c.7.

Decline of Apprenticeship

The Statute of Artificers required anyone setting up in trade to serve a seven year apprenticeship. Although the Statute remained in force through the 18th century, the restrictions it imposed conflicted with the rise in belief in free trade and were increasingly ignored. Legal opinion supported the idea that every man should be free to practise his trade whether or not he had served an apprenticeship, and craft companies (successors to the medieval guilds) were unable to enforce their monopoly. Practitioners of trades which had not existed at the time of the Statute claimed that in any case the act did not apply to them. Successive acts of parliament removed some of the restrictions. From 1757[1] indentures ceased to be legally necessary and were replaced by a stamped deed; from 1768[2] the term of service was to end at the age of 21 not 24 and eventually in 1814[3] the Statute of Artificers was repealed and it became lawful for anyone to set up in any trade in which he considered himself capable and for anyone to take or retain or become an apprentice. This act did not however abolish apprenticeship and contained the caveat that it was not intended to infringe ancient custom or the privileges of any city, town, corporation, or company.

One of these privileges was for a municipal corporation to grant the right to trade in the town only to its freemen. Serving an apprenticeship was one route to becoming a freeman and provided an incentive for many boys. This restriction too ran contrary to the prevailing belief in free trade and in 1835 the Municipal Corporations Act[4] abolished exclusive trading rights in corporate cities.

Freemen

In Gloucester in 1700, apprenticeship was one of the routes to acquiring the privileges of a freeman and the enrolling of apprentices was closely supervised by the municipal authorities. For a claim to be valid the apprenticeship had to be served within the city,[5] the apprentice had to live 'at bed and board' with his master or mistress,[6] the master had to belong to one of a specified list of trades, and the indentures had to be enrolled.[7] Some tried to claim the freedom without fulfilling these conditions and in

---

[1] 30 Geo. II c.24.
[2] 8 Geo. III c.28.
[3] 54 Geo. III c.96.
[4] 5 & 6 Wm. IV c.76.
[5] GBR B3/8 p. 275.
[6] GBR B3/9 f. 120.
[7] GBR B3/9 f. 317.

1708 the common council passed an act 'for the preventing of frauds in binding apprentices':

> 'And that all such persons to be so bound shall be bound and placed every Monday and Friday at the Tolsey and at no other time and the Master and Apprentices to be both present and the Indentures to be subscribed by the Mayor and two such Aldermen. And that if any dispute or account shall be brought for not doing or doing anything contrary to this act the charge thereof shall be borne by the Corporation.'[1]

The trade companies too had an interest in ensuring that only properly qualified apprentices became freemen. In 1709 the Company of Cordwainers 'suggested' that because a master lived in Huntley and not in the city, his apprentice was 'incapable of being free at the end of his term'. The entry was deleted from the register (**3**/523). Again in 1720 the Master and Wardens of the Company of Barbers complained that an apprentice had not properly served his time and his name was crossed out (**3**/536). In 1719 the glovers took their complaint against Walter Nash, who had been apprenticed six years earlier, to Quarter Sessions and the court decided that he should not be made a freeman (**3**/548).

In 1732 frauds were still proving a problem to the corporation, 'the claims of serving apprenticeship requiring much more time and pains thoroughly to examine into than the mayors of the said city for the time being have had leisure to bestow'.[2] The common council's attempted solution was to vote to fine the mayor £50 if ever he was 'prevailed on by such representations and claims to admit any persons to the freedom of the city and to swear them who had no right to the same'.

In the same year the council again ruled that only apprentices bound to masters belonging to a 'composition fraternity or company'[3] were entitled to have their indentures enrolled in the register and to claim the freedom of the city by apprenticeship.[4] In 1755 these rights were extended to include upholders, booksellers, brushmakers, woolcombers, woolstaplers, clock and watchmakers, hatters, curriers, vintners and distillers.[5] In Gloucester, as elsewhere, the traditional trade companies were becoming less powerful and the number of new trades was growing. Concerned by the number of applicants refused the freedom 'by reason of their not

---

[1] GBR B3/8 p. 267.

[2] GBR B3/9 f. 325.

[3] These included mercers, weavers, bakers, tanners, haberdashers, innkeepers, tailors, butchers, shearmen, glovers, shoemakers, barbers, metalmen and joiners.

[4] GBR B3/9 f. 317.

[5] GBR B3/10 f. 200v.

belonging to trades formerly incorporated,' the council in 1787 extended the freedom to all 'who have served regular apprenticeships to freemen resident in this city'.[1]

Even this failed to halt the decline in the number of apprentices enrolled in the register and therefore theoretically entitled to claim the freedom by apprenticeship. At the start of the 18th century there were on average 50 per year. By the end of the century the average was only ten. Although freemen still had trading privileges, it was the right to vote which was now more important and election years saw a surge in the number of new freemen admitted. In 1727 there were over 300 admissions, almost 80 of them by apprenticeship. Nearly all the names appeared in the apprenticeship register (apart from Joseph Jeanes who was later disfranchised for making a fraudulent claim).[2] In addition 49 registered apprentices claimed by patrimony. In 1789, when more than 400 new freemen were admitted, only half the 60 claimants by apprenticeship appeared in the register. Eleven of the new freemen whose names were not in the register had been apprenticed with money from charities administered by the city council. Many of the former apprentices had moved away from Gloucester, a high proportion of them to London, and some were admitted more than 20 years after they were apprenticed. Thomas Friend of Hadlow, Kent, had been apprenticed to a collarmaker in 1766 (**4**/1) and William Dorsett of Chertsey, Surrey, apprenticed to an apothecary in 1768 (**4**/3). Not only was apprenticeship becoming less important as a route to the freedom of the city, but the apprenticeship register was no longer being used as the authority for deciding whether claimants were qualified.

The apprentices

Numbers of apprentices

Between 1700 and 1742 there was a steady decline in the number of apprentices registered, from an average of 49 a year in the 1700s to 28 a year in the 1730s. The later register records far fewer apprentices, the numbers dropping from an annual average of 16 in the 1760s to only four a year in the 1820s. This however is not an accurate reflection of the total number of apprentices. In the second half of the 18th century up to 20 boys a year were awarded money by municipal charities to become apprentices. Only a small proportion appear in the apprenticeship register and yet some of the names are recorded in the Register of Freemen. The Apprenticeship Books, the national registers kept by the Commissioners of

---

[1] GBR B3/12 f. 86.
[2] Juřica, p. 90.

Stamps to record the duty paid on apprentice premiums, list an average of 11 a year in Gloucester in the 1750s. This does not include charity apprentices who did not have to pay the tax.

Origins of apprentices

Information on the homes and occupations of the apprentices' fathers is given in the volume covering the years to 1742[1] but not in the following volume. Between 1700 and 1742, 1546 apprentices were registered. The trend noted previously[2] for an increasing proportion of boys to come from the city of Gloucester continued. In the 17th century it rose from 23% to 53% and in the first four decades of the 18th from 53% to 61%. There was a marked drop in the number coming from Herefordshire and Worcestershire. The only two long-distance travellers were both sons of yeomen who came from Ireland (Bartholomew Ragon, apprenticed to Richard White, cordwainer, in March 1710 and William Wright, apprenticed to Henry Corr, tailor, in July 1716).

TABLE I: *Place of origin of apprentices 1700–1739*

	1700s	1710s	1720s	1730s
Total	**493**	**340**	**350**	**279**
Gloucester city	261 (53%)	181 (53%)	197 (56%)	170 (61%)
Cheltenham	15	4	5	5
Tewkesbury	8	3	0	2
Rest of county	137	130	116	86
Herefordshire	29	8	9	3
Worcestershire	28	4	8	3
Wiltshire	6	1	3	1
Other counties	5	5	6	7
London	3	1	6	1
Bristol	1	1	0	1
Ireland	0	2	0	0

[1] GBR C10/3.
[2] Barlow, pp. xxiv–xxv.

Between 1700 and 1742 the occupation of 1515 fathers is given. Overall 23% were yeomen or farmers but the term husbandman, formerly a common description, had disappeared. 5% (72) were gentlemen or aldermen, the same percentage as in the previous century. 194 boys were recorded as being apprenticed to their fathers, many with charity money (see below). Several men took two of their sons as apprentices and the weaver William Garn took three: Matthew in 1721, William in 1722 and John in 1728. All three became freemen. The 1765–1834 register does not routinely record whether boys were apprenticed to their fathers and lists only three. There are cases where master and apprentice have the same surname but such is the duplication of names that it is impossible to be sure of the relationship. The James Parry apprenticed to John Parry, baker and confectioner, in 1814 with 'love and affection' given as the only premium was probably apprenticed to his father, as was the William Hatton apprenticed in 1768 to William Hatton, glover. In 1780 William Hatton son of William Hatton, breechesmaker, was made a freeman.

Trade learned

The removal in 1755 and 1787 of the restrictions on the trades giving the right to the freedom of the city allowed apprentices in many new trades to appear in the registers. The traditional weaving trades virtually disappeared although there were several woolcombers and, in the 1770s, woolstaplers (who checked the length and quality of raw wool and graded the wool fibres).

TABLE II: *Comparison of trade groups over time*

	1595–1700	1700–1742	1765–1834
Number of apprentices	4246	1456	724
	%	%	%
leather	24	21	17
metal	16	20	17
food	13	12	12
distribution	13	7	18
textiles	11	6	0
clothing	10	10	7
wood	6	6	8
professional	3	8	9
building	1	6	6
other	4	4	6

Cordwainers had the largest number of apprentices (310 overall) and were the most numerous leatherworkers. There were 15 apprentice tanners registered between 1700 and 1733 but only one is recorded after 1765.

Pinmaking continued to provide employment in Gloucester. 234 apprentices were bound to 80 masters. John Holder in the first half of the century and Newton Brabant in the second each had a dozen apprentices. The other metalworkers were blacksmiths and coopers. There were 32 apprentice blacksmiths registered before 1742 but none after 1765.

Butchers, bakers and maltsters continued to appear, but bakers began to describe themselves in addition as confectioners and biscuitmakers. Similarly barbers became hairdressers, perukemakers and perfumers; grocers were also seedsmen, tea dealers and wine merchants, and cabinetmakers came to outnumber joiners.

TABLE III: *Declining and rising trades*

Trades appearing 1700–1742 but not 1765–1834	Trades appearing 1765–1834 but not 1700–1742
barber surgeon	banker
bellfounder	bookbinder
blacksmith	bread- & biscuitmaker
bodicemaker	brushmaker
buttonmaker	breechesmaker
cardmaker	cabinetmaker
crape weaver	cheese factor
distiller	chemist & druggist
dyer	coach harnessmaker
feltmaker	confectioner
glazier	grocer & seedsman
hatter	grocer & soapboiler
horn turner	grocer & tallowchandler
innholder	grocer & tea dealer
pewterer	grocer & winemerchant
ropemaker	hairdresser
serge weaver	hairdresser & perfumer
shagmaker	hairdresser & perukemaker
silkweaver	hairdresser & umbrella- & parasolmaker
staymaker	man midwife
weaver	printer
	tinplate worker
	upholder

There are no barber surgeons in the second list because in 1745 the surgeons separated from the barbers to form the Company of Surgeons which later became the Royal College of Surgeons. Man midwives, fashionably known as accoucheurs, were trained in anatomy and in the use of the newly introduced forceps. Thomas Parker described himself as 'apothecary and man midwife' and Charles Cooke as 'apothecary, surgeon and man midwife'.

The printer Robert Raikes, founder of the *Gloucester Journal* (or possibly his son Robert) appears in the Stamp Duty records as master of an apprentice in 1750 (**51**/5). The *Journal* was bought in 1802 by David Walker[1] and between 1805 and 1812 he and his sons David and Alexander took five apprentices. John Selwyn Pytt who published the *Gloucester Gazette* took three between 1791 and 1795. John Washbourn also described himself as a printer in addition to being a bookbinder, bookseller and stationer.

The appearance of bankers signals a shift in the way in which both businessmen and private individuals managed their finances. Among the bankers named are James (Jemmy) Wood the well-known eccentric and miser, and Thomas Turner. The grocer Samuel Niblett and mercer Merrot Stephens also ran banks.[2]

Brushmakers were among the trades given the right to claim the freedom of Gloucester in 1755. Between 1767 and 1813 nine masters took 32 apprentices. Pettat Gardiner, who took ten apprentices, was described in the 1791 *Universal Register* as 'brushmaker and brandy merchant', so there was scope for a little diversification.

Upholders, also given the right to claim the freedom of Gloucester in 1755, were dealers in small and secondhand wares and were often auctioneers. Upholder is also the archaic name for an upholsterer; the London livery company is still called the Worshipful Company of Upholders.

Premiums

The Stamp Act of 1709 introduced a tax on the premium paid when an apprentice was bound. The amount of the premium had to be recorded on the indenture but unfortunately it appears regularly in the apprenticeship register only after 1765. The only references to the tax in the earlier volume are in 1712 when William Lander, grocer, was given the indentures 'and he to pay duty' (**3**/545) and Richard Harris, barber surgeon, paid 7s. 6d. duty (**3**/546). A premium of £32 5s. was paid to the grocer, John Bonner, in the same year (**3**/544).

---

[1] Herbert, p. 159.
[2] Herbert, p. 133.

Of the 727 entries in the later register, 148 either do not mention a premium, or specify that no money is to be paid, the master expecting to receive only 'service' or 'faithful service'. 234 are recorded as receiving charity money on which tax would not be payable. The wealthier trades naturally charged the highest premiums. The two highest amounts, both of £210, went to the mercers Edwin Jeynes, in 1788, and Elisha Farmer Sadler, in 1793.

TABLE IV: *Masters charging a premium of £100 or over, 1765–1834*

mercer	19
grocer	8
apothecary	2
cabinetmaker	2
ironmonger	2
banker	1
bookseller	1
brushmaker	1
chemist & druggist	1

At the other end of the scale, of 78 pinmakers, 32 had no premium, 36 had charity money, four received £10 or less and only three had more than £10.

Stamp Duty

The standard rate of duty introduced in 1709 was 6d. in the pound but it was doubled on premiums over £50 and on duty paid more than two months after the date of indenture. Later acts introduced a scale of charges with upper levels reflecting the rise in the size of premiums. In 1804[1] the scale ranged from 15s. on premiums less than £10 to £20 on those over £300. By 1815[2] there was a tax of £60 on premiums of £1000 or more. Even when no consideration was given there was £1 to pay although the exemption for poor children was retained.

The payments were made to a local collector who travelled to London every six months to hand over all the money from his county. Tax from Gloucestershire was collected by Samuel Worrall from 1742 to 1745, and then by Peter Cocks. In most years they appeared before the Commissioners of Stamps in May and November with about 50 indentures from the whole of the county. Payments for Gloucester apprentices were occasionally made in Bristol where the collector was again Samuel Worrall. In March 1754 he took 53 indentures to London, including those of six boys

---

[1] 44 Geo. III c.98.
[2] 55 Geo. III c.184.

apprenticed in the city of Gloucester. In 1764 the 92 indentures taken by Joshua Green, the Worcestershire collector, included that of John Millward apprenticed to John Crump, a Gloucester cabinetmaker, with a premium of £30. These payments were recorded in the Apprenticeship Books now kept at the National Archives as IR 1. As noted above, entries for Gloucester have been transcribed to provide names for the years missing from the Gloucester apprenticeship registers: see Appendix.

The duty was payable on the premiums given with servants and articled clerks as well as apprentices. The 275 Gloucester names included 13 girls apprenticed to mantuamakers and 8 to milliners, many of them for terms of three, four or five years. Girls were also indentured to a gardener, a pastry cook, a pinmaker, a plasterer, a rugmaker and a shoemaker, five of them for seven years and the other two for shorter terms.

Four of the five boys learning to be attorneys were bound for less than seven years and probably had articles rather than apprenticeship indentures. One of the three boys trained by Martin Smith the cathedral organist[1] is also described as doing articles.

TABLE V:
Premiums in IR 1 1742–65 (including servants and articled clerks)

under £10	81
£10	47
£10 10s.–£19	69
£20–59	53
£60–99	10
£100 or more	10

Of the ten premiums of £100 or more, five were paid to mercers, three to attorneys, one to a goldsmith and one to a surgeon.

Apprenticing charities

The corporation administered the money from several apprenticing charities. Those of Alderman William Holliday, Mrs Sarah Browne, Alderman Powell and Sir Thomas Rich were established in the 17th century.[2]

Alderman Powell's charity awarded £5 a year to one boy who was often chosen on the personal recommendation of a member of the council.

---

[1] Gloucester Cathedral organist 1740–82 and father of John Stafford Smith who wrote the tune now famous as that of the national anthem of the United States: Welander, p. 435.
[2] Barlow, pp. xx–xxii.

At the start of the 18th century the recipient was frequently listed in the corporation minutes together with those receiving money from Alderman Holliday's charity. The two charities appear to have been merged and the last named recipient of Alderman Powell's charity was James Gunn in 1726.

William Holliday's charity gave £5 a year to six boys. One of the conditions imposed by the council was that recipients should not be apprenticed to their fathers. However, this had been ignored in the 17th century[1] and it was still ignored in the 18th. Of 194 boys listed as being bound to their fathers, 76 received money from the Holliday charity. All six of those granted the money in December 1709 were apprenticed to their fathers in January 1710.

In 1705 the council voted to increase the number of boys given £4 a year from Mrs Sarah Browne's charity from three to five,[2] but in most years only four boys received the money.

In her will of 2 July 1767, Mrs Jane Punter left the residue of her estate (a total of £2522 13s. 9d.) to the council for 'binding and placing out and apprenticing every year so many poor boys of the City of Gloucester to some manual trade or occupation as the interest shall allow'.[3] The boys were not to be bound to their fathers and masters were to give the same securities to the corporation as for the other charities. The first distribution was in 1775 when there were nine eligible candidates. Boys were given £10 though it is not always clear from the minutes how many boys received the money. The number of votes given to each candidate was recorded, but not necessarily where the line between successful and unsuccessful candidates was drawn.

Boys applying for money from these charities had to appear in person at a council meeting, usually in September of each year. In the early years of the 18th century they had to take an oath that they were aged over 14. Later they had to produce a certificate of age. This did not deter many younger boys from lining up hopefully each year and being sent away. Boys were also rejected for not being 'freeborn', not living in the city or, in one case in 1784, for being in the workhouse.[4] Members of the council voted for the boys they considered most deserving and the mayor frequently had to use his casting vote. Not all the boys turned out to be worthy of the gift. In 1722 Master King went to sea without being bound

---

[1] Barlow, p. xxi.
[2] GBR B3/8 p. 167.
[3] GBR B3/11 f. 169.
[4] GBR B3/11 f. 359.

apprentice[1] and in 1775 Charles Greening, one of the first successful applicants for Mrs Punter's money, was transported before receiving it.[2]

Boys who were unsuccessful in obtaining money from either the Browne or the Holliday charity frequently applied to the other, but £4 or £5 was proving insufficient to pay the premium for a good position and money from other sources sometimes had to be added (James Keele in 1766 received £4 from Sarah Browne's charity and £4 'not charity', **4/1**). The numbers applying to these two charities were already falling by the 1740s and from 1775, when Mrs Punter's charity began offering gifts of £10, they fell even further. In 1792 the council decided to add together the money from the two charities and give successful boys £9.[3] As a further incentive to persuade masters to take boys with charity money, the requirement for them to give a bond to the council for the faithful performance of their contract was dispensed with in 1821.[4] The full premium was to be paid to the master, half on the execution of the indentures and half after two years.

However, there was still a shortage of suitable candidates and by 1825 the Punter charity had an undistributed surplus of £715 13s. 4d. and the Holliday charity a surplus of £58 16s. It was decided that all the charities should be administered together and additional money given to 'meritorious and deserving' boys leaving Sir Thomas Rich's school in the hope of obtaining for them 'more eligible situations'.[5]

Each year six boys leaving Sir Thomas Rich's school on St Thomas's Day (21 December) were to be given £10 to be bound apprentice. However, this could be affected by the school's financial difficulties as in 1715 when no boys were sent out.[6] Some boys made themselves ineligible for the gift by 'grossly misconducting' themselves. The optimistic mother of John Ambrose Heath petitioned the council for his £10 in 1804 even though he had been expelled for desertion and misconduct.[7] She was unsuccessful. When boys leaving the school began to receive additional money from the other charities, the school found another way to save money. From 1831 the charge for the stamps for the indentures for these boys (£2 5s. 6d. per indenture) was transferred to the master.[8] The school also saved £25 a year by no longer giving clothes to the boys who were leaving.

[1] GBR B3/9 f. 120.
[2] GBR B3/11 f. 182v.
[3] GBR B3/12 f. 168v.
[4] GBR B3/14 f. 25.
[5] GBR B3/14 f. 25.
[6] GBR B3/8 p. 629.
[7] GBR B3/12 f. 383.
[8] GBR B3/14 f. 178.

Other boys were helped by the Gloucestershire Society which was established in 1657 by 50 Gloucestershire gentlemen living in Bristol. Their declared aim was to provide benefactions and apprenticeships to those in need, though it is now thought that their real purpose was to support the restoration of Charles II to the throne. This was quickly achieved but the charitable donations continue to this day. The Gloucestershire Society is now believed to be the oldest existing county charitable organisation.[1]

Between 1798 and 1824 the Gloucestershire Society paid premiums of £7 10s., £10 or £15 for five Gloucester apprentices. Applicants to the charity had to fulfil very stringent conditions: the petition from the boy had to be signed by six members of the society; the intended master had to be a respectable tradesman, a married man and resident in the county of Gloucestershire; the boy had to be aged between 13 and 16; the petition had to be accompanied by the parents' marriage certificate and by baptism certificates to show that at least one of the parents and the son were born in Gloucestershire; the father, son and proposed master had to attend the committee meeting when the ballot was to be held for the awards.[2]

In 1818 the Gloucestershire Society in London gave a premium of £15 for an apprentice carpenter. This society was established in 1767; although its aims and many of its supporters were the same as those of the Gloucestershire Society, the two seem to have been organised entirely separately.[3] The London society apparently came to an end in 1848 when its bank account was closed, but an 'offshoot' did appear in 1924.[4]

The Registers

The registers of Gloucester apprentices are in four volumes, covering the years 1595–1742 and 1765–1834. They are held among the Gloucester borough records in the Gloucestershire Archives as GBR C10/1–4. This volume calendars the latter part of C10/3 and all of C10/4.

The registers have been rebound in dark brown leather and are stamped 'RESTORED BY MALTBY, OXFORD' inside the front cover. The page size of both the third and fourth registers is approximately 310mm x 200mm. C10/3 has the dates 1668–1742 stamped in gold on the upper part of the spine and 1458B at the foot; C10/4 has APPRENTICE REGISTER 1765–1834 on the upper part of the spine and 1458C at the foot.

---

[1] The Gloucestershire Society Report and Accounts, 353rd year ended 31 Dec. 2009.
[2] Rules of the Gloucestershire Society reproduced in the Report and Accounts for 1907: GA JX11.1.
[3] *Gloucestershire Notes and Queries* vol. 3, p. 450.
[4] Correspondence relating to the Gloucestershire Society in London: GA JX11.3.

Entries in C10/3 are in Latin until 1733, although occupations are frequently given in English. Thereafter entries are in English. Most marginal notes are in English but some are in Latin. Both Latin and English entries are in the same standard form:

Cornelius Fifield son of William Fifield of Minety in the County of Gloucester, clerk, hath put himself an apprentice to Matthew Weaver of the City of Gloucester, baker, and Susannah his wife for the term of seven years to begin from the five and twentieth day of May in the year of our Lord one thousand seven hundred and thirty three.

Although C10/4 has been ruled throughout in red with columns stretching across the double spread, only the first 39 pages have been used. The column headings are:

Time of the Inrollment, Date of the Indenture, The Apprentice's Name, Master's name and place of abode, Sums given, Trade the apprentice is to learn, Commencement of the apprenticeship

The entry for each apprentice takes only one line and a line has been ruled under each except on the last few pages where the entries become more cramped.

Editorial Method

The two registers calendared here contain slightly different information, but a standard format has been maintained as far as possible. The volume number and the number of the page within the volume are given at the left-hand margin, followed by the date of the indenture. The first line of each entry gives the name of the apprentice. This is followed by the name, occupation and place of origin of his father when this appears in the register and, in later entries, by the amount paid as a premium when the indentures were enrolled. The second line gives the master's name and occupation, the term to be served and the date on which the apprenticeship was to begin.

Entries in the Appendix are in the same format but the page numbers within each volume are not consecutive because only those entries relating to the city of Gloucester were selected. These entries also record in the first line whether double tax was due and in the second the date on which tax was paid to the collector.

The county has been omitted for places in Gloucestershire and for county towns elsewhere. Notes which appear in the MS as additions to the entries first registered are set in the calendar in italic. Text supplied to fill omissions in the MS is enclosed in square brackets. Roman numerals have been converted to arabic.

Footnotes referring to awards of charity money are appended to the name of the mayor in whose year of office the decisions were made.

The spelling (other than that of surnames) has been modernised. A place-name spelling notably different from the modern form is given in brackets after the modern form. Place-names which have not been identified are enclosed in single quotation marks.

For the whole period, the new year is deemed to begin on 1 January.

CALENDAR OF
GLOUCESTER APPRENTICESHIP REGISTERS
GBR C10/3: 1700–1742

Nicholas Webb, mayor 1700–1[1]

3/400	1700	12 Oct.	Razor, George son of John, yeoman of Newent Pace, Francis & Susannah, cordwainer, 7 yrs from 19 Oct.
		24 Oct.	Cowles, Joseph son of Joseph, glover of Gloucester Brocke, John & Mary, glover, 7 yrs from 1 Sept.
		4 Nov.	White, John son of William, yeoman of Huntley Rogers, John & Elizabeth, baker, 7 yrs
3/401		8 Nov.	Twyning, William son of John jr, gentleman, dec'd, of Quedgeley Fowler, William & Sarah, baker, 7 yrs from 30 Sept.
			Coopy, Joseph son of John, tanner of Gloucester Parlour, John & Joan, cutler, 7 yrs from 5 Nov.
		12 Nov.	Hathway, William son of William, horn turner, dec'd, of Gloucester Browne, William & Joan, cordwainer, 7 yrs from 5 Nov. *22 July 1706: turned over to Richard Wells, cordwainer.* *Before Samuel Lye, mayor*
		4 Dec.	Lea, John son of John, tailor, dec'd, of Gloucester Lea, Elizabeth, his mother, 7 yrs from 29 Sept.
3/402		6 Dec.	Mamby, John son of John, cordwainer of Gloucester Davis, Samuel, butcher, 7 yrs from 29 Sept.
			Long, George son of Andrew, yeoman of Ashleworth Wells, John & Anne, cordwainer, 7 yrs from 17 Nov. [*Entered again on p. 403 and crossed out*]
		12 Dec.	Bryan, Joshua son of Joshua, cordwainer, dec'd, of Bristol Bryan, Daniel & Anne, cordwainer, 7 yrs
		4 Dec.	Glover, Thomas son of Lawrence, yeoman of Earl's Croome, Worcs. Heming, William & Anne, ropemaker, 7 yrs
3/403	1701	6 Feb.	Ball, Samuel son of Samuel, clothier of Stonehouse Gammond, John & Sarah, baker, 7 yrs from feast of St Thomas the apostle [*21 Dec.*]

[1] 29 Apr. 1701: To receive £4 of Mrs Sarah Browne's money: Thomas Sinnocks, John Cooke, William Hutchins. GBR B3/8 p. 14.

8 Aug. 1701: To receive £5 of Mr William Holliday's money: Thomas Stephens, Thomas Birch, Nicholas Nott, Mr Merrett's son, Isaac Medway, Charles Jones. GBR B3/8 p. 22.

25 Sept. 1701: To leave Sir Thomas Rich's hospital and receive £10: John Baker, Thomas Symon, Thomas Perry, Thomas Morris, Matthew Phelps, William Deane. GBR B3/8 p. 43.

	1701	14 Feb.	Gill, Richard son of William, yeoman of Barton Street, Gloucester Gill, William jr & Mary, ropemaker, 7 yrs
		21 Feb.	Palmer, John son of Edward, baker of Gloucester Palmer, Samuel jr, bookseller, 7 yrs from 21 Dec.
3/404		28 Feb.	Stait, Grey son of Richard, innholder, dec'd, of Gloucester Jennings, Jeremiah & Anne, tailor, 7 yrs from 24 Feb.
		10 Mar.	Gooding, Joseph son of Richard, yeoman of Linton, Churcham Cowles, Alice, widow, 7 yrs from 2 Feb.
			Jones, John son of John, yeoman, dec'd, of Newent Skynner, William & Mary, cordwainer, 7 yrs from 4 Mar.
		17 Mar.	Nott, Lawrence son of George, carpenter, dec'd, of Gloucester Nest, John jr & Barbara, carpenter, 7 yrs from 2 Feb.
3/405		19 Mar.	Bosley, James son of Robert, miller of Redmarley d'Abitot, Worcs. Whittingham, Edward & Abigail, baker, 7 yrs from 24 Feb.
		25 Mar.	Gwynett, George son of George, yeoman of 'Elstone' [Alstone or Elkstone?] Veysey, Thomas & Elizabeth, mercer, 7 yrs
		1 Apr.	Aldridge, Thomas son of Thomas, yeoman, dec'd, of Gloucester Beedle, John & Jane, collarmaker, 7 yrs from the last feast of the apostle [*not identified*]
		5 Apr.	Powell, John son of John, yeoman of Dowdeswell Randle, William & Elizabeth, barber surgeon, 7 yrs *The apprentice went away from his master & by consent of all parties the indentures were cancelled*
3/406		28 Apr.	Wheeler, John son of John, miller, dec'd, of Walford Freeman, Robert & Frances, joiner, 7 yrs from 25 Mar.
		6 May	Phelps, Thomas son of Joseph, feltmaker, dec'd, of Gloucester Gwillim, John, feltmaker, 7 yrs from 10 Mar.
		13 May	Lord, John son of Thomas, baker, dec'd, of Barnwood Mathews, John & Anne, butcher, 7 yrs from 25 Mar.
		14 May	Edwards, Richard son of Anthony, gentleman of Shurdington Webb, Thomas & Anne, mercer, 7 yrs from 25 Mar.
		20 May	Drinkwater, Richard son of James, yeoman of Churcham Drew, Thomas & Hannah, cordwainer, 7 yrs from 1 May
3/407		22 May	Edwards, James son of Richard, cordwainer of Gloucester Prynn, William & Margaret, tailor, 7 yrs
		30 May	Mills, Richard son of Richard, silkweaver of Gloucester Collericke, Daniel & Elizabeth, bodicemaker, 7 yrs from 29 Sept.
		13 June	Fitchew, Josiah son of Thomas, feltmaker of Purton Stoke, Wilts. Oatley, Francis & Sarah, feltmaker, 7 yrs from 23 May
			Oatley, Isaac son of John, mercer of Ashton Keynes, Wilts. Oatley, Francis & Sarah, feltmaker, 7 yrs from 23 May
3/408		17 June	Greene, John son of Richard, gentleman of Gloucester Lane, Richard & Anne, grocer, 7 yrs from St Thomas
		30 June	Synocks, Thomas son of Thomas, labourer, dec'd, of Gloucester King, William & Elizabeth, pinmaker, 7 yrs from 1 May

	1701	9 July	Worrall, Joshua son of Joshua, silkweaver of Gloucester Colericke, Daniel & Elizabeth, bodicemaker, 7 yrs
		17 July	Bradford, George son of Thomas, mariner of Newnham Brabant, Francis jr & Margaret, cooper, 7 yrs
3/409		21 July	Longden, Thomas son of Thomas, gent. & alderman of Gloucester Hyett, John & Elizabeth, sheriff & alderman, 7 yrs from 25 Dec.
		18 Aug.	Lodge, Stephen son of Trustram, cooper, dec'd, of Gloucester Lodge, William & Mary, cooper, 7 yrs from 1 Aug.
		27 Aug.	Lugg, Thomas son of John, pinmaker of Gloucester Price, Alice, widow, 8 yrs from 25 Mar.
		21 Aug.	Archer, Thomas son of Sampson, silkweaver of Gloucester Farley, Thomas & Elinor, cutler, 7 yrs [later insertion]
		1 Sept.	Williams, Evan son of Thomas sr, farmer of Llanbedr Painscastle, Herefs. [recte Radnorshire] Till, Richard & Mary, cutler, 7 yrs
3/410		8 Sept.	Lovett, John son of James, weaver of Gloucester Rowles, Timothy & Mary, basketmaker, 7 yrs
		15 Sept.	Merrett, Henry son of Thomas, clerk of Gloucester Merrett, Thomas & Jane, baker, 7 yrs from 1 Aug.
		19 Sept.	Stephens, Thomas son of Thomas, pinmaker, dec'd, of Gloucester Gardner, William & Hannah, pinmaker, 7 yrs
		1 Oct.	Meadway, Isaac son of Abraham, bricklayer of Gloucester Meadway, Abraham, his father, & Mary, 7 yrs
3/411		4 Oct.	Greene, Richard son of Richard, gentleman of Gloucester Greene, Richard, his father, & Elizabeth, gentleman, 7 yrs from 24 June
		26 Sept.	Cage, John son of Edward, yeoman, dec'd, of Frampton on Severn Jones, Joseph & Frances, barber surgeon, 7 yrs from 1 Sept.

Thomas Webb, mayor 1701–2[1]

3/411	1701	13 Oct.	Young, Giles son of Giles, yeoman, dec'd, of Churchdown Church, Roger & Sarah, tailor, 7 yrs from 24 June
		20 Oct.	Hayes, John son of William, cordwainer of Gloucester Mutlow, Anthony & Elinor, tailor, 7 yrs from 29 Sept.
3/412		9 Oct.	Yarnell, Richard son of Richard, yeoman of Sollers Hope, Herefs. Lane, Nicholas jr & Hester, apothecary, 7 yrs from 3 May
		24 Oct.	Jackson, Daniel son of Edward, pinmaker of Gloucester Hall, John, tiler & plasterer, 7 yrs *16 Aug. 1702: turned over to Thomas Brotherton, tiler & plasterer*

[1] 20 Jan. 1702: To receive £5 of Alderman Powell's money: Mr Meadway's son. GBR B3/8 p. 49.
9 Apr. 1702: To receive £4 of Mrs Sarah Browne's money: John Bishopp, John Eastam, John Spillman. To receive £5 of Mr William Holliday's money: Charles Turner, Joseph Hobson, Thomas Sanders, James Lumbard, George Philipps, Thomas Watt's son. GBR B3/8 pp. 54, 62.
25 Sept. 1702: To leave Sir Thomas Rich's hospital and receive £10: William Hartland, John Hawkes, John Hartland, Charles Williams, Joseph Harris, William Ham. GBR B3/8 p. 73.

	1701	30 Oct.	Man, Edward son of Edward, yeoman, dec'd, of Barnwood Ravener, Joseph & Mary, weaver, 7 yrs from 1 Dec.
		10 Nov.	Thurstone, Joseph son of Nathaniel, yeoman of Thornbury Bliss, Samuel & Mary, tanner, 7 yrs
3/413		20 Nov.	Gunn, James son of Arthur, cordwainer, dec'd, of Painswick Church, Roger & Mary, glazier, 7 yrs
		13 Nov.	Rogers, William son of Mary, widow, of Newport Corsnett, Richard & Martha, vintner, 7 yrs from 29 Sept.
		10 Dec.	Walker, James son of Anthony, blacksmith of Gloucester Walker, Anthony, his father, & Mary, 7 yrs
		21 Oct.	Tyler, John son of Edward, cordwainer of Gloucester Bicknell, William & Abigail, tailor, 7 yrs from 21 Apr.
3/414	1702	15 Jan.	Kemis, Samuel son of Samuel, butcher of Gloucester Barrett, William, woolcomber, 7 yrs
		26 Jan.	Burgis, James son of Thomas, gentleman of Gloucester Niccolls, Thomas, sheriff of Gloucester, & Elizabeth, 7 yrs
		2 Feb.	Haynes, Thomas son of John, tailor of St Clements, Oxford Wood, Isaac & Sarah, tailor, 7 yrs
		10 Feb.	Baker, John son of James, butcher of Gloucester Nest, John jr & Barbara, carpenter, 7 yrs from 2 Feb.
		13 Feb.	Hornage, Thomas son of William, pinmaker, dec'd, of Gloucester Price, Brian & Joyce, pinmaker, 7 yrs
3/415		23 Feb.	Burdocke, William son of William, yeoman, dec'd, of Miserden Davis, Jonathan & Elizabeth, tailor, 7 yrs
		27 Feb.	Cooke, John son of John, tailor of London Sparry, Samuel & Margaret, baker, 7 yrs from 25 Mar. next
		6 Mar.	Meadway, Henry son of Edward, hosier of Gloucester Meadway, Edward, his father, & Elizabeth, 7 yrs
		3 Apr.	Fielder, Benjamin son of George, farrier of Gloucester Fielder, George, his father, & Sarah, 7 yrs from 10 Oct.
			Birch, Thomas son of Thomas, feltmaker of Gloucester Jones, Giles, of Boddington, tailor, 7 yrs from 17 Feb.
3/416		10 Apr.	Perry, Thomas son of Thomas, innholder, dec'd, of Gloucester Kent, Samuel & Jane, joiner, 7 yrs from 1 Apr.
		25 Feb.	Remmington, Daniel son of Thomas, yeoman of South Cerney Rodway, Giles, alderman, 7 yrs from 2 Feb.
		21 Apr.	Dunn, William son of William, victualler of Gloucester Savory, Robert & Mary, farrier, 7 yrs from 24 June *Crossed out by mayor's order*
		22 Apr.	Mason, Adam son of Adam, glassmaker of Gloucester Browne, Thomas, esquire, 7 yrs from 20 Apr.
3/417		1 May	Cole, George son of John, yeoman, dec'd, of Shurdington Cooke, Thomas & Susannah, tailor, 7 yrs
		27 Apr.	Bishop, John son of John, silkweaver of Gloucester Carill, Thomas & Mary, hosier, 7 yrs

	1702	2 May	Edwards *alias* Welsh, George son of Welsh, [—] of Charlton Kings Cross, Thomas & Frances, lastmaker, 7 yrs
		4 May	Tomlins, William son of John, pinmaker, dec'd, of Gloucester Davis, Henry & Mary, pinmaker, 7 yrs
			Smith, Henry son of Henry, yeoman of Lydney Madocks, Thomas, saddler, 7 yrs from 1 May
3/418		4 May	Matthews, John son of John, buttonmaker of Gloucester Davis, John & Margaret, pinmaker, 7 yrs
		13 May	Webb, William son of George, labourer of St Mary de Lode, Barton Street, Gloucester Howell, Joseph & Elizabeth, blacksmith, 7 yrs from 24 June
		25 May	Stephens, William son of Thomas, tailor, dec'd, of Gloucester Randle, William & Susannah, serge weaver, 7 yrs
		28 May	Howells, Abraham son of Abraham, blacksmith of Barton Street, Gloucester Evenis, William & Catherine, cordwainer, 7 yrs from 1 May
			Gazard, Richard son of Richard, feltmaker, dec'd, Gloucester Nash, Jesse, feltmaker, 7 yrs
3/419			Stratford, John son of John, yeoman of Hucclecote Launder, James jr & Hester, baker, 7 yrs from 1 May
		1 June	Heath, Thomas son of Thomas, gardener of Gloucester Joseph, Thomas & Margaret, tanner, 7 yrs from 25 Apr.
			Clissold, John son of John, gentleman, dec'd, of Quedgeley Payne, Capel & Katherine, mercer, 7 yrs
		2 June	Nott, Nicholas son of George, carpenter, dec'd, of Gloucester Nest, William & Mary, carpenter, 7 yrs from 1 Apr.
		5 June	Burford, Samuel son of George, yeoman of Tewkesbury Bell, John & Mary, mercer, 7 yrs
3/420		6 June	Jennings, Henry son of Henry, carpenter of Gloucester Rudhall, Abraham & Elinor, carpenter, 7 yrs
		8 June	Cother, Joseph son of Joseph, farmer of Newent Wells, Richard & Mary, cordwainer, 7 yrs
		2 June	Hill, Thomas son of Robert, clerk of Condicote Lane, Nicholas jr & Hester, apothecary, 7 yrs from 1 May
		22 June	Philipps, Philip son of John, butcher of Gloucester Lucas, Samuel & Elizabeth, joiner, 7 yrs
		2 July	Beard, Henry son of Henry, yeoman of Stonehouse Evenis, William & Katherine, cordwainer, 7 yrs
3/421		6 July	Hathway, Thomas, son of William, horn turner, dec'd, of Gloucester Williams, John & Margaret, glover, 7 yrs
		9 July	Miles, Henry son of Henry, yeoman, dec'd, of Birdlip Fletcher, Thomas & Sarah, baker, 7 yrs
		11 July	Mayoe, Richard son of John, yeoman of Huntley Pace, Francis & Susannah, cordwainer, 7 yrs
		16 July	Wellavise, John son of William, feltmaker, dec'd, of Gloucester Greene, John & Joan, cordwainer, 7 yrs from 24 June

	1702	17 July	Humphris, Thomas son of Richard, cordwainer, dec'd, of Guiting Power Humphris, Edward & Elizabeth, currier, 7 yrs
3/422		24 July	Pheasant, James son of Thomas, buttonmaker of Gloucester Pheasant, Thomas, his father, & Elizabeth, 7 yrs
			Emes, John son of John, yeoman of Great Hampton, Worcs. Wiggett, Samuel & Alice, glover, 7 yrs from 25 July
		8 Aug.	Stocke, Samuel son of John, gentleman of Chaceley, Worcs. Perkins, George, baker, 7 yrs
		10 Aug.	Halford, Edward son of Edward, yeoman of Maisemore Halford, John, cordwainer, 7 yrs from 10 Nov. last
		14 Aug.	Nanfan, John son of Bridges, gentleman of Tewkesbury Harris, Richard & Hester, barber, 7 yrs from 1 Aug.
3/423		21 Sept.	Fords, Thomas son of Thomas, jacksmith of Newent Fords, Thomas, his father, & Anne, 7 yrs
		25 Sept.	Young, Joseph son of Joseph, pinmaker, dec'd, of Gloucester Pitt, Joyce, widow, 7 yrs
		28 Sept.	Nest, Richard son of John jr, carpenter of Gloucester Nest, John jr & Barbara, carpenter, 7 yrs from 10 Oct. last
			Symon, Thomas son of David, innholder, dec'd, of Gloucester Robins, James, currier, 7 yrs
			Still, William son of Edward, yeoman of Cheltenham Still, Francis, maltster, 7 yrs from 24 June
3/424		2 Oct.	Rolfe, Jasper son of Jasper, carpenter of Gloucester Randle, James & Jane, joiner, 7 yrs from 8 Apr.

Sir Samuel Eckley, mayor 1702–3[1]

3/424	1702	6 Oct.	Barrow, Thomas son of Stephen, tailor, dec'd, of Gloucester Cowcher, Richard & Margaret, pinmaker, 7 yrs
		13 Oct.	Turner, Charles son of John, cordwainer of Gloucester Turner, John, his father, & Margaret, 7 yrs
		20 Oct.	Phillips, George son of Thomas, tailor of Gloucester Hannis, Thomas & Anne, pinmaker, 7 yrs from 30 Sept. *25 Sept. 1704: turned over to Henry Davies, pinmaker, and Mary. Before John Hyett, alderman and justice*
		22 Oct.	Lea, Daniel son of Henry, cordwainer of Gloucester Lea, Henry, his father, 7 yrs
3/425		29 Oct.	Eastam, John son of Christopher, yeoman, dec'd, of Gloucester Holton, Richard & Elizabeth, serge weaver, 7 yrs from 1 Nov.

---

[1] 24 May 1703: To receive £4 of Mrs Sarah Browne's money: James Maverley, Peter Mason, Israel Powell's son. GBR B3/8 p. 92.

16 Aug. 1703: To receive £5 of Mr William Holliday's money: Christopher Hayes, Edward Hayward, William King, James Arnold, Joseph Atkins, William Cooke. To receive £5 of Alderman Powell's money: Thomas Matthews. GBR B3/8 pp. 103–4.

27 Sept. 1703: To leave Sir Thomas Rich's hospital and receive £10: Walter Myles, Thomas Wyly, Thomas Rolfe, John Mower, George Meighen, James Workman. GBR B3/8 p. 105.

	1702	11 Dec.	Hill, Thomas son of William, glover of Ross-on-Wye, Herefs. Hornage, James & Mary, blacksmith, 8 yrs
		15 Dec.	Hyeron, Nathaniel son of Nathaniel, bodicemaker of Wotton-under-Edge Freeman, Thomas, bodicemaker of Wotton but late of Gloucester, 7 yrs from 29 Sept.
		18 Dec.	Lumbard, Isaac son of James, serge weaver of Gloucester Till, Richard, cutler, 7 yrs
3/426		22 Dec.	Sanders, Thomas son of Thomas, tanner of Gloucester Matthews, John & Dorcas, tanner, 7 yrs
	1703	6 Jan.	Dowell, John son of John, labourer, late of Minsterworth Marshfield, James, fisherman, 8 yrs
		14 Jan.	Ady, William son of Ralph, cook of Painswick Jeanes, Thomas & Martha, feltmaker, 7 yrs
	1702	17 Dec.	Cowdall, Francis son of John, grocer of Gloucester Cowdall, John, his father, & Sarah, 7 yrs
	1703	23 Jan.	Newman, John son of Richard, carpenter, dec'd, of Cheltenham Smith, John jr & Frances, currier, 7 yrs from 1 Oct. 1702
3/427		4 Feb.	Hayward, John son of Samuel, gentleman of Gloucester Johnson, Samuel & Dorothy, mercer, 7 yrs from 15 Jan.
		5 Feb.	Kearsy, William son of William, yeoman of Kilcot, Newent Horrold, William & Jane, pewterer, 7 yrs from 25 Mar.
		11 Feb.	Humphries, Thomas son of Thomas, barber, dec'd, of Gloucester Hague, James & Hester, chandler, 7 yrs
		15 Mar.	Blanch, Daniel son of Trustram, pinmaker of Gloucester Ricketts, John & Bridget, pinmaker, 7 yrs
3/428		17 Feb.	Hartland, William son of Thomas, pinmaker of Gloucester Hartland, Thomas, his father, & Mary, 7 yrs
			Spillman, John son of John, tiler & plasterer of Gloucester Cowles, Thomas, tiler & plasterer, 7 yrs
		20 Feb.	Pitt, Rowland son of John, gentleman of Colwall, Herefs. Tayler, William & Dorothy, alderman, 7 yrs from 1 Jan.
		1 Mar.	Edwards, James son of James, yeoman of Hanley Castle, Worcs. Weale, Thomas & Margery, baker, 7 yrs from 2 Feb.
3/429		9 Mar.	Ham, William son of William, butcher of Gloucester Kent, Hannah, widow, 7 yrs
		16 Mar.	Webley, Richard son of Giles, feltmaker of Gloucester Shipton, Cowcher, pinmaker, 7 yrs
		13 Mar.	Horniel, John son of Horniell, William, gentleman, dec'd, of London Nest, John & Barbara, carpenter, 7 yrs
		30 Mar.	Elliott, John son of Edward, yeoman of Barton Street, Gloucester Perris, Richard & Mary, butcher, 7 yrs
3/430		3 Apr.	Payne, Thomas son of Joseph, cutler, dec'd, of Cirencester Tyler, Charles & Hester, plumber & glazier, 7 yrs from 11 Feb.
		6 Apr.	Elliott, John son of John, upholsterer, dec'd, of Gloucester Elliott, Jane, widow, 7 yrs

	1703 6 Apr.	Barnes, Benjamin son of John, plumber of Upton upon Severn, Worcs. Dowle, Job & Anne, mercer, 7 yrs from 1 Mar.
	7 Apr.	Cugley, Thomas son of William, cardmaker of Stroud Cugley, William, his father, & Anne, 7 yrs
3/431	12 Apr.	Window, John son of John, yeoman, dec'd, of Haresfield Webb, Thomas & Anne, alderman, 7 yrs
	14 Apr.	Gilding, Thomas son of John, yeoman, dec'd, of Mathern [MS Mathon], Worcs. Burroughs, Samuel & Elizabeth, gentleman, 7 yrs from 1 Feb.
	1 May	Cother, Thomas son of Joseph, yeoman of Newent Bryan, Daniel & Anne, cordwainer, 7 yrs
	1 June	Wilton, Henry son of Henry, woolcomber of Gloucester Trow, John, pinmaker, 7 yrs from 25 Mar.

[*There are no pages numbered 432 and 433*]

3/434	12 June	Man, Richard son of John, yeoman, dec'd, of Upleadon Capper, Matthew & Anne, innholder, 7 yrs
	14 June	Corsnett, William son of Richard, gentleman, dec'd, of Gloucester Branch, Thomas & Rachel, grocer, 7 yrs from 1 June
	21 June	Holder, Joseph son of Edward, woolcomber of Gloucester Benson, William & Mary, tiler & plasterer, 7 yrs from 26 May
	25 June	Young, Henry son of Giles, yeoman, dec'd, of Brockworth Hornage, William & Anne, cordwainer, 7 yrs from 29 June
3/435	2 July	Gundimore, Joseph son of Walter, cordwainer of London Gundimore, Tobias & Anne, tailor, 7 yrs from 24 June
	22 July	Powell, William son of Francis, yeoman, dec'd, of St Margaret's, Gloucester Nicolls, Thomas & Elizabeth, gentleman, 7 yrs from 5 Nov. 1697[1]
	27 July	Greening, Daniel son of Jeremiah, yeoman of Hardwicke Heard, Humphrey & Jane, butcher, 7 yrs from 29 Sept. 1700
		Maverly, James son of James, buttonmaker of Gloucester Berwick, Thomas & Barbara, buttonmaker, 7 yrs from 24 June
3/436	28 Aug.	Phewterell, Richard son of Richard, yeoman, dec'd, of Hempsted Jennings, Michael & Abigail, butcher, 7 yrs from 25 Mar.
	2 July	Lawrence, Obadiah son of William, yeoman of Bromsberrow Lodge, William & Mary, cooper, 7 yrs from 2 July
	4 July	Hardwicke, Thomas son of Thomas, pinmaker, dec'd, of Barton Street, Gloucester Cowcher, Richard & Margaret, pinmaker, 7 yrs
	4 Aug.	Long, Edward son of Andrew, yeoman of Ashleworth Jaques, Aaron & Mary, baker, 7 yrs from 24 June
3/437	9 Aug.	Powell, John son of Israel, yeoman of Gloucester Rodway, Thomas & Edith, butcher, 7 yrs from 24 June

[1] 21 July 1703: William Powell, who dwelt with and served Mr Thomas Nicholls as an apprentice from 5 Nov. 1697 although not bound by indenture according to the custom of the city, to be bound and enrolled in the Town Clerk's office. GBR B3/8 p. 97.

	1703	14 Aug.	Blake, Thomas son of Thomas, yeoman of Up Hatherley Lawrence, William, baker, 7 yrs from 23 Apr.
		21 Aug.	Dowding, George son of John, silkweaver of Fownhope, Herefs. Rickards, Samuel & Hannah, carpenter, 7 yrs from 24 June
		24 Aug.	Hayward, Edward son of Edward, silkweaver of Gloucester Hayward, Edward, his father, & Anne, 7 yrs
3/438		2 Sept.	Allen, Andrew son of Joseph, maltster, dec'd, of Pershore, Worcs. Farmer, Samuel & Anne, apothecary, 7 yrs from 2 Aug.
		6 Sept.	Boss, Thomas son of Thomas, barber, dec'd, of London Best, John, tailor, 7 yrs
		9 Sept.	Harris, Joseph son of Joseph, baker of Gloucester Harris, Joseph, his father, & Elizabeth, 7 yrs from 1 May
		27 Sept.	Roberts, John son of John, cordwainer of Tewkesbury Bubb, William, barber surgeon, 7 yrs from 12 Aug.
3/439		29 Sept.	Wilkins, Nicholas son of Thomas, butcher, dec'd, of Gloucester Porter, Anthony & Sarah, butcher, 7 yrs from 24 June
			Hayes, Christopher son of Christopher, cordwainer of Gloucester Hayes, Christopher, his father, & Margaret, 7 yrs

Robert Payne, esquire, mayor 1703–4[1]

3/439	1703	8 Oct.	Weeksy, Richard son of Richard, clerk of Sherston, Wilts. Longdon, Anne, widow, 7 yrs from 23 Sept.
		6 Nov.	Serjeant, James, son of John, gentleman of Mitcheldean Elliott, Jane, widow, 7 yrs from 1 Aug.
3/440		9 Nov.	Cooke, Samuel son of John, worsted comber of Tetbury late of Gloucester Cooke, John, his father, & Elizabeth, 7 yrs
			Atkins, Joseph son of Walter, cordwainer of Gloucester Atkins, Walter, his father, & Mary, 7 yrs from 29 Sept.
			Grigg, Henry son of William, silkweaver of Gloucester Trow, John, pinmaker, 7 yrs from 29 Sept.
			Niccolls, Thomas son of Henry, maltster of Gloucester Niccolls, Henry, his father, & Hester, 7 yrs from 29 Oct.
3/441		10 Nov.	Shatford, John son of Thomas, silkweaver of Gloucester Hopkins, Theophilus & Susannah, joiner, 7 yrs from 29 Oct.
		16 Nov.	Layton, John son of John, waterman of Gloucester Parker, John & Martha, tailor, 7 yrs from 29 Sept.
		17 Nov.	Watts, John son of Edward, farmer of Prestbury Bryan, Richard & Mary, brazier, 7 yrs

---

[1] 2 May 1704: To receive £4 of Mrs Sarah Browne's money: Edward Addis, Philip Price's son, Richard Archer. GBR B3/8 p. 134.

3 Aug. 1704: To receive £5 of Mr William Holliday's money: Ralph Brymyard, Richard Webb, Robert Cooke, Samuel Welavise, Thomas Jones, William Benson. To receive £5 of Alderman Powell's money: Dennis Jones's son. GBR B3/8 pp. 137–8.

14 Aug. 1704: To leave Sir Thomas Rich's hospital and receive £10: Daniel Mason, Little Wintle, James Hornage, James Pinnocke, Thomas Bowler, Robert Stephens. GBR B3/8 p. 142.

1703   17 Nov.   Mathews, Thomas son of Thomas, baker of Gloucester
                                 Mathews, Thomas, his father, & Margaret, 7 yrs

3/442   15 Dec.   Smith, Abraham son of Thomas, yeoman of Tockenham Wick, Wilts.
                                 Smith, James, cooper, 7 yrs from 29 Sept.

1704   6 Jan.   Cowley, Job son of Job, bricklayer of Gloucester
                                 Church, Roger & Mary, glazier, 7 yrs from 6 Dec. 1703

                 13 Jan.   Griffin, Thomas son of John, combmaker, dec'd, of Gloucester
                                 Higgins, Ephraim & Anne, bricklayer, 7 yrs

                                 Haynes, William son of William, yeoman of Malswick, Newent
                                 Rogers, John & Jane, baker, 7 yrs from 5 Nov. 1703

3/443   17 Jan.   Barnard, John son of Daniel, clothworker of Cam
                                 Ingley, Richard & Anne, bricklayer, 7 yrs

                 29 Jan.   Marshall, William son of Thomas, yeoman, dec'd, of Longhope
                                 Maude, John & Mary, glover, 7 yrs

                 2 Feb.   Rolfe, Thomas son of John, yeoman, dec'd, of Gloucester
                                 Browne, Thomas & Martha, sievemaker, 7 yrs

                                 Pearce, William son of William, pinmaker of Mitcheldean
                                 Dunn, Lawrence, cordwainer, 7 yrs

3/444   5 Feb.   Hawkins, James son of James, baker of Newent
                                 Skinner, William & Mary, cordwainer, 7 yrs from 10 Jan.

                 14 Feb.   Cowdall, James son of John, gentleman of Gloucester
                                 Cowdall, John, his father, & Sarah, 7 yrs from 29 Sept. 1703

                 4 Feb.   Lovell, Joseph son of John, silkweaver of St John the Baptist, Gloucester
                                 Davis, John & Margaret, pinmaker, 7 yrs

                 14 Feb.   Young, James son of James, pinmaker of Gloucester
                                 Holder, John & Sarah, pinmaker, 7 yrs from 21 Dec. 1703

3/445   17 Feb.   Keyse, William son of Patrick, tailor, dec'd, of Gloucester
                                 Sayer, James sr & Margaret, tailor, 7 yrs from 29 Sept.

                 23 Feb.   Miles, Walter son of Walter, baker of Gloucester
                                 Miles, Walter, his father, & Elizabeth, 7 yrs

                 24 Feb.   Nelmes, Edmund son of Ellis, yeoman, dec'd, of Newent
                                 Castle, Nathaniel & Hannah, baker, 7 yrs from 1 Nov. 1703

                 18 Mar.   Roberts, Joshua son of George, yeoman, dec'd, of Shipton Sollers
                                 Veysey, Thomas & Elizabeth, gentleman, 7 yrs from 20 Dec. 1703

3/446   23 Mar.   Brotherton, Thomas son of Thomas, tiler & plasterer of Gloucester
                                 Randle, John, tiler & plasterer, 7 yrs from 29 Feb.

                 4 Apr.   Dickes, Daniel son of Thomas, farmer, dec'd, of Gloucester
                                 Spencer, Thomas & Beata, cooper, 7 yrs from 29 Sept. 1703

                 8 Apr.   Harding, Robert son of John, haberdasher, dec'd, of Ross-on-Wye, Herefs.
                                 Heaven, John & Deborah, barber surgeon, 7 yrs from 25 Mar.

                 12 Apr.   Beal, Charles son of Thomas, yeoman, dec'd, of Staunton
                                 Rickards, Samuel & Hannah, carpenter, 7 yrs from 1 Nov. 1703

3/447   14 Apr.   King, William son of John, scrivener of Gloucester
                                 Jones, Charles & Anne, cooper, 7 yrs from 25 Mar.

	1704	18 Apr.	Randle, Thomas son of Giles, silkweaver of Gloucester Brotherton, Thomas & Mary, tiler & plasterer, 7 yrs from 25 Dec. 1703
		9 May	Toney, Henry son of Charles, yeoman of Gloucester Way, John & Susannah, butcher, 8 yrs from 1 May
		8 May	Stone, Thomas son of Hester, widow of Stonehouse Jeffryes, Henry, joiner, 7 yrs
3/448		12 May	Fisher, James son of John, yeoman of Ross-on-Wye, Herefs. Endall, Thomas & Martha, barber surgeon, 7 yrs from 25 Mar.
		18 May	Pembruge, John son of Thomas, grocer of Gloucester Pembruge, Thomas, his father, & Elbeata, 7 yrs from 10 Oct. 1703
		27 May	Niccolls, William son of William, gentleman of Gloucester Niccolls, William, his father, & Elizabeth, 7 yrs from 1 Jan.
		1 June	Price, John son of Philip, maltmaker of Gloucester Heming, Richard & Mary, tailor, 7 yrs
3/449		2 June	Archer, Sampson son of Sampson, silkweaver of Gloucester Weaver, Henry & Sarah, blacksmith & farrier, 7 yrs
		7 June	Smith, John son of Thomas, yeoman of Taynton Williams, Anthony & Mary, barber surgeon, 7 yrs from 8 May [entered again on p. 450 and crossed out]
			Addis, Edward son of Edward, buttonmaker of Gloucester Puckeridge, Thomas, tailor, 7 yrs [entered again on p. 450 and crossed out]
		10 June	Bamford, William son of William, broadweaver of Westbury-on-Severn Craft, Samuel & Martha, silkweaver, 7 yrs
3/450		24 June	Colchester, Joshua son of Joshua, yeoman of Ashleworth Hoare, Thomas & Elizabeth, grocer, 7 yrs from 6 Apr.
		26 June	Sparkes, John son of John, innholder of Cheltenham Burroughes, Samuel & Elizabeth, gentleman, 7 yrs
3/451		5 July	Roberts, William son of Edward, farmer, of Dumbleton Rickets, Samuel & Hannah, carpenter, 7 yrs from 1 May
		10 July	Gorton, William son of Thomas, brewer of Gloucester Selwyn, Thomas & Mary, cordwainer, 8 yrs from 24 June
		12 July	Dunn, George son of Francis, mason, dec'd, of Gloucester Ravener, Joseph & Mary, serge weaver, 8 yrs
		17 July	Baker, Thomas son of Thomas, barber surgeon of Gloucester Baker, Thomas, his father, & Mary, 7 yrs from 14 Apr.
3/452		28 Aug.	Field, Samuel son of Samuel, cordwainer of Gloucester Freeman, Robert & Frances, joiner, 7 yrs from 25 July
			Brooks, John son of William, farmer of Over Pace, John & Anne, cordwainer, 7 yrs from 4 Aug.
		29 Aug.	Hare, Edward son of Roger, farmer of Leominster, Herefs. Fletcher, William & Elizabeth, butcher, 7 yrs from 19 June
3/453		30 Aug.	Fryer, John son of John, mason, dec'd, of Arlingham Archer, Abraham & Mary, bricklayer, 7 yrs from 25 Mar.

	1704	1 Sept.	Humphris, William son of William, mercer of Cheltenham Humphris, William, his father, & Sarah 7 yrs from 25 July
			Ady, Ralph son of Ralph, cook of Painswick Graffstocke, John & Sarah, butcher, 7 yrs from 1 July
		25 Dec.	Shatford, James son of Thomas, innholder of Gloucester Harris, David & Katherine, chandler of Bewdley, Worcs., 7 yrs
3/454		16 Aug.	Greene, Robert son of [—], weaver of Gloucester Randle, William & Sarah, serge weaver, 7 yrs from 16 Feb.
		27 July	Hall, John son of Richard, farmer of Linton, Herefs. Ady, Edward & Elizabeth, baker, 7 yrs from 5 June
		4 Sept.	Stirt, Thomas son of Thomas, fishmonger of Gloucester Mathews, John jr, butcher, 7 yrs *16 Apr. 1707: turned over to Richard Mathews, butcher.* *Before Ald Rodway*
		27 Sept.	Turner, John son of Richard, labourer, dec'd, of Longhope Jones, Thomas & Jane, glover, 7 yrs

John Hyett, mayor 1704–5[1,2]

3/454	1704	7 Oct.	Emes, Thomas son of John, yeoman of Hampton, Worcs. Smith, James, cooper, 7 yrs from 25 Aug.
3/455			Mayoe, Guy son of William, yeoman of The Leigh Greene, John & Joan, cordwainer, 7 yrs from 29 Sept.
		10 Oct.	Rudhall, William son of Abraham, bellfounder of Gloucester Jones, Joseph & Frances, barber surgeon, 7 yrs
		11 Oct.	Whitfield, Andrew son of Andrew, innholder of Thornbury Bishopp, Anne, widow, 7 yrs from 1 Sept.
			Draper, Richard son of Thomas, yeoman of Huntley Drew, Thomas & Hannah, cordwainer, 7 yrs 29 Sept.
3/456		13 Oct.	Brimyard, Ralph son of William, pipemaker of Gloucester Mutlow, Anthony & Frances, tailor, 7 yrs from 1 Oct.
		13 Nov.	Jones, Thomas jr son of Thomas sr, glover of Gloucester Jones, Thomas, his father, & Jane, 7 yrs
			Jones, Thomas son of Denis, yeoman of Gloucester Carter, John & Susannah, cordwainer, 7 yrs
		15 Nov.	Ball, William son of William, barber of Ross-on-Wye Bossome, Thomas & Mary, barber surgeon, 7 yrs from 1 Aug.

---

[1] From this point on, mayoral dates are not given in the MS, and are here supplied editorially.

[2] 7 June 1705: To receive £4 of Mrs Sarah Browne's money: John Bicke, Samuel Ashmead, Griffantius Philipps, Thomas Jones, William Maverly. GBR B3/8 p. 167.

1 Aug. 1705: To receive £5 of Mr William Holliday's money: John Hornage, William Hale, Zachariah Stephens, Jacob Lumbard, [—] Grindall, Thomas Philipps. To receive £5 of Alderman Powell's money: Joseph Davis. GBR B3/8 p. 172.

26 Sept. 1705: To leave Sir Thomas Rich's hospital and receive £10: John Hickman, Nathaniel Nott, Thomas Andrews, Joseph Hale, Samuel Bishopp, Richard Hathway. GBR B3/8 p. 178.

3/457	1704	8 Dec.	Pritchard, Owen, of St Katherine's, Gloucester Swayne, Thomas, tiler & plasterer of St Mary de Lode parish, 7 yrs
		21 Dec.	Beckett, Richard son of James, yeoman of Cheltenham Gregory, John & Hester, mercer, 7 yrs
	1705	2 Jan.	Cooke, Robert son of Robert, cordwainer of Gloucester Collericke, Adam & [—], barber surgeon, 7 yrs from 8 Dec. 1704
			Hartland, John son of William, cordwainer of Over in Churcham Pace, John jr, cordwainer, 7 yrs from 17 Dec. 1704
3/458		5 Jan.	Dolloman, Thomas son of George, tanner of Gloucester Higgins, Ephraim & Anne, bricklayer, 7 yrs from 1 Jan.
		13 Jan.	Bonner, John son of Thomas, yeoman of Weston under Penyard, Herefs. Lane, John & Sarah, grocer, 7 yrs
		19 Jan.	Mason, Daniel son of Richard, labourer of Gloucester Pace, John jr & Anne, cordwainer, 7 yrs
		22 Jan.	Dyer, Moses son of John, wiredrawer of Gloucester Shingler, John & Sarah, pinmaker, 7 yrs from 1 Nov. 1704
3/459			Bragger, Nathaniel son of William, chandler, dec'd, of Ellesmere, Salop. Hone, John, tailor, 7 yrs *Crossed out by order of the mayor*
			Veysey, John son of Nathaniel, tailor of Gloucester Lea, Robert & Grace, cordwainer, 7 yrs from 2 Jan.
		1 Feb.	Woodward, Francis son of Thomas, horner of Upton upon Severn, Worcs. Bird, Daniel & Anne, horner, 7 yrs
		5 Mar.	Perry, William son of William, tailor, dec'd, of Gloucester Pruin, William & Margaret, tailor, 7 yrs from 21 Dec. 1704
		7 Mar.	Benson, William son of William, tiler & plasterer of Gloucester Benson, William, his father, & Mary, 7 yrs from 1 Nov. 1704
3/460		10 Mar.	Sermon, Joseph son of Samuel, yeoman of Cheltenham Wells, Richard & Mary, cordwainer, 7 yrs
		13 Mar.	Cooke, Florice son of Florice, gentleman, dec'd, of Eldersfield, Worcs. Sayer, James jr & Catherine, writing master, 7 yrs from 25 Dec.
			Bowler, Thomas son of Thomas, collarmaker of Gloucester Bowler, Thomas, his father, & Katherine, 7 yrs from 21 Dec. 1704
		14 Mar.	Millard, Samuel son of Robert, yeoman, dec'd, of Gloucester Price, John & Elizabeth, gardener, 7 yrs from 15 Feb.
3/461		15 Mar.	Edwards, Anthony son of John, gentleman of Bentham Edwards, Thomas, gentleman, 7 yrs from 21 Dec. 1704
		16 Mar.	Man, John son of James, glover & hosier of Gloucester Man, James, his father, & Mary, 7 yrs
		7 Mar.	Draper, Thomas son of Thomas, blacksmith of Huntley Draper, Henry & Anne, blacksmith, 7 yrs from 1 Nov. 1704
		16 Mar.	Jones, Nathaniel son of Walter, tiler & plasterer of Gloucester Braddis, Edward, bricklayer, 7 yrs from 25 Dec. 1704
3/462		19 Mar.	Pinnocke, Thomas son of John, glassmaker of Gloucester Aram, Arnold & Elizabeth, gentleman, 7 yrs from 1 Jan.

	1705	7 Apr.	Window, Richard son of John, yeoman, dec'd, of Haresfield Niblett, Daniel & Deborah, baker, 7 yrs from 25 Dec.
		8 Apr.	Woodward, John son of Richard, pinmaker of Gloucester Woodward, Richard, his father, & Sarah, 7 yrs
		20 Apr.	Birt, Peter son of Peter, gentleman of Wallingford, Berks. Barker, John & Anne, barber surgeon, 7 yrs from 25 Mar.
3/463		9 May	Herring, William son of John, yeoman, dec'd, of Apperley Pegler, Joseph & Jane, tanner, 7 yrs from 25 Mar.
		12 May	Skey, Richard son of William, yeoman of Great Washbourne Humphris, Edward & Elizabeth, currier, 7 yrs from 22 Mar.
		21 May	Gazard, Richard son of Richard, feltmaker, dec'd, of Gloucester Jones, John, combmaker, 7 yrs
		31 May	Banister, George son of Peter, yeoman of Down Hatherley Atkins, Benjamin & Elizabeth, shipwright, 7 yrs from 31 May
3/464		11 June	Kirby, Jacob son of William, weaver of Gloucester Summers, Thomas & Elizabeth, silkweaver, 7 yrs from 1 Mar.
		12 June	Perks, William son of William, pinmaker, dec'd, of Barton Street, Gloucester Shipton, Cowcher & Martha, pinmaker, 7 yrs from 11 June
		18 June	Jefferyes, Samuel son of Henry, joiner of Gloucester Jefferyes, Henry, his father, & Mary, 7 yrs from 14 Nov. 1704
		21 June	Wheeler, Wintour son of Edward, gentleman of Droitwich, Worcs. Webb, Thomas, esquire, & Anne, alderman, 7 yrs from 1 June
3/465		5 July	Bicke, John son of William, tiler & plasterer of Gloucester Bicke, William, his father, & Sarah, 7 yrs
			Hopkins, John son of Edward, weaver, dec'd, of Taynton Rickards, Samuel & Hannah, carpenter, 8 yrs from 9 Apr.
		10 July	Welladvise, Samuel son of William, feltmaker, dec'd, of Gloucester Browne, Samuel & Hester, glazier, 7 yrs
		27 June	Wood, Richard son of John, yeoman of Gloucester Best, John, tailor, 7 yrs from 24 June
3/466		30 July	Cooke, William son of William, tailor of Gloucester Rush, John & Catherine, barber surgeon, 7 yrs from 24 June
			Ady, George son of Ralph, cook of Painswick Cox, Thomas & Mary, baker, 7 yrs
		7 Aug.	Symonds, Thomas son of Thomas, labourer of Gloucester Wooding, William & Margaret, buttonmaker, 7 yrs
			Maverly, William son of James, buttonmaker of Gloucester Hone, John, tailor, 7 yrs
3/467		9 Aug.	Monnington, John son of Thomas, woolcomber of Gloucester Humphris, Edward & Elizabeth, currier, 7 yrs from 17 June
		21 Aug.	Hornage, John son of John, pinmaker of Gloucester Hornage, John, his father, & Elizabeth, 7 yrs
		22 Aug.	Tench, Stephen son of Stephen, silkweaver of Tewkesbury Tench, Stephen, his father, burgess of Gloucester, & Hester, 7 yrs

	1705	6 Sept.	Long, Robert son of John, buttonmaker of Gloucester Sparks, Richard & Ellen, ropemaker, 7 yrs from 29 Sept.
3/468			Bradgate, Matthew son of William, buttonmaker of Gloucester Cox, John, barber surgeon, 7 yrs from 29 Sept.
		27 Aug.	Knowles, James son of James, pinmaker of Gloucester Howell, Joseph & Elizabeth, blacksmith, 7 yrs
		7 Sept.	Lisle, William son of William, grocer of Bristol Allen, William, grocer, 7 yrs from 4 Apr.
		21 Sept.	Hellyard, John son of John, butcher, dec'd, of Poulton, Wilts. [*now* Glos.] Savory, Robert & Mary, farrier, 7 yrs

3/469			Sharp, John son of John, labourer, dec'd, of Lower Southgate
			    Street, Gloucester
			    Holder, Joseph & Mary, barber surgeon, 7 yrs from 6 Aug.

			Philipps, Griffith son of Samuel, silkweaver, dec'd, of Gloucester Watts, Robert & Mary, tailor, 7 yrs
			Jeffes, John son of William, sawyer, dec'd, of Barton Street, Gloucester Weaver, Richard & Mary, blacksmith, 7 yrs from 25 Mar.
			Gold, William son of John, fishmonger, dec'd, of Chipping Campden Tyler, Eleanor, widow, 7 yrs from 25 Dec.
3/470		1 Sept.	Brotherton, Samuel son of Jeremiah, cordwainer, dec'd, of Gloucester Archer, Abraham & Mary, bricklayer, 7 yrs

Samuel Lye, mayor 1705–6[1]

3/470	1705	3 Oct.	Rooke, Thomas son of William, yeoman, dec'd, of Charlton Kings Collett, John & Mary, joiner, 7 yrs from 17 Sept.
		10 Oct.	Pegler, Joseph son of Joseph, tanner of Gloucester Pegler, Joseph, his father, & Jane, 7 yrs from 20 Mar.
		11 Oct.	Ashmead, Samuel son of Francis, saddletreemaker late of Gloucester Wilmott, Robert, saddler, 7 yrs from 29 Sept.
3/471		12 Oct.	Grindall, John son of John, feltmaker of Gloucester Carter, John & Susannah, cordwainer, 7 yrs from 29 Sept.
		16 Oct.	Dunn, William son of William, innholder, dec'd, of Gloucester Cowles, Thomas & Anne, tiler & plasterer, 7 yrs from 29 Sept.
		27 Oct.	Stephens, Zachariah son of Robert, innholder, dec'd, of Gloucester Church, Roger & Sarah, tailor, 7 yrs from 1 Sept.
		29 Oct.	Newton, Thomas son of Thomas, innholder of Newent Sayer, Daniel & Mary, ropemaker, 7 yrs from 17 Sept.
3/472		30 Oct.	Wood, John son of William, cordwainer of Newent Reeves, John & Sarah, blacksmith, 7 yrs from 25 Mar.

[1] 23 May 1706: To receive £4 of Mrs Sarah Browne's money: William Wattes, John Spiller, Thomas Greene, Thomas Mills. GBR B3/8 p. 191.

6 Aug. 1706: To receive £5 of Mr William Holliday's money: William Webley, Francis Lye, Joseph Brimyard, William Pace, John Birch, John Mason. To receive £5 of Alderman Powell's money: John Ward. To leave Sir Thomas Rich's hospital and receive £10: Thomas Browne, Thomas Lea, Joseph Winniatt, Samuel Bradley, Thomas Pembruge, Daniel Colericke. GBR B3/8 pp. 202, 206.

	1705	31 Oct.	Harris, Thomas son of Joseph, baker of Gloucester Harris, Richard & Hester, barber surgeon, 7 yrs
		3 Nov.	Jarrett, Thomas son of Thomas, cordwainer of Tewkesbury Wiggett, Samuel & Alice, glover, 7 yrs from 5 Nov.
		6 Nov.	Bishopp, Thomas son of John, silkweaver of Gloucester Gregory, John & Elizabeth, barber surgeon, 7 yrs from 1 Nov.
3/473		9 Nov.	Bennett, Thomas son of Richard, yeoman of Barton Street, Gloucester Ady, Thomas & Margery, gentleman, 7 yrs from 29 Sept.
		14 Nov.	Russell, Robert son of Thomas, silkweaver of Gloucester Drinkwater, Richard & Mary, pinmaker, 7 yrs from 24 June
		29 Oct.	Jones, Thomas son of Thomas, tanner of Gloucester Higgins, Ephraim & Anne, bricklayer, 7 yrs from 29 Sept.
		15 Nov.	Archer, John son of John, buttonmaker, dec'd, of Gloucester Archer, Abraham & Mary, bricklayer, 7 yrs from 29 Sept.
3/474		19 Nov.	Price, Charles son of Richard jr, gardener of Gloucester Baker, Edward & Elizabeth, wiredrawer, 7 yrs
		20 Nov.	Williams, William son of Thomas, gardener, dec'd, of Gloucester Swayne, Thomas & Joyce, tiler & plasterer, 7 yrs from 29 Sept.
		25 Nov.	Philipps, Thomas son of Thomas, tailor of Gloucester Stephens, Thomas & Elizabeth, pinmaker, 7 yrs
		10 Dec.	Williams, Anthony son of Anthony, barber surgeon of Gloucester Williams, Anthony, his father, & Mary, 7 yrs
3/475		29 Dec.	Myles, William son of Armell, miller of Boddington Ady, Edward & Elizabeth, baker, 7 yrs from 24 Dec.
	1706	3 Jan.	Lander, John son of James, maltster of Gloucester Lander, William & Hester, grocer, 7 yrs from 25 Mar. 1705
			Keyse, William son of Patrick, tailor, dec'd, of Gloucester Sysemore, William, barber surgeon, 7 yrs from 1 Sept. 1705
		4 Jan.	Davis, Joseph son of Joseph, cordwainer of Gloucester Davis, Joseph, his father, & Mary, 7 yrs
3/476		8 Jan.	King, Samuel son of Giles, woolcomber of Gloucester Benson, John jr & Joan, plasterer, 7 yrs from 1 Sept. 1705
		15 Jan.	Sparrow, William son of Thomas, yeoman of Evington, The Leigh Bryan, Daniel & Anne, cordwainer, 7 yrs from 2 Feb.
		19 Jan.	Witcombe, Thomas son of Samuel, serge weaver of Gloucester Witcombe, Samuel & Elizabeth, serge weaver, 7 yrs from 2 Jan.
		21 Jan.	Church, Richard son of Richard, tailor, dec'd, of Sandhurst Mutlow, James & Margaret, glover, 7 yrs
3/477		25 Feb.	Whittingham, Thomas son of Edward, baker of Westbury-on-Severn Whittingham, Edward, his father, & Abigail, 7 yrs from 1 Nov. 1705
			Perry, William son of Thomas, innholder, dec'd, of Gloucester Cowles, John, tailor, 7 yrs from 2 Feb.
			Lewis, George son of George, silkweaver of Gloucester Holder, John & Sarah, pinmaker, 7 yrs from 1 Feb.
		26 Feb.	Shatford, William son of Thomas, weaver of Gloucester Jones, Thomas & Jane, glover, 7 yrs from 9 Feb.

3/478	1706	5 Mar.	Hale, William son of William, pinmaker of Gloucester Hone, John, tailor, 7 yrs from 2 Feb.
		11 Mar.	Deane, Thomas son of William, labourer of Barton Street, Gloucester Cripps, Edward & Deborah, butcher, 7 yrs from 25 Mar.
		13 Mar.	Davis, John son of John, yeoman, dec'd, of Westbury-on-Severn Halford, John & Margaret, cordwainer, 7 yrs from 1 Oct. 1705
		27 Mar.	Wheeler, William son of John, yeoman, dec'd, of Walford, Herefs. Higgins, Ephraim & Anne, bricklayer, 7 yrs from 2 Feb.
3/479		30 Mar.	Fisher, Thomas son of Richard, yeoman, dec'd, of Hardwicke Brymyard, Henry & Sarah, cordwainer, 7 yrs
		22 Mar.	A'Deane, Lewis son of Thomas, of Guiting Hendy, Samuel & Sarah, mercer, 7 yrs
		8 Apr.	Webb, John son of Macklin, yeoman of Malvern, Worcs. Powell, Samuel, baker, 7 yrs from 21 Dec. 1705
		11 Apr.	Perkins, Samuel son of Samuel, cordwainer, dec'd, of Gloucester Benson, John jr & Joan, tiler & plasterer, 7 yrs from 1 Mar.
3/480		12 Apr.	Parks, William son of William, yeoman of Lee, Salop Engly, John & Alice, bricklayer, 7 yrs from 8 Feb.
		15 Apr.	Cowcher, Thomas son of Thomas, woolcomber of Gloucester Elliott, Thomas, cordwainer, 7 yrs from 29 Feb.
		17 Apr.	Pawling, Samuel son of John, clothier of Painswick Pawling, Daniel & Mary, baker, 7 yrs from 1 Jan.
		22 Apr.	Baker, James son of James, butcher of Gloucester Sparrowhawke, William, cordwainer, 7 yrs from 1 Apr.
3/481		23 Apr.	Lewis, Richard son of Thomas, gentleman, dec'd, of Gloucester Lewis, Bridget, widow, 7 yrs from 1 May
			Punter, Joseph son of Robert, mercer of Gloucester Punter, Robert, his father, & Mary, 7 yrs
		2 May	Watts, William son of William, cordwainer, dec'd, of Gloucester Savory, Robert & Mary, farrier, 7 yrs
		11 May	Preece, John son of Henry, yeoman, dec'd, of Upton Bishop, Herefs. Heaven, John & Deborah, barber surgeon, 7 yrs from 1 Apr.
3/482		13 May	Lewis, Philip son of Philip, yeoman of Ross-on-Wye, Herefs. Ravener, George & Elizabeth, butcher, 7 yrs from 13 May
		17 May	Hill, George son of John, gentleman of Painswick Skynner, Thomas & Sarah, baker, 7 yrs from 25 Mar.
		18 May	Blake, Giles son of Thomas, yeoman of Up Hatherley Nurse, John & Mary, blacksmith, 7 yrs from 2 Apr.
		25 May	Jones, Thomas son of William, yeoman of Hope Mansell, Herefs. Voyce, Jonathan, glover, 7 yrs from 6 May
3/483		27 May	Pool, John son of John, plasterer of Gloucester Pace, John & Anne, cordwainer, 7 yrs from 25 Mar.
		28 May	Puxon, William son of William, silkweaver of Gloucester Cooke, Thomas & Susannah, tailor, 7 yrs from date of indenture

	1706	18 Apr.	Watts, Robert son of Robert, tailor of Gloucester Watts, Robert, his father, & Mary, 7 yrs from 1 Nov.
		1 June	Fido, Richard son of James, combmaker of Tenbury, Worcs. Green, William, clothworker, 7 yrs
3/484		14 June	Harris, Walter son of Edward, yeoman of Walford, Herefs. Hardwicke, Nathaniel & Esther, baker, 7 yrs
		17 June	Williams, John son of Thomas, gardener, dec'd, of Gloucester Darke, Richard & Mary, gunsmith, 7 yrs from 23 Apr.
		19 June	Nurse, John son of John, innholder of Gloucester Bosom, Thomas & Mary, barber surgeon, 7 yrs from 25 Dec. 1705
		19 Aug.	Skynner, Stephen son of William, [—] of Ledbury, Herefs. Beard, Richard, of Dymock, burgess of Gloucester, [—], 7 yrs
3/485		24 Aug.	Bradford, John son of John, gentleman, dec'd, of Newent Payne, Capel & Catherine, gentleman & alderman, 7 yrs
		30 Aug.	Peynard, Thomas son of John, woollen draper of Hereford Lane, Nicholas jr & Hester, gentleman, 7 yrs from 22 June
		16 Sept.	Pullen, Thomas son of Richard, woolcomber of Gloucester Jennings, Margaret, widow, 7 yrs
			Mills, Thomas son of Richard, silkweaver of Gloucester Ricketts, John & Bridget, pinmaker, 7 yrs
3/486		19 Sept.	Webley, William son of Joseph, tailor of Gloucester Webley, Joseph, his father, & Anne, 7 yrs
		4 Sept.	Little, John son of William, labourer, dec'd, of Gloucester Singleton, John & Sarah, pinmaker, 7 yrs
		23 Sept.	Pace, William son of William, tailor, dec'd, of Gloucester Shipton, Cowcher & Martha, pinmaker, 7 yrs from 29 Sept.
			Merry, Thomas son of John, baker, dec'd, of Gloucester Tyler, John & Anne, cordwainer, 7 yrs from 24 June
3/487		26 Sept.	Heath, Samuel son of Samuel, silkweaver of Gloucester Lucas, Samuel & Elizabeth, joiner, 7 yrs
		28 Sept.	Kingman, John son of John, wiredrawer of Gloucester Kingman, John & Anne, wiredrawer, 7 yrs from 25 Mar.

John Bell, mayor 1706–7[1]

3/487	1706	12 Oct.	Greene, Thomas son of Robert, weaver of Gloucester Stephens, Thomas & Elizabeth, pinmaker, 7 yrs
		21 Oct.	Andrews, William son of William, saddler of Gloucester Randle, Daniel & Alice, tailor, 7 yrs

[1] 13 May 1707: To receive £4 of Mrs Sarah Browne's money: Abraham Hale, Samuel Cane, Joseph Horwood, [–] Kirby. GBR B3/8 p. 228.

11 July 1707: To receive £5 of Alderman Powell's money: John son of Richard Ingly. To receive £5 of Mr William Holliday's money: William Hornage, Thomas Harding, John Wells, John Reband, William Weaver, James Wintle. GBR B3/8 p. 236.

9 Sept. 1707: To leave Sir Thomas Rich's hospital and receive £10: Richard Swayne, Thomas Wells, John Merrett, Jacob Medway, Richard Holton, Edward Butter. GBR B3/8 p. 242.

3/488	1706	27 Oct.	Hickman, John son of John, tailor, dec'd, of Gloucester Wells, Richard & Mary, cordwainer, 7 yrs from 29 Sept.

		25 Oct.	Bennett, Edward son of Edward, gentleman, of Shelwick Court,
			    Holmer, Herefs.
			    Matthews, Thomas, apothecary, 7 yrs from 27 Sept.

		27 Oct.	Mason, John son of Richard, bricklayer of Gloucester Ingly, John & Alice, bricklayer, 7 yrs from 2 Sept.

		30 Oct.	Mason, John son of William, tanner of Gloucester
			    Mason, William jr & Elizabeth, tailor, 7 yrs from 1 Oct.
			    He served but about 3 years & was apprenticed to a shoemaker
			    in London

		8 Nov.	Ward, John son of John, yeoman of Gloucester
			    Atkins, Walter & Mary, cordwainer, 7 yrs
			    Town clerk gave his fees

3/489		12 Nov.	Mitchell, Joseph son of Israel, collarmaker of Gloucester Benson, John & Mary, plasterer, 7 yrs from 25 Mar.
		11 Dec.	Spiller, John son of James, haulier of Gloucester Wadley, John, baker, 7 yrs from 7 Dec.
		26 Dec.	Fletcher, Edward son of Robert, yeoman of Postlip Barker, John & Anne, barber surgeon, 7 yrs from 15 Oct.
		[—]	Lye, Francis son of Henry, brewer, dec'd, of Gloucester Spencer, Thomas & Beata, cooper, 7 yrs from 23 Dec.
3/490		23 Dec.	Hopley, Titus son of Thomas, labourer of Gloucester Baker, Richard & Anne, haulier, 7 yrs from 1 Dec.
			Ward, John son of John, wheelwright of Barton Street, Gloucester Pitt, Roger, carpenter, 7 yrs from 29 Sept.
			Darke, Isaac son of Richard, gentleman, dec'd, of Alstone Lane, Richard & Anne, grocer, 7 yrs from 16 Oct.
		30 Dec.	Webb, Giles son of Giles, collarmaker of Cheltenham Vernon, Henry, apothecary, 7 yrs from 25 Dec.

3/491	1707	2 Jan.	Nest, William son of William, carpenter of Gloucester
			    Hooke, Jonathan & Rebecca, joiner, 7 yrs
			    8 Apr. 1709: These indentures were cancelled, the boy being but
			    seven years old

		6 Jan.	Hobbs, Richard son of Thomas, haulier of Gloucester Ravener, George, butcher, 7 yrs
			Brimyard, Joseph son of William, pipemaker of Gloucester Harrison, Thomas & Elizabeth, feltmaker, 7 yrs from 15 Nov. 1706
		11 Jan.	Pruin, William son of William, labourer, dec'd, of Newent Bower, Thomas & Mary, tanner, 7 yrs

3/492		24 Jan.	Moore, Humphrey son of Thomas, mason of Stratford upon Avon,
			    Warws.
			    Engly, Henry & Sarah, bricklayer, 7 yrs from 29 Sept. 1706

		1 Feb.	Badger *alias* Bale, Nathaniel son of Nathaniel, yeoman of Barnwood Swayne, Thomas & Rejoyce, tiler & plasterer, 7 yrs from 1 Jan.
		4 Mar.	Bishopp, Samuel son of Daniel, barber surgeon, dec'd, of Gloucester Hayward, Samuel & Hannah, barber surgeon, 7 yrs from 1 Feb.

	1707 4 Mar.	Birch, John son of Thomas, feltmaker, dec'd, of Gloucester Beale, John & Dinah, cordwainer, 7 yrs from 20 Feb.
3/493	15 Mar.	Wilks, John son of John, yeoman, dec'd, of Eckington, Worcs. Ravener, Joseph & Mary, serge weaver, 7 yrs from 1 Apr.
	11 Jan.	Hawker, Samuel son of Edward, labourer late of The Leigh Benson, William & Mary, plasterer, 7 yrs
	29 Mar.	Skey, Thomas son of William, yeoman of Great Washbourne Fletcher, Thomas & Sarah, baker, 7 yrs from 14 Feb.
	17 Apr.	Browne, Thomas son of Thomas, cordwainer of Gloucester Browne, Thomas, his father, & Alice, 7 yrs from 1 May
3/494	23 Apr.	Gardner, Nathaniel son of Nathaniel, cordwainer late of Minchinhampton Skillerne, William & Anne, tailor, 7 yrs
	6 May	Cull, Richard son of Stephen, wheelwright of Barton Street, Gloucester Conklin, Thomas & Susannah, writing master, 7 yrs
	17 May	Smith, Charles son of Charles, yeoman of Huntley Pace, Francis & Susannah, cordwainer of Newent, 7 yrs
	19 May	Bullocke, John son of Thomas, yeoman of Hartpury Bryan, Daniel & Anne, cordwainer, 7 yrs
3/495	21 May	Howlett, William son of William, gentleman of Winchcombe Harris, John & Elizabeth, mercer, 7 yrs from 16 May
	22 May	Parrott, Thomas son of John, innholder of Tewkesbury Randle, William & Elizabeth, barber surgeon, 7 yrs from 1 May *Thomas Parrott left his service by departing from his master at Michaelmas 1710, therefore he will have no right to his freedom*
	22 May	Martin, David son of John, yeoman, dec'd, of Down Hatherley Greene, Joan, cordwainer [*deleted*] widow, 7 yrs from 5 May
	27 May	Pytt, Joseph son of Joseph, feltmaker of Gloucester Kent, Samuel & Jane, joiner, 7 yrs
3/496	4 June	Arcoll, John son of John, cooper of Cheltenham Cheesman, Paul & Anne, joiner, 7 yrs
	13 June	Wadley, William son of John, gentleman of Tewkesbury Jordan, William & Elizabeth, apothecary, 7 yrs from 1 May
	16 June	Billings, William son of Richard, sievemaker of the Magdalens, Gloucester Charles, John & Mary, cordwainer, 7 yrs from date of indenture
	1 July	Ferreby, John son of John, tailor of Uley Ferreby, John, his father, & Sarah, 7 yrs from 25 Mar.
3/497	17 June	Rolfe, John son of John, yeoman, dec'd, of Gloucester Jennings, Jeremiah & Anne, tailor, 7 yrs [*deleted*] 9 yrs from 1 May
	19 June	Hale, Abraham son of John, yeoman of Gloucester Evenis, William & Mary, cordwainer, 7 yrs
	24 June	Young, Richard son of Joseph, yeoman of Westbury-on-Severn Rowles, Robert & Elizabeth, butcher of Minsterworth, 7 yrs from 10 May
	1 July	Banister, William son of Willoughby, gentleman of Starton *alias* Staverton Gammond, John & Sarah, baker, 7 yrs from 11 June

3/498	1707	4 July	Mills, William son of Thomas, yeoman of Hope Mansell, Herefs. Voyce, Jonathan jr, glover, 7 yrs from 14 June
		9 July	Kane, John son of John, innholder, dec'd, of Gloucester Wyman, John & Anne, cordwainer, 7 yrs from 25 June
			Kane, Samuel son of John, innholder, dec'd, of Gloucester Young, Walter & Margaret, cordwainer, 7 yrs from 24 June
		17 July	Engly, John son of Richard, bricklayer of Gloucester Jones, Nathaniel & Alice, tailor, 7 yrs
3/499		4 Aug.	Hobbs, Thomas son of Thomas, haulier of Gloucester Nest, John & Barbara, carpenter, 7 yrs from 1 July
		15 Aug.	Hornage, William son of William, cordwainer of Gloucester Hornage, William, his father, & Anne, 7 yrs from 1 Aug.
		12 Aug.	Niccolls, John son of Henry, maltster of Gloucester Niccolls, John, his father, & Hester, 7 yrs
		13 Aug.	Rathband, John son of Richard, pipemaker of Gloucester Russell, Thomas & Joan, farrier, 7 yrs
3/500		21 Aug.	Harding, Thomas son of John, pinmaker of Gloucester Davis, Henry & Mary, pinmaker, 7 yrs from 11 Aug.
		27 Aug.	Baylis, Joseph son of William, yeoman of Eldersfield, Worcs. Man, John & Mary, glover, 7 yrs
		28 Aug.	Bradley, Samuel son of John, grocer of Gloucester Bowler, George & Mary, tailor, 7 yrs from 10 Aug.
		4 July	Wintle, John son of John, yeoman of Blaisdon Hooper, John, of Hartpury, burgess of Gloucester, cordwainer, 7 yrs from 29 June
3/501		11 Sept.	Kemmis, John son of John, woolcomber of Gloucester Puckeridge, Thomas, tailor, 7 yrs
		18 Sept.	Weaver, William son of Richard, butcher of Gloucester Weaver, Richard, his father, & Anne, 7 yrs
		2 Oct.	Curtis, Richard son of William, innholder of Winchcombe Hayes, Henry & Alice, tailor, 7 yrs from 1 Sept.
		3 Oct.	Phipps, Richard son of William, farmer of Barton Street, Gloucester Steel, Francis, maltster, 7 yrs from 24 June
3/502		4 Oct.	Wells, John son of Richard, cordwainer of Gloucester Wells, Richard, his father, & Mary, 7 yrs from 29 Sept. 1706
		6 Oct.	Cooke, John son of Charles, butcher of Gloucester Cooke, Charles, his father, & Joan, 7 yrs from 29 June

---

[1] 13 July 1708: To receive £4 of Mrs Sarah Browne's money: Edward Armitage, William Winniatt, Robert Bicke, [—] Marshfield. GBR B3/8 p. 278.

12 Aug. 1708: To receive £5 of Mr William Holliday's money: John Jones, Abraham Archer, Thomas Nest, John Hornage, James Freeman, George Ireland. To receive £5 of Alderman Powell's money: Stephen Reeve. GBR B3/8 p. 281.

14 Sept. 1708: To leave Sir Thomas Rich's hospital and receive £10: Samuel Horsington, Joseph Freeman, Henry Browne, William Freame, John Aylway, Anthony Mutlow. GBR B3/8 p. 287.

Caple Payne, mayor 1707–8[1]

3/502	1707	7 Oct.	Jennings, Edward son of Thomas, gardener of Kingsholm, Gloucester Best, Thomas & Elizabeth, gardener, 7 yrs
		7 Nov.	King, John son of Giles, woolcomber of Gloucester Engly, Richard, bricklayer, 7 yrs from 29 Sept.
3/503		18 Oct.	Millard, William son of Robert, yeoman of Gloucester Price, Henry & Elizabeth, gardener, 7 yrs

		31 Oct.	Clayton, Henry son of Lawrence, yeoman of Dumbleton
			    Wiltshire, John & Mary, tailor, 7 yrs from 18 Oct.
			    [*Marginal note: nil received*]

		29 Sept.	Davis, Richard son of Richard, yeoman, dec'd, of Brockworth Nest, William, carpenter, 7 yrs from 29 Sept.
		3 Nov.	Harris, William son of Richard, labourer, dec'd, of Littleworth Stephens, Thomas & Elizabeth, pinmaker, 7 yrs
3/504		5 Nov.	Halling, William son of William, bricklayer, dec'd, of Gloucester Engly, Thomas & Mary, butcher, 7 yrs from 24 June
		6 Nov.	Arnold, Charles son of William of Gloucester Swayne, Thomas & Rejoice, tiler & plasterer, 7 yrs from 29 Sept.
		10 Nov.	Horwood, Joseph son of Joseph, bricklayer of Gloucester Barton, John & Elizabeth, bricklayer, 7 yrs from 29 Sept.
			Window, Richard son of Christopher, farmer of Churcham Hayes, William & Sarah, cordwainer, 7 yrs from 1 Oct.
3/505		11 Nov.	Caldwell, James son of John, yeoman, dec'd, of Churcham Carter, John & Susannah, cordwainer, 7 yrs
		17 Nov.	Jelfe, John son of Elizabeth of Littleworth Engly, Richard & Alice, bricklayer, 7 yrs
			Milton, William son of Richard, maltster, dec'd, of Cheltenham Hopkins, Theophilus & Susannah, joiner, 7 yrs from 4 Nov.
		22 Nov.	Davis, Robert son of John, yeoman of Cam Bound, Thomas & Rachel, grocer, 7 yrs from 8 Nov.
3/506		3 Dec.	Greene, William son of John, yeoman of Churcham Drew, Thomas & Hannah, cordwainer, 7 yrs from 29 Sept.
	1708	5 Jan.	Owen, Francis son of Francis, clerk, dec'd, of Cheltenham Aram, Arnold & Elizabeth, gentleman, 7 yrs from 1 Oct. 1707
		2 Feb.	Gunter, James son of James, innholder of Gloucester Lucas, Samuel & Elizabeth, joiner, 7 yrs
		4 Feb.	Swayne, Richard son of Richard, collarmaker of Gloucester Swayne, Richard, his father, & Katherine, 7 yrs from 1 Feb.
3/507		9 Feb.	Merrett, John son of Thomas, clerk of Gloucester Cleevly, Henry & Jane, tailor, 7 yrs
		16 Feb.	Cooke, William son of William, dec'd, of Cheltenham Niccolls, Thomas & Elizabeth, plumber, 7 yrs
		23 Feb.	Keylocke, Jasper son of Thomas, joiner, dec'd, of Newent Holford, John & Margaret, cordwainer, 7 yrs

	1708	1 Mar.	Holton, Richard son of Richard, weaver of Gloucester Holton, Richard, his father, & Elizabeth, 7 yrs from 1 Jan.
3/508		3 Mar.	Nott, Nathaniel son of Nathaniel, glazier of Gloucester Nest, William, carpenter, 7 yrs from 10 Oct. 1707
		4 Mar.	Applegath, Roger son of John, gentleman, dec'd, of Dowdeswell Longden, Thomas, mercer, 7 yrs
		15 Mar.	Deane, William son of William, farmer of Gloucester Nest, John & Barbara, carpenter, 7 yrs
		17 Mar.	Trotman, William son of Daniel, yeoman, dec'd, of Quedgeley Jennings, Jeremiah & Anne, tailor, 7 yrs
3/509		9 Apr.	Eldridge, Thomas son of John, yeoman, dec'd, of Ashleworth Cowles, John, butcher, 7 yrs from 6 Feb.
		12 Apr.	Medway, James son of Abraham, bricklayer, dec'd, of Gloucester Mann, James & Mary, glover, 7 yrs from 25 Mar.
		19 Apr.	Little, Adam son of Mark, carpenter, dec'd, of Highnam Pace, John sr & Anne, cordwainer, 7 yrs from 25 Mar.
		7 May	Perryn, Richard son of Nathaniel, woolcomber of Gloucester Hayward, Edward, weaver, 7 yrs from 1 May
3/510		4 June	Tompkins, Job son of Thomas, cordwainer, dec'd, of Churcham Drinkwater, Richard, cordwainer, 7 yrs
		7 June	Cooke, William son of William, yeoman of Newent Robins, James jr, currier, 7 yrs from 25 Mar.
		8 June	Mutlow, John son of John, gentleman of Winchcombe Bell, John, alderman, 7 yrs from 9 Apr.
		28 May	Trinder, Thomas son of John, baker of Ashton Keynes, Wilts. Oatley, Francis & Sarah, feltmaker, 7 yrs
3/511		14 June	Vickeridge, Richard son of Richard, labourer of Wichenford, Worcs. Bird, Daniel & Anne, horn turner, 7 yrs
		28 June	Okey, Benjamin son of John, yeoman of Churchdown Church, Roger & Sarah, tailor, 7 yrs from 24 June
		21 July	Mashfield, Thomas son of James, fisherman of Gloucester Grigg, Edward & Sarah, basketmaker, 7 yrs
		23 July	Roberts, Thomas son of Nicholas, brazier, dec'd, of Wood Stanley Reeve, John & Sarah, gunsmith, 7 yrs from 26 July
3/512			Dower, Richard son of Richard, farmer of Minsterworth Hayes, William & Sarah, cordwainer, 7 yrs from 12 May *7 Apr. 1712: Richard Dower, by his master's consent, turned over to serve the residue of his term with Hannah Drew, widow*
		2 Aug.	Ball, Richard son of Richard, cordwainer of Ross-on-Wye, Herefs. Brabant, Francis jr & Margaret, cooper, 7 yrs
		27 Aug.	Reeve, Stephen son of Stephen, mason of Gloucester Reeve, Stephen, his father, & Anne, 7 yrs from 1 Aug.
			Humphryes, John son of Richard, cordwainer, dec'd, of Lower Guiting Heard, Humphrey & Jane, butcher, 7 yrs from 1 May

	1708	30 Aug.	Jones, John son of Charles, cooper of Gloucester Jones, Charles, his father, & Anne, [7 *deleted*] 10 yrs
3/513		3 Sept.	Nest, Thomas son of John, carpenter of Gloucester Nest, John, his father, & Barbara, carpenter, 7 yrs
		6 Sept.	Archer, Abraham son of Abraham, bricklayer of Gloucester Archer, Abraham, his father, & Mary, 7 yrs
		13 Dec.	Winniat, William son of Richard, pinmaker of Gloucester Feilder, George & Sarah, farrier, [7 *deleted*] 8 yrs
		24 Sept.	Barker, Thomas son of Thomas, gentleman of Worcester Webb, Thomas esquire, & Anne, alderman, 7 yrs from 24 May
			Smart, Giles son of Giles, miller, dec'd, of Barton Street, Gloucester Carill, Thomas & Mary, hosier, 7 yrs from 25 Mar.
3/514		1 Oct.	Freeman, James son of Tobias, tailor of Gloucester Hayes, Henry & Alice, tailor, 7 yrs from 1 Sept.
			Armitage, Edward son of Edward, cordwainer of Gloucester Mutloe, Anthony & Frances, 7 yrs from 1 Sept.

Giles Rodway, mayor 1708–9[1]

3/514	1708	8 Oct.	Phelps, John son of William, farmer, dec'd, of Minsterworth Corr, Henry & Elizabeth, tailor, 7 yrs from 29 Sept.
		1 Nov.	Bick, Robert son of William, salter of Gloucester Rawlings, William & Frances, joiner, 7 yrs from 29 Sept.
3/515		15 Nov.	Worrall, Samuel son of Joshua, mercer of Gloucester Worrall, Joshua, his father, & Elizabeth, 7 yrs
			Butt, Samuel son of John, dyer of Evesham, Worcs. Sparrowhawke, William, cordwainer, 7 yrs
	1709	7 Jan.	Mills, John son of Thomas, plasterer of Gloucester [—] Mills, his brother, plasterer, 7 yrs from 29 Sept.
			Elliott, Edward son of Edward, yeoman of Barton Street, Gloucester Freeman, Robert & Frances, joiner, 7 yrs from 1 Jan.
		17 Jan.	Etheridge, Samuel son of Robert, farmer of Badgeworth Smith, James & Sarah, cooper, 7 yrs from 7 Nov. 1708
3/516		10 Feb.	Arnold, Michael son of William, carpenter of Gloucester Haynes, Edward & Mary, pinmaker, 7 yrs from 10 Jan.
		18 Feb.	Cole, Joseph son of John, innholder of Gloucester Hale, John, barber, 7 yrs
		24 Dec.	Carter, John son of William, yeoman, dec'd, of Hartpury Weale, Thomas & Margery, baker, 7 yrs from 21 Dec.

---

[1] 16 May 1709: To receive £4 of Mrs Sarah Browne's money: John Layton's son, John Halling, Charles Philipps. GBR B3/8 p. 305.

16 Dec. 1709: To receive £5 of Mr William Holliday's money: Anthony Workman, Thomas Burridge, Samuel Spencer, John Randle, John Price, Thomas Ellis. To leave Sir Thomas Rich's hospital and receive £10: Edward Church, John Hayward, John Jeffryes, John Beard, John Clifford, William Browne. GBR B3/8 p. 336.

	1709	11 Mar.	Farmer, Samuel son of Samuel, apothecary of Gloucester Farmer, Samuel, his father, & Anne, 7 yrs

1709   11 Mar.   Farmer, Samuel son of Samuel, apothecary of Gloucester
Farmer, Samuel, his father, & Anne, 7 yrs

30 Mar.   Horsenton, Samuel son of Samuel, silkweaver of Gloucester
Finch, Richard, bodicemaker, 7 yrs

3/517   18 Mar.   Wheeler, John son of John, yeoman of Newent
Hornidge, James & Mary, blacksmith, 7 yrs

28 Mar.   Bowyer, Humphrey son of John, innholder of Gloucester
Rowles, Timothy & Mary, basketmaker, 7 yrs from 21 Dec.

Arnold, Robert son of Thomas, waggoner of Gloucester
Davis, John & Margaret, pinmaker, 7 yrs from 25 Mar.

4 Apr.   Dunn, William son of Francis, bricklayer, dec'd, of Gloucester
Lumbard, James & Mary, serge weaver, 7 yrs from 1 Apr.

3/518   8 Apr.   Pulton, Thomas son of Thomas, gentleman, dec'd, of Hartpury
Furney, James & Sarah, ironmonger, 7 yrs from 25 Mar.

Allen, William son of Edmund, gentleman, dec'd, of Maisemore
Mathews, John & Anne, butcher, 7 yrs from 2 Feb.

15 Apr.   Mamby, Thomas son of John, cobbler, dec'd, of Gloucester
Greene, Philip, horn turner, 7 yrs from 8 Oct. 1708

Jordan, Thomas son of Thomas, weaver of Burford, Oxon.
Vaughan, John & Merriam, vintner, 7 yrs from 1 Jan.

18 Apr.   Mutlow, Anthony son of Anthony, tailor of Gloucester
Mutlow, Anthony, his father, & Frances, 7 yrs from 1 Jan.

3/519   13 May   Gardner, Thomas son of Thomas, yeoman of Aconbury, Herefs.
Wygatte, Samuel & Alice, 7 yrs from 8 Oct.

15 Apr.   Wood, James son of James, maltster of Cheltenham
Burroughs, Samuel & Elizabeth, mercer, 7 yrs from 1 Jan.

13 May   Street, John son of Charles of Tibberton
Hayes, Christopher & Margaret, cordwainer, 7 yrs
29 Sept. 1710: crossed out by order of Edmund Gregory, esq., mayor

16 May   Spillman, Thomas son of John, plasterer of Gloucester
Rogers, Thomas, feltmaker, 7 yrs

3/520   23 May   Leyton, Richard son of John, fisherman of Gloucester
Hale, William & Elizabeth, pinmaker, 7 yrs

27 June   Sparks, William son of Sparkes, Richard, innholder of Gloucester
Young, Walter & Margaret, cordwainer, 7 yrs from 24 June

Mountague, John son of Charles, victualler of Over
Drinkwater, Richard, cordwainer, 7 yrs from 20 June

Lewis, John son of George, silkweaver of Gloucester
Haynes, Edward & Mary, pinmaker, 7 yrs from 20 June

Holder, Joseph son of Joseph, barber of Gloucester
Holder, John & Sarah, pinmaker, 7 yrs from 2 Feb.

3/521   4 July   Hornage, John son of James, blacksmith of Gloucester
Hornage, James, his father, & Mary, 7 yrs

Ireland, George son of Richard, labourer of Gloucester
Hayes, John & Elizabeth, cordwainer, 7 yrs from 24 June

	1709	18 July	Phillipps, Charles son of Samuel, silkweaver late of Gloucester Long, William & Mary, cordwainer, 7 yrs
		12 Aug.	Cowles, John son of Richard, innholder, dec'd, of Cheltenham Tyler, Charles & Hester, plumber, 7 yrs from 1 July
3/522		1 Aug.	Bishopp, Hugh son of Thomas, of Barton Street, Gloucester Tyler, John & Elinor, tailor, 7 yrs from 14 July
		22 July	Bubb, Nathaniel son of Daniel, blacksmith of Barnwood Niccolls, Thomas, saddler, 7 yrs from 24 June
		22 Aug.	Smart, William son of Giles, miller, dec'd, of Barton Street, Gloucester Wells, Mary, widow, cordwainer, 7 yrs from 14 Aug.
		5 Sept.	Halling, John son of Walter, labourer of Gloucester Jackson, Daniel & Margaret, pargiter, 7 yrs
			Roberts, Edward son of Edward, labourer of Dumbleton Jones, Charles & Anne, cooper, 7 yrs
3/523			Plaister, John son of Robert, dec'd, of Westbury-on-Severn Hayes, Josiah & Elizabeth, cordwainer, 7 yrs
		23 Sept.	Bishopp, Daniel son of Daniel, barber surgeon, dec'd, of Gloucester Drew, John, barber surgeon, 7 yrs

Edmund Gregory, mayor 1709–10 [1]

3/523	1709	5 Oct.	Scott, Thomas son of William, clothier of Wotton-under-Edge Lane, Nicholas & Hester, apothecary, 7 yrs from 1 Sept.
		14 Oct.	Bullocke, James son of Henry, labourer of Blaisdon Mutlow, Miles & Martha, cordwainer, 7 yrs *6 Feb. 1709: Suggested by the Company of Cordwainers that the master, Miles Mutlow, dwells at Huntley in Gloucestershire so the apprentice is incapable of being free at the end of his term* [entry crossed out]
		24 Oct.	Cale, Francis son of John, innholder, dec'd, of Tewkesbury Rogers, John & Jane, baker, 7 yrs from 12 Apr.
3/524		4 Oct.	Salcombe, William son of James, yeoman of Norton Greene, John, cordwainer, 7 yrs from 1 Oct.
		4 Nov.	Bonnett, John son of Charles, bricklayer of Gloucester Engly, Richard & Elinor, bricklayer, 7 yrs
		23 Dec.	Winniatt, William son of Richard, pinmaker of Gloucester Filder, George & Sarah, farrier, 7 yrs from 13 Dec.
3/525			Weston, John son of John, fisherman of Gloucester Swayne, Jonathan & Blanche, 7 yrs from 29 Sept.
	1710	20 Jan.	Workman, Anthony son of Anthony, butcher of Gloucester Workman, Anthony, his father, & Anne, 7 yrs
		23 Jan.	Price, John son of William, cordwainer of Gloucester Price, William, his father, & Jane, cordwainer, 7 yrs

[1] 1 June 1710: To receive £4 of Mrs Sarah Browne's money: John Barton, John Baldwyn, Moses Davis, William Jeffs and Thomas Lambeth in place of Young who was chosen last year but was under age. GBR B3/8 p. 354.

	1710	23 Jan.	Burridge, Thomas son of Thomas, weaver of Gloucester Burridge, Thomas, his father, & Frances, 7 yrs
			Randell, John son of William, serge weaver of Gloucester Randell, William, his father, & Susannah, 7 yrs
3/526		27 Jan.	Cowles, Robert son of Robert, butcher of Gloucester Cowles, Robert, his father, & Joan, 7 yrs
			Spencer, Samuel son of Thomas, cooper of Gloucester Spencer, Thomas, his father, & Beata, 7 yrs
		13 Feb.	Rogers, James son of John, shearman of Tortworth Engly, Henry & Sarah, bricklayer, 7 yrs from 23 Dec.
			Engly, Arthur son of John, bricklayer, dec'd, of Gloucester Engly, Henry & Sarah, bricklayer, 7 yrs from 23 Dec.
3/527		6 Feb.	Church, Edward son of John, pinmaker of Gloucester Jeenes, Thomas & Martha, hatter, 7 yrs
		27 Mar.	Ragon, Bartholomew son of Cornelius, yeoman of Bandon Bridge, Co. Cork White, Richard & Mary, cordwainer, 7 yrs
		18 Apr.	Bullock, John son of Richard, yeoman of Blaisdon Pegler, Joseph & Jane, tanner, 7 yrs
		26 Apr.	Iremonger, John son of John, gentleman of Buckingham Bryan, Daniel, surgeon & apothecary, 7 yrs from 10 Mar.
		27 Mar.	Browne, William son of Joseph, painter, dec'd, of Gloucester Acocke, John & Tabitha, painter, 7 yrs *Charity money*
3/528		28 Apr.	Tranter, Thomas son of Nathaniel, chandler, dec'd, of Newent Haynes, Peter & Susannah, grocer, 7 yrs from 25 Mar.
		8 May	Weal, Richard son of John, yeoman of Dymock Weal, Thomas & Margery, baker, 7 yrs from 1 May
		17 June	Jones, Philip son of Thomas, labourer of Newent Atkins, Walter & Mary, cordwainer, 7 yrs from 27 May *29 Sept. 1710 crossed [out] by order of Edmund Gregory, esq., mayor*
		16 June	Ricketts, John son of Samuel, carpenter of Gloucester Ricketts, Samuel, his father, & Hannah, 7 yrs from 29 Sept.
			Bennett, Isaac son of John, tailor, dec'd, of Tirley Ricketts, Samuel & Hannah, carpenter, 7 yrs from 29 Sept.
3/529		19 June	Goodwyn, Joseph son of Joseph, cordwainer of Minsterworth Luter, John & Elizabeth, butcher, 7 yrs from 3 May
			Birt, Philip son of Philip, feltmaker of Newent Dark, Richard & Mary, gunsmith, 7 yrs from 11 June
			Evenis, James son of Thomas, yeoman of Whaddon Evenis, William & Mary, cordwainer, 7 yrs from 25 Mar.
		7 July	Humphrys, Richard son of Humphris, Richard, cordwainer, dec'd, of Guiting Power Humphris, Thomas & Hannah, currier, 7 yrs from 24 June
3/530		14 Oct.	Davis, Moses son of Howell, labourer of Gloucester White, Richard & Mary, cordwainer, 7 yrs from 14 July

	1710	17 July	Barton, Richard son of Thomas, labourer of Gloucester Barton, John & Elizabeth, bricklayer, 7 yrs
		28 July	Maul, Richard son of Lawrence, yeoman of Notgrove Cooke, James & Anne, joiner, 7 yrs from 24 July *Date altered to 28 October 1710*
			Lambeth, Thomas son of John, pipemaker of Gloucester Brymyard, Henry & Sarah, cordwainer, 7 yrs from 24 June
3/531			Prestbury, Thomas son of William, gentleman late of Churcham Branch, Thomas & Edith, grocer, 7 yrs from 24 June *Date altered to 28 October 1710*
		7 Aug.	Hale, Joseph son of Joseph, yeoman of Berrow, Worcs. Gardner, Anthony & Sarah, baker, 7 yrs from 1 May *Date altered to 28 October 1710*
		11 Sept.	Warne, John son of John, butcher of Newent Lea, Robert & Grace, cordwainer, 7 yrs from 1 Aug. *Date altered to 28 October 1710*
		25 Sept.	Baldwyn, John son of John, waggoner of Gloucester Pawling, Daniel & Mary, baker, 7 yrs *Date altered to 28 October 1710*

Caple Payne, mayor 1710–1[1]

	1710	27 Oct.	Hunt, Benjamin son of John, yeoman, dec'd, of 'Welham' [Welland?], Worcs. Lawrence, Obadiah, cooper, 7 yrs from 18 Oct.
3/532		29 Oct.	Yeend, William son of John, gentleman of Ashchurch Williams, Anthony & Mary, barber surgeon, 7 yrs
		1 Dec.	Ellis, Thomas son of John, farrier of Gloucester Ellis, John, his father, & Elizabeth, 7 yrs *City money*
		18 Dec.	Reeve, John son of Stephen, stonecutter of Gloucester Engly, John & Alice, bricklayer, 7 yrs
3/533		15 Dec.	Brotherton, John son of Jeremiah, cordwainer of Gloucester Brotherton, Jeremiah & Marian, cordwainer, 7 yrs *City money*
	1711	15 Jan.	Dancey, William son of John, labourer of Kingscote Engley, Henry & Sarah, bricklayer, 7 yrs from 21 Dec. 1710
		19 Jan.	Hopkins, John son of John, cooper of Tetbury Hopkins, John, his father, a burgess of Gloucester, cooper, 7 yrs *City money by order of the mayor.* [entry crossed out]

[1] 6 Nov. 1710: To receive £5 of Mr William Holliday's money: John Reeve, Thomas Bradley, John Brotherton, John Shipton's son, Richard Overthrow, Thomas Hale, Giles Ham's son. To leave Sir Thomas Rich's hospital and receive £10: Thomas Collins, Richard Weaver, John Price, George Marshfield, Richard Jones, Jesse Jelfe. GBR B3/8 p. 373.

23 Aug. 1711: To receive £5 of Alderman Powell's money: Benjamin Beal. To leave Sir Thomas Rich's hospital and receive £10: George Bowler, John Stephens, William Gravestock, Thomas Cooke, John Cudd, John Parlour. GBR B3/8 pp. 405–6.

6 Sept. 1711: To receive £4 of Mrs Sarah Browne's money: Henry Barrett, Thomas Wheeler, William Williams, Thomas Hampton. To receive £5 of Mr William Holliday's money: Myles Mutlow, Daniel Bishop, Thomas Bromley, [—] Pace, Thomas Hayward, John Greene. GBR B3/8 p. 411.

	1711	3 Feb.	Jeffes, William son of William, yeoman of Barton Street, Gloucester Ball, Samuel, baker, [*no term given*] from 2 Feb. *City money*
		26 Feb.	Hale, Thomas son of Joseph, pinmaker of Gloucester Corr, Henry & Elizabeth, tailor, 7 yrs from 21 Dec. 1710
3/534		2 Mar.	Mitchell, William son of James, yeoman, dec'd, of Tortworth Perkins, George & Martha, baker, 7 yrs
	1710	6 Nov.	Bennett, Adam son of Adam, yeoman, dec'd, of Highnam Williams, Richard & Elizabeth, glover, 7 yrs
	1711	19 Jan.	Window, James son of William, silkweaver of Gloucester White, Richard & Mary, cordwainer, 7 yrs from 5 Nov. 1710
		26 Jan.	Carpenter, John son of Thomas, yeoman, dec'd, of Hucclecote Niccolls, Thomas & Mary, saddler, 7 yrs
3/535		27 Apr.	Haynes, Joseph son of Nathaniel, yeoman of Wheatenhurst Gregory, John & Elizabeth, barber surgeon, 7 yrs from 25 Mar.
		30 Apr.	Hayns, Samuel son of Haynes, Samuel, blacksmith of Minsterworth Savory, Robert & Mary, farrier, 7 yrs
		4 May	Overthrow, Richard son of William, carpenter of Minsterworth Weaver, Richard & Mary, blacksmith, 7 yrs from 25 Mar.
			Weyman, Ambrose son of Wyman, Thomas, yeoman of Ashleworth Wadley, John & Sarah, baker, 7 yrs from 25 Mar.
3/536		18 May	Surman, Thomas son of Samuel, maltster of Cheltenham Beard, Richard & Mary, barber & periwigmaker, 7 yrs from 13 Apr. 16 Sept. *1720: upon the complaint of the Master and Wardens and company of barbers against Thomas Surman for the non-service of his time the Mayor and Aldermen ordered his enrolment to be crossed out and he to have no benefit of the freedom of the Corporation*
		28 May	Garrett, John son of John, innholder, dec'd, of Gloucester Symon, Thomas & Elizabeth, currier, 7 yrs
			Phelps, Joseph son of William, tanner of Gloucester Phelps, William, his father, & Sarah, 7 yrs
		15 June	Locke, Thomas son of Walter, tailor of Cheltenham Stocke, Samuel & Hannah, baker, 7 yrs
		30 May	Cother, John son of William, yeoman of Tibberton Cook, Thomas & Susannah, tailor, 7 yrs
3/537		20 July	Wintle, Richard son of Richard, yeoman of Westbury Humphryes, Thomas & Hannah, currier, 7 yrs from 24 June
		27 July	Webb, Nicholas son of Thomas, alderman of Gloucester Webb, Thomas, his father, & Anne, 7 yrs from 25 Mar.
		30 July	Collins, Thomas son of James, grocer of Gloucester Collins, James, his father, & Sarah, 7 yrs
		13 Aug.	Gifford, Thomas son of Thomas, carpenter, dec'd, of Maisemore Long, William & Mary, cordwainer, 7 yrs from 1 Aug.
		10 Sept.	Wheeler, Thomas son of Thomas, carpenter of Gloucester Wheeler, Samuel & Anne, carpenter, 7 yrs from 25 Mar.
3/538			Etheridge, Samuel son of Robert, labourer of Badgeworth Lodge, William & Mary, cooper, 7 yrs from 25 Mar. 1710

	1711	14 Sept.	Barrett, Henry son of Henry, innholder of Gloucester Elliott, Thomas & Grace, cordwainer, 7 yrs

Samuel Hayward, mayor 1711–2[1]

3/538	1711	15 Oct.	Greene, John son of Richard, woolcomber of Gloucester Greene, Joan, widow, 7 yrs
		19 Oct.	Brampton, Thomas son of Brian, yeoman of Painswick Draper, Henry & Anne, blacksmith, 7 yrs
3/539		2 Nov.	Mutlow, Miles son of Anthony, tailor of Gloucester Mutley, William & Joan, blacksmith of Walford, Herefs., 7 yrs
		3 Dec.	Bromly, Thomas son of Thomas, fisherman Partridge, Robert & Mary, cordwainer, 7 yrs
	1712	11 Jan.	Williams, William son of John, yeoman of Gloucester King, John & Susannah, dyer, 7 yrs from 21 Dec. 1711
		28 Jan.	Locke, Thomas son of Walter, baker of Cheltenham Cook, John & Elizabeth, baker, 7 yrs from 25 Mar.
3/540		4 Feb.	Ball, John son of John, cardmaker of Gloucester Ball, John, his father, & Margaret, 7 yrs
			Cole, Benjamin son of John, innholder of Gloucester Jakeman, William, baker, 7 yrs from 1 Jan.
			Beale, Benjamin son of Benjamin, blacksmith of Gloucester Beale, Benjamin, his father, & Anne 7 yrs
		11 Feb.	Harris, James son of Joseph, baker, dec'd, of Gloucester Lander, James & Hester, baker, 7 yrs
3/541		25 Feb.	Bowler, George son of George, tailor of Gloucester Sparry, Samuel & Margaret, baker, 7 yrs from 2 Feb.
		28 Feb.	Ellis, John son of Guy, ironmonger, dec'd, of Gloucester Ellis, [—], his mother, ironmonger, 7 yrs from 23 July
		18 Feb.	Tomlins, Samuel son of John, pinmaker, dec'd, of Gloucester Engly, Richard & Eleanor, bricklayer, 7 yrs from 10 Feb.
		21 Mar.	Driver, Jonathan son of Thomas, gentleman of Hereford Webb, Thomas & Anne, alderman, 7 yrs from 1 Nov. 1711
3/542		11 Apr.	Bishopp, George son of Thomas, tailor of St Mary de Lode, Gloucester Heaven, John & Deborah, barber surgeon, 7 yrs from 1 Mar.
		14 Apr.	Fowle, Samuel son of Joseph, yeoman, dec'd, of Longhope Brymiard, Henry & Sarah, cordwainer, 7 yrs from 14 Apr.
		11 Apr.	Onyon, John son of John, surgeon, dec'd, of Berkeley Harris, Richard & Hester, barber surgeon, 7 yrs from 1 Mar.
		28 Apr.	Rayer, George son of William, yeoman of Cutsdean Barker, John & Anne, barber surgeon, 7 yrs

---

[1] 19 Aug. 1712: To receive £4 of Mrs Sarah Browne's money: Richard Rogers, Richard Meeke, Sampson Glendall, Jarrett Smith. To receive £5 of Mr William Holliday's money: John Bowler, James Brody, Charles Butter, [—] Church, Francis Lea, William Barrett. To receive £5 of Alderman Powell's money: John Roberts. GBR B3/8 p. 456.

	1712	9 May	Mills, Nathaniel son of Thomas, plasterer of Gloucester Dowdy, George & Eleanor, carpenter, 7 yrs from 1 May
		27 June	Overthrow, Richard son of William, carpenter of Minsterworth Weaver, Richard & Mary, blacksmith, 7 yrs from 25 Mar.
3/543		30 June	Holder, John son of Josiah, yeoman, dec'd, of Huntley Holford, Edmund, cordwainer, 7 yrs
		19 July	Hampton, Thomas son of John, innholder of Gloucester Church, Roger, tailor, 7 yrs from 25 Mar.
		21 July	Stephens, John son of Robert, innholder, dec'd, of Gloucester Browne, Samuel, alderman, & Hester, to be instructed in the art of glazier, 7 yrs from 1 May
		30 July	White, John son of Joseph, silkweaver, dec'd, of Donnington, Herefs. Prinn, William & Margaret, tailor, 7 yrs
		28 Aug.	Prestbury, Thomas son of William, yeoman, dec'd, of Churcham Stocke, John & Susannah, grocer, 7 yrs
3/544		1 Sept.	Rogers, Richard son of John, yeoman of Gloucester Mathews, Richard & Hester, 7 yrs
			Window, Richard son of William, tailor of Gloucester Williams, Thomas & Jane, gardener, 7 yrs
		19 Sept.	Porter, John son of Paul, maltster of Gloucester Bonner, John & Elizabeth, grocer, 7 yrs *Sol mro [paid to master] £32 5s.*
		22 Sept.	Lee, Thomas son of John, tailor, dec'd, of Gloucester Lee, John & Sarah, tailor, 7 yrs from 2 Feb. *Charity money*
		26 Sept.	Gulliford, Thomas son of George, innholder, dec'd, of Gloucester Drinkwater, Richard & Sarah, cordwainer, 8 yrs *Charity money*

James Furney, mayor 1712–3[1]

3/544	1712	10 Nov.	Bowler, John son of George, tailor of Gloucester Bowler, George, his father, & Mary, 7 yrs £5 *Charity money*
		21 Nov.	Smith, Jarrett son of John, dyer of Gloucester Heaven, John & Deborah, barber surgeon, 7 yrs *£4 boy*
3/545		24 Nov.	Barrett, William son of William, woolcomber, dec'd, of Gloucester Stephens, Thomas & Elizabeth, pinmaker, 7 yrs [*deleted*] 8 yrs *£5 boy*
		28 Nov.	Hardwicke *alias* Mason, Walter son of Mason, Elizabeth single woman of Awre Lander, William & Hester, grocer, 7 yrs from 18 Oct. *Indentures to the master and he to pay duty*

[1] 11 Sept. 1713: To leave Sir Thomas Rich's hospital and receive £10: William Pembruge, William Window, James Kingman, Thomas Hornidge, Thomas Davis, John Collins. GBR B3/8 p. 515.

18 Sept. 1713: To receive £5 of Mr William Holliday's money: William Randle, John Clarke, Thomas Hossington, John Winston, Francis Goodwyn, John Price. To receive £5 of Alderman Powell's money: James Brotherton. To receive £4 of Mrs Sarah Browne's money: William Barrett, John Griffin, William Howell, Thomas Taylor. GBR B3/8 p. 519.

| | 1712 | 28 Nov. | Cooke, Thomas son of Thomas, tailor, dec'd, of Gloucester |
| | | | Wells, Mary, widow, 7 yrs *Sir Thomas Rich Hospital boy* |

3/546   1 Dec.   Hawkins, Jeremiah son of Thomas, yeoman of Abloads Court, [Sandhurst]
Harris, Richard & Hester, barber surgeon, 7 yrs from 20 Oct.
Sol [*paid*] *7/6 duty Mr Palmer*

22 Dec.   Beard, Henry son of Andrew, innholder, dec'd, of Gloucester
Hayward, Samuel jr & Hannah, barber surgeon, 7 yrs

22 Dec.   Porter, Thomas son of Paul, maltster, dec'd, of Gloucester
Hill, Thomas, apothecary, 7 yrs from 19 Nov.

1713   5 Jan.   Rodway, Thomas son of Thomas, mercer of Gloucester
Rodway, Thomas, his father, & Hester, 7 yrs from 24 June

3/547   23 Jan.   Bicke, Thomas son of Hugh, yeoman of Hartpury
Greene, Joan, widow, 7 yrs

2 Feb.   Buckle, John son of William, yeoman of Haresfield
Lawrence, William & Elizabeth, baker, 7 yrs from 24 June   *£8 paid*

4 Feb.   Lea, Francis son of John, tailor, dec'd, of Gloucester
Jones, Thomas, of Ross-on-Wye, Herefs. & Margaret, cordwainer,
7 yrs from 2 Feb.

19 Jan.   Bishopp, George son of Thomas, barber surgeon, dec'd, of Gloucester
Bishopp, Thomas, barber surgeon, 7 yrs from 10 Jan.   *£6 received*

3/548   13 Feb.   Nash, Walter son of Walter, skinner of Cheltenham
Williams, Richard & Elizabeth, glover, 7 yrs

*26 Aug. 1717: On application this day made to the Mayor and
Justices by the Company of Glovers it was ordered that Walter
Nash the apprentice be not admitted a burgess before satisfaction
be given that he hath duly served his time and that notice be
given to the Master of the Company of Glovers when Walter
Nash comes to be admitted a burgess.*

*26 Feb. 1719: Upon hearing of a second complaint of the Glovers to the
Mayor and Aldermen present at an adjournment of the Quarter Sessions
it is the opinion of the court that this apprentice ought not to be made a
burgess and freeman of this corporation at the end of his term.*

Freame, John son of John, feltmaker of Gloucester
Freame, John, his father, & Elizabeth, 7 yrs

28 Feb.   Clarke, George son of Richard, labourer, dec'd, of Lower Southgate
Street, Gloucester
Holder, John & Sarah, pinmaker, 7 yrs

30 Mar.   Wheeler, Richard son of Richard, yeoman, dec'd, of Longhope
Halford, John & Margaret, cordwainer, 7 yrs from 28 Feb.

14 Apr.   Read, John son of Richard, yeoman of Bulley
Drew, Hannah, widow, 7 yrs from 2 Mar.

3/549   24 Apr.   Clarke, William son of Richard, brazier, dec'd, of Lower Southgate
Street, Gloucester
Shipton, Cowcher & Martha, pinmaker, 7 yrs

20 Apr.   Townly, William son of Martin, yeoman of Winchcombe
Cowles, John & Anne, tailor, 7 yrs from 25 Mar.

	1713	1 May	Offlett, Thomas son of Thomas, yeoman, dec'd, of Churchdown Collett, John & Mary, joiner, 7 yrs
		8 May	Smith, Aaron son of Aaron, weaver of Uley Smith, Abraham & Susannah, cooper, 7 yrs from 28 Feb.
		20 Apr.	Haynes, Henry son of William, butcher, dec'd, of Newent Rogers, John & Jane, baker, 7 yrs from 25 Mar.
3/550		27 Apr.	Glendall, Sampson son of Thomas, combmaker of Gloucester Jones, Thomas & Elizabeth, glover, 7 yrs from 25 Mar.
		15 May	Butt, Thomas son of John, yeoman, dec'd, of Elmstone Hardwicke Haynes, William & Phoebe, mercer, 7 yrs from 12 Mar.
		1 June	Townsend, Richard son of Richard, tailor of Gloucester Pruin, William & Mary, tailor, 7 yrs from 4 Apr.
		18 May	Baker, Richard son of Richard, yeoman of Gloucester Freeman, Robert & Frances, joiner, 7 yrs from 25 Mar.
		8 June	Layton, Anthony son of Alice, single woman of Tuffley Davis, Joan, widow, 7 yrs
3/551		19 June	Bird, Joseph son of Daniel, combmaker, dec'd, of Gloucester Pace, Thomas & Jane, cordwainer, 7 yrs from 24 June
		27 June	Young, James son of Samuel, pinmaker, dec'd, of Holy Trinity parish, Gloucester Winniatt, Thomas & Arabella, pinmaker, 7 yrs from 24 June
		31 Aug.	Wilcox, George son of George, dec'd, of Gloucester Lane, Nicholas jr & Hester, gentleman, 7 yrs from 1 Aug.
		31 July	Meek, Richard son of Richard, labourer of Gloucester Best, John & Mary, tailor, 7 yrs from 24 June
		23 Oct.	Taylor, Thomas son of Thomas, pipemaker, dec'd, of Gloucester Smith, Joseph & Rebecca, pipemaker, 7 yrs

Richard Greene, mayor 1713–4[1]

3/552	1713	16 Oct.	Hayward, Thomas son of Edward, weaver of Gloucester Hayward, Edward jr & Apphia, weaver, 7 yrs [2]
			Randle, William son of William, weaver of Gloucester Randle, William, his father, & Anne, 7 yrs
			Barrett, William son of Henry, innholder of Gloucester Swett, William & Bridget, tobacco pipemaker, 7 yrs
			Bradley, Thomas son of Thomas, butcher of Gloucester Ward, Thomas & Margaret, pinmaker, 7 yrs

---

[1] 28 May 1714: To receive £4 of Mrs Sarah Browne's money: John Meighen, Abraham Barrett, Thomas Brotherton, Thomas Lugg. GBR B3/8 p. 540.

14 Aug. 1714: To receive £5 of Mr William Holliday's money: William Price, William Dawes, Edward Haynes, [—] Elliott, John Meeke, John Swayne. To receive £5 of Alderman Powell's money: James Lambeth. GBR B3/8 p. 555.

[2] 25 Sept. 1713: £5 granted to Thomas Hayward [*in 1711*] now to be paid to him. GBR B3/8 p. 523.

	1713	30 Oct.	Clarke, John son of Walter, pinmaker, dec'd, of Gloucester Winniatt, Thomas & Arabella, pinmaker, 7 yrs
3/553		2 Nov.	Howell, William son of William, weaver, dec'd, of Gloucester Mason, William & [—], tailor, 7 yrs
		9 Nov.	Brotherton, James son of Jeremiah, cordwainer of Gloucester Brotherton, Jeremiah & Marian, cordwainer, 7 yrs
			Greenway, Charles son of Walter, pinmaker of Gloucester Sparrowhawk, William, cordwainer, 7 yrs
		18 Dec.	Clarke, Thomas son of Thomas, yeoman, dec'd, of Huntley Hall, John & Sarah, baker, 7 yrs
	1714	29 Jan.	Price, Thomas son of John, pinmaker of Gloucester Price, Thomas, his father, & Elizabeth, 7 yrs
3/554			Hossington, Thomas son of Samuel, silkweaver of Gloucester Woodward, John & Barbara, pinmaker, 7 yrs
		1 Feb.	Griffin, John son of John, labourer of Gloucester Hale, William & Elizabeth, pinmaker, 7 yrs
		5 Feb.	Bell, Miles son of John, gentleman & alderman of Gloucester Bell, John, his father, & Hester, 7 yrs
		8 Feb.	Gooding, Francis son of William, baker of Gloucester Perris, Richard & Mary, butcher, 7 yrs from 2 Feb.
3/555		22 Feb.	Collins, John son of John, baker, dec'd, of Gloucester Hale, John & Anne, barber surgeon, 7 yrs from 22 Feb.
		19 Mar.	Blackwell, John son of John, yeoman, dec'd, of Chedworth Powell, Samuel & Hannah, baker, 7 yrs from 8 Mar.
		12 Apr.	Mitchell, Lewis son of James, yeoman, dec'd, of Tortworth Reeve, John & Sarah, gunsmith, 7 yrs from 25 Mar.
			Matthews, Thomas son of Edward, glover of Ross-on-Wye, Herefs. Church, Richard & Elizabeth, glover, 7 yrs from 25 Mar.
3/556			Graffstocke, Samuel son of John, butcher of Gloucester Haynes, Thomas & Mary, tailor, 7 yrs from 25 Mar.
		16 Apr.	Nokes, John son of Richard, yeoman, dec'd, of Hartpury Bryan, Daniel & Anne, cordwainer, 7 yrs from date of indenture
		24 May	Pembruge, William son of William, baker of Gloucester Cooke, Samuel & Sarah, saddler, 7 yrs from 1 Apr.
		28 May	Broughton, Thomas son of Thomas, farrier of *iuxta le castle* [near the castle. *See 3/578*] Wells, Mary, widow, 7 yrs from 29 May
3/557		14 June	Cooke, Richard son of Richard, labourer, dec'd, of Newent Howell, Joseph & Elizabeth, blacksmith, 7 yrs from 10 May
			Small, Joseph son of John, mercer of Cirencester Driver, Richard & Dorothy, haberdasher of hats, 7 yrs from 12 Mar.
		9 July	Everard, Joseph son of Mark, clothier, dec'd, of Hammersmith, Middx. Ashmead, John & Sarah, mercer, 7 yrs from 24 June
		30 July	Batchford, John son of John, innholder of Winchcombe Fletcher, Edward & Sarah, barber surgeon, 7 yrs from 28 June

3/558	1714	3 Sept.	Perrin, Nathaniel son of Nathaniel, woolcomber of Gloucester Harris, Nathaniel & Hannah, woolcomber, 7 yrs
		13 Sept.	Ellis, Guy son of Guy, ironmonger, dec'd, of Gloucester Haynes, Peter & Susannah, grocer, 7 yrs from 25 Mar.
		20 Sept.	Browne, Thomas son of Charles, gentleman, dec'd, of The Leigh Lea, Daniel & Elizabeth, cordwainer, 7 yrs from 1 Aug.
		24 Sept.	Price, William son of William, cordwainer of Gloucester Price, William, his father, & Jane, 7 yrs
3/559		13 Sept.	Wood, Thomas son of John, yeoman, dec'd, of Gloucester Window, William & Elizabeth, tailor, 7 yrs from 1 Aug.

Samuel Browne, mayor 1714–5[1]

3/559	1714	25 Oct.	Makepeace, John son of Samuel, baker, dec'd, of Gloucester Evenis, William & Mary, cordwainer, 7 yrs from 20 Oct.
		8 Nov.	Tranter, John son of Nathaniel, grocer, dec'd, of Newent Lovett, James & Martha, barber surgeon, 7 yrs from 29 Sept.
		29 Oct.	Winston, John son of Thomas, tailor of Gloucester Tyler, John & Elizabeth, plumber, 7 yrs from 29 Sept.
3/560		19 Nov.	Haynes, Edward son of Edward, pinmaker of Gloucester Puckeridge, Thomas & Mary, tailor, 7 yrs
		26 Nov.	Davis, Thomas son of Thomas, pinmaker, dec'd, of Gloucester Whittington, John & Sarah, white wiredrawer, 7 yrs from 29 Sept.
		1 Dec.	Bonner, Josiah son of Thomas, gent. of Weston under Penyard, Herefs. Barnes, Nicholas & Elizabeth, mercer, 7 yrs from 4 Oct.
		10 Dec.	Hayward, Samuel son of Clement, tailor, dec'd, of Gloucester Oatley, Sarah, widow, 7 yrs from 29 Sept.
3/561		17 Dec.	Lambert, James son of William, pipemaker, dec'd, of Gloucester Stephens, Thomas & Elizabeth, pinmaker, 7 yrs
		20 Dec.	Swayne, John son of Thomas, tiler & plasterer of Gloucester Swayne, Jonathan & Blanche, tiler & plasterer, 7 yrs
	1715	7 Jan.	Meighen, John son of Ferdinand, gentleman, dec'd, of Gloucester Engley, John & Alice, bricklayer, 7 yrs
		17 Jan.	Hayford, John son of John, pavior, dec'd, of Gloucester Shatford, John & Mary, joiner, 7 yrs
3/562		11 Feb.	Brotherton, Abraham son of Thomas, tiler & plasterer of Gloucester Freame, John & Elizabeth, feltmaker, 7 yrs from 6 Feb.

[1] 15 Nov. 1714: To leave Sir Thomas Rich's hospital and receive £10: Samuel Bower, Giles Smith, Robert Mutlow, William Nest, Charles Bidwell, Thomas Greene. GBR B3/8 p. 578.

22 July 1715: To receive £4 of Mrs Sarah Browne's money: John Wilton, Richard Collier, John Maverly, James Middleton. GBR B3/8 p. 600.

26 Aug. 1715: To receive £5 of Mr William Holliday's money: Henry Davis, Charles Hannis, Joseph Hornedge, William Ricketts, Joseph Jones, William Warnford. To receive £5 of Alderman Powell's money: Henry Weaver's son. GBR B3/8 p. 608.

	1715	18 Feb.	Hornage, Thomas son of William, cordwainer, dec'd, of Gloucester Burroughs, Samuel, mercer, 7 yrs
		28 Feb.	Beal, John son of Benjamin, gentleman of Longdon, Worcs. Payne, Capel, gentleman & alderman, & Catherine, 7 yrs
		4 Mar.	Lugg, Thomas son of Jasper, combmaker of Gloucester Lugg, Jasper, his father, & Mary, 7 yrs
3/563		4 Apr.	Hankins, William son of John, yeoman of Dymock Edwards, James & Mary, baker, 7 yrs from 25 Mar.
		16 May	Long, Giles son of Thomas, yeoman of Ashleworth Dowdy, George & Eleanor, carpenter, 7 yrs from 10 Apr.
			Watts, Thomas son of William, yeoman of Highnam Veysey, Nathaniel & Elizabeth, tailor, 10 yrs
		13 June	Ellis, John son of John, blacksmith of Gloucester Cole, George & Elizabeth, tailor, 7 yrs
3/564			Phipps, George son of William, clerk of Duntisbourne Abbotts Beard, John & Elizabeth, cutler, 7 yrs from 20 Apr.
			Williams, John son of John, yeoman of Newent Long, John, cordwainer, 7 yrs
		27 June	Woodward, William son of William, waterman, dec'd, of Tewkesbury Niccolls, Thomas jr & Mary, saddler, 7 yrs
		4 July	Weaver, Matthew son of Henry, smith of Gloucester Gardner, Anthony & Sarah, baker, 7 yrs from 24 June
		15 July	Mills, John son of Thomas, yeoman, of Hope Mansell, Herefs. Oatley, Sarah, widow, 7 yrs from 24 June
3/565		18 July	Bubb, John son of John, yeoman, dec'd, of Maisemore Cowles, John, butcher, 7 yrs from 7 June
			Luter, John son of John, butcher, dec'd, of Gloucester Ady, Ralph & Dorothy, butcher, 7 yrs
		29 July	Eades, Thomas son of Thomas, yeoman of Mitcheldean Baker, James & Margaret, cordwainer, 7 yrs from 14 Apr.
		12 Aug.	Herring, Richard son of John, yeoman, dec'd, of Apperley, Deerhurst Pegler, Andrew, saddler, 7 yrs from 1 Aug.
3/566			Wingate, John son of John, labourer, dec'd, of Barnwood Greenway, Charles & Elizabeth, cordwainer, 7 [*deleted*] 8 yrs from 24 June
		15 Aug.	Nurse, John son of John, yeoman of the Rea, Hempsted Weal, Thomas & Margery, baker, 7 yrs
		5 Aug.	Wilton, John son of Henry, woolcomber of Gloucester Shingler, John & Sarah, pinmaker, 7 yrs
		19 Aug.	Watts, Thomas son of John, labourer of Gloucester Workman, James & Hester, butcher, 7 yrs from 14 Aug.
3/567			Holder, William son of Josiah, yeoman of Huntley Drew, Hannah, widow, 7 yrs from 11 June
			Collier, Richard son of Richard, labourer, dec'd, of Gloucester Carill, Thomas & [—], hosier, 7 yrs

	1715	26 Aug.	Bower, Samuel son of Samuel, pipemaker, dec'd, of Gloucester Shatford, John & Mary, joiner, 7 yrs
		30 Sept.	Ashmead, Francis son of Francis, gentleman of Campden Dymocke, Charles & Anne, mercer, 7 yrs from 29 Sept.

Thomas Ludlow, mayor 1715–6[1]

3/568	1715	7 Oct.	Corr, John son of John, surgeon, dec'd, of Gloucester Wantner, Charles & Anne, barber surgeon, 7 yrs
		17 Oct.	Davis, Henry son of Henry, pinmaker of Gloucester Davis, Henry, his father, & Mary, 7 yrs from 29 Sept.
			Ricketts, William son of John, pinmaker of Gloucester Ricketts, John, his father, & Dinah, 7 yrs from 29 Sept.
			Hannis, Charles son of Charles, blacksmith, dec'd, of Gloucester Long, George, cordwainer, 7 yrs
			Kingman, James son of James, wiredrawer of Gloucester Kingman, John & Anne, wiredrawer, 7 yrs from 21 Dec. 1714
3/569		21 Oct.	Midleton, James son of George, labourer of Gloucester Rawlings, William & Frances, joiner, 7 yrs from 29 Sept.
			Jones, Joseph son of Thomas, glover of Gloucester Jones, Thomas, his father, & Elizabeth, 7 yrs
		24 Oct.	Richards, John son of David, yeoman of Elmore Young, Walter & Margaret, cordwainer, 7 yrs
	1715	31 Oct.	Ireland, Giles son of Giles, yeoman of Bisley Knowles, James & Hester, blacksmith, 7 yrs from date of indenture
3/570		18 Nov.	Daws, William son of Daw, Eleazer, carpenter of Gloucester Walker, Richard & Dinah, carpenter, 7 yrs
			Puxon, John son of William, silkweaver of Gloucester Lumbard, James & Mary, serge weaver, 7 yrs from 24 June
		12 Dec.	Elliott, William son of Nathaniel, yeoman, dec'd, of Stonehouse Hale, Joseph, cordwainer, 7 yrs
		19 Dec.	Mutlow, Robert son of Miles, cordwainer of Gloucester Mutlow, Miles, his father, & Martha, 7 yrs from 1 Jan. 1715
3/571	1716	10 Feb.	Jeffs, Joseph son of William, sawyer, dec'd, of Barton Street near Gloucester Merry, Thomas & Elizabeth, cordwainer, 7 yrs from 21 Dec. 1715
		17 Feb.	Gears, Thomas son of John, labourer of Hucclecote Draper, Richard & Grace, cordwainer, 7 yrs
		20 Feb.	Farmer, John son of Anne, widow of Gloucester Dymocke, Charles & Anne, mercer, 7 yrs

---

[1] 17 June 1716: To receive £4 of Mrs Sarah Browne's money: John Sheppard, Thomas Meeke, Joseph Bloxsome, John Smith. GBR B3/8 p. 645.

7 Aug. 1716: To receive £5 of Mr William Holliday's money: John Man, John Greene, Amity Medway, Edward Haynes, Daniel Sayer, Joseph Price. To receive £5 of Alderman Powell's money: Thomas Spencer. GBR B3/8 p. 648.

| | 1716 | 1 Mar. | Brotherton, Jeremiah son of Jeremiah, cordwainer of Gloucester
Watts, Robert & Mary, tailor, 7 yrs |

3/572   5 Mar.   Man, William son of James, tailor of Tirley
                   Wadley, John & Sarah, baker, 7 yrs

                23 Mar.   Fowles, Joseph son of Joseph, yeoman of Longhope
                   Stayte, Grey & [—], tailor, 7 yrs

                16 Apr.   Weaver, Thomas son of Henry, farrier of Gloucester
                   Holder, [—] & Sarah, pinmaker, 7 yrs

                11 May   Furney, William son of James, ironmonger of Gloucester
                   Furney, James, his father, & Sarah, 7 yrs from 25 Mar.

3/573   17 Apr.   Swayne, James son of Richard, collarmaker of Gloucester
                   Perris, John & Margaret, butcher, 7 yrs from 25 Mar.

                30 Apr.   Cor, Richard son of Edward, blacksmith of London
                   Cor, Henry & Elizabeth, tailor, 7 yrs from 23 Apr.

                14 May   Ireland, John son of Giles, labourer of Bisley
                   Kemis, Samuel jr, woolcomber, 7 yrs from 1 May

                          Boyce, William son of John, yeoman of Brockworth
                   Pauling, Samuel & Mary, baker, 7 yrs from 6 Apr.

3/574   8 June   Jones, Thomas son of Thomas, bricklayer, dec'd, of Tirley
                   Lovett, James & Martha, barber surgeon, 7 yrs

                11 June   Hawkins, John son of Samuel, clothworker of Stonehouse
                   Sparrowhawke, William & Hannah, cordwainer, 7 yrs from 28 May

                15 June   Luter, Samuel son of John, butcher, dec'd, of Gloucester
                   Perry, William & Elizabeth, tailor, 7 yrs

                22 June   Phipps, Joseph son of Joseph, yeoman, dec'd, of Broadwell
                   Lodge, William & Mary, cooper, 7 yrs

3/575   23 July   Browne, Joseph son of Joseph, painter, dec'd, of Gloucester
                   Wintle, Philip & Mary, joiner, 7 yrs

                23 July   Corr, John son of John, surgeon, dec'd, of Gloucester
                   Randle, William & Anne, serge weaver, 7 yrs

                27 July   Wright, William son of James, yeoman of Antrim, Ireland
                   Corr, Henry & Elizabeth, tailor, 7 yrs

                6 Aug.   Sheppard, John son of John, labourer, dec'd, of Gloucester
                   Randle, William, weaver, 7 yrs

                20 Aug.   Mason, John son of William, tanner of Gloucester
                   Mason, William & Mary, tanner, 7 yrs from 10 Oct. 1715

3/576   10 Aug.   Hornidge, Joseph son of James, blacksmith of Gloucester
                   Hornidge, James, cordwainer, 7 yrs from 1 July
                   [*the next entry, identical except that the name is spelt Hornage*
                   and the start date omitted, has been crossed out]

                10 Sept.   Haynes, John son of Edward, pinmaker, dec'd, of Gloucester
                   Ricketts, John & Dinah, pinmaker, 7 yrs

                14 Sept.   Smith, John son of John, currier, dec'd, of Gloucester
                   Woodward, John & Mary, pinmaker, 7 yrs from 10 Sept.

	1716	24 Sept.	Bloxom, Joseph son of Joseph, labourer of Gloucester Stephens, William & Mary, crape weaver, 7 yrs
3/577			Mann, John son of Richard, cordwainer, dec'd, of Gloucester Stephens, William, pinmaker, 7 yrs
		28 Sept.	Brooks, Freeman son of Thomas, tailor of Bristol Ward, Thomas & Margaret, pinmaker, 7 yrs from 25 July
			Spencer, Thomas son of Thomas, cooper of Gloucester Spencer, Thomas & Beata, cooper, 7 yrs

Thomas Niccolls, mayor 1716–7[1]

3/577	1716	19 Oct.	Gyttens, Charles son of George, butcher of Ashleworth Pace, Thomas & [—], cordwainer, 7 yrs from 1 Aug.
3/578		22 Oct.	Meeke, Thomas son of Richard, yeoman of Gloucester Evenis, William & Mary, cordwainer, 7 yrs from 15 Oct.

			Braughton, William son of Thomas, blacksmith of 'le Bowle' near
			    the castle, Gloucester
			    Ellis, John & Elizabeth, farrier, 7 yrs

		26 Oct.	Worrall, George son of Joshua, pin merchant of Gloucester Worrall, Joshua, his father, 7 yrs
		29 Oct.	Lilly, Robert son of Matthew, yeoman, dec'd, of Dymock Jones, Anne, widow, 7 yrs from 15 Oct.
3/579			Gregory, William son of William, yeoman, dec'd, of Brimpsfield Heaven, John & Deborah, barber surgeon, 7 yrs from 24 Sept.
		9 Nov.	Tomkins, James son of Isaac, brazier of Leominster, Herefs. Bryan, Daniel & Mary, apothecary, 7 yrs
	1717	18 Jan.	Myles, William son of Martha, of Tirley Kirby, Jacob & Sarah, serge weaver, 7 yrs
		11 Jan.	Woodcocke, James son of Giles, yeoman, dec'd, of Barton Street, Gloucester Jennings, Jeremiah, tailor, 7 yrs
3/580		18 Jan.	Fuller, Thomas son of John, labourer of Whitchurch, Oxon. Benson, John & Joan, tiler & plasterer, 7 yrs
		28 Jan.	Burton, Hester daughter of William, yeoman, dec'd, of Ruardean Jennings, Jeremiah & Elizabeth, tailor, 7 yrs from 19 Nov. 1716
		1 Feb.	Hayward, William son of Jeremiah, grocer of Gloucester Hayward, Jeremiah, his father, & Elizabeth, 7 yrs
		14 Feb.	Gregory, Francis son of Francis, cutler of Marlborough, Wilts. Jeans, Thomas & Martha, feltmaker, 7 yrs
3/581			Gardner, Andrew son of Andrew, woolcomber of Gloucester Stephens, Zachariah & Margaret, tailor, 7 yrs

---

[1] 21 June 1717: To receive £4 of Mrs Sarah Browne's money: Thomas Jobbins, William Hyett, John Lynsy, Augustine Oldham. GBR B3/9 f. 14.

9 Aug. 1717: To receive £5 of Mr William Holliday's money: John Pace, Richard Charles, John Drinkwater, Walter Smith, William Chewett, John Pitt. Nominated by Mr Pleydell to receive £5 of Alderman Powell's money: John Herbert. GBR B3/9 f. 17.

1717   25 Feb.   Rudge, Thomas son of William, fisherman of Westbury
          Ricketts, Samuel & Martha, carpenter, 7 yrs from 29 Sept. 1716

8 Mar.   Phelton, Joseph son of Joseph, barber, dec'd, of Gloucester
          Baker, James, cordwainer, 7 yrs

Coleborne, Joseph son of John, mercer of Stroud
          Lane, Nicholas jr & Hester, apothecary, 7 yrs from 2 Feb.

5 Apr.   Parker, Thomas son of James, yeoman of Minchinhampton
          Bishopp, Samuel & Alice, barber surgeon, 7 yrs

3/582   4 Apr.   Burton, Ann daughter of William, yeoman of Ruardean
          Jennings, Jeremiah, tailor, 7 yrs

13 May   Powell, Thomas son of Thomas, labourer of Gloucester
          Shingler, John & Sarah, pinmaker, 7 yrs

20 May   Drew, Thomas son of Thomas, yeoman of Hartpury
          Pawling, Daniel & Mary, baker, 7 yrs from 27 Mar.

27 May   Cooke, Thomas son of William, tailor of Gloucester
          Smith, John & Mary, barber surgeon, 7 yrs from 1 May

3/583   5 July   Price, Joseph son of John, blacksmith of Gloucester
          Groves, Samuel & Hannah, cordwainer, 7 yrs from 8 Apr.

Harris, Jeremiah son of Nathaniel, woolcomber of Gloucester
          Harris, Nathaniel, his father, 7 yrs

Arnold, William son of William, carpenter of Gloucester
          Archer, Abraham & Abigail, bricklayer, 7 yrs from 1 Feb.

Lynsey, John son of Charles, pinmaker, dec'd, of Gloucester
          Arnold, Robert & Margaret, pinmaker, 7 yrs

22 July   Reeve, Nathaniel son of Stephen, stonecutter of Gloucester
          Wintle, Philip & Mary, joiner, 7 yrs from 24 June

3/584   Holiday, Henry son of Henry, carpenter of Gloucester
          Hutchings, Francis & Elizabeth, tailor, 7 yrs from 25 Mar.

9 Aug.   Gythens, Richard son of George, butcher of Ashleworth
          Wells, Mary, widow, 7 yrs from date of indenture

12 Aug.   Baylis, John son of Edward, woolcomber of Gloucester
          Baylis, Edward, his father, & Hester, 7 yrs

Skillerne, Joseph son of Isaac, furrier of Gloucester
          Bullocke, Thomas & Anne, tailor, 7 yrs

3/585   22 Aug.   Wickham, John son of Joseph, yeoman late of Great Witcombe
          Smith, James & Sarah, distiller & maltster, 7 yrs from 24 June

2 Sept.   Skinner, Luke son of John, labourer of Tewkesbury
          Pegler, Joseph & Jane, tanner, 7 yrs from 24 July

Clarke, William son of [—], carpenter, dec'd, of [—], Gloucester
          Cowcher, Richard & Margaret, pinmaker, 7 yrs

30 Mar.   Taylor, Richard son of Richard, weaver of Ross-on-Wye, Herefs.
          Gregory, John, barber, 7 yrs

John Bell, mayor 1717–8[1]

3/586   1717   11 Oct.   Charles, Richard son of John, pinmaker of Gloucester
Wilton, Henry & Mary, pinmaker, 7 yrs

4 Oct.   Pytt, John son of Roger, carpenter & joiner of Gloucester
Pytt, John, his father, & Mary, 7 yrs

28 Oct.   Piffe, Benjamin son of Joseph, yeoman, dec'd, of Hatherley
Cooke, William & Anne, barber surgeon, 7 yrs from 29 Sept.

4 Nov.   Dowle, John son of Job, mercer, dec'd, of Gloucester
Webb, Thomas & Anne, mercer, 7 yrs from 24 July

3/587   Smith, William son of John, labourer of Gloucester
Church, Roger & Mary, glazier, 7 yrs from 1 Aug.
8 Aug. 1720: William Smith was in due form of law turned over to serve the remainder of his time with Nathan Not of the city of Gloucester, glazier, by the consent of all parties and before alderman Rodway and others

Ellis, Daniel son of William, yeoman of Longney
Corr, Henry & Elizabeth, tailor, 7 yrs from 29 Sept.
[1718–19] Turned over to serve the residue of his term to John Best of the city of Gloucester. Before James Furney, mayor

Chewett, William son of Thomas, labourer of Gloucester
Dark, Richard & Mary, gunsmith, 7 yrs from 1 Nov.

15 Nov.   Pace, John son of William, tailor, dec'd, of Gloucester
Pace, William & Hester, pinmaker, 7 yrs

3/588   Lawson, Hugh son of Edward, tailor late of London
Lumbard, Jacob, weaver, 7 yrs from 14 Oct.

22 Nov.   Jack, John son of William, mercer of Kemble
Longden, Thomas & Mary, mercer, 7 yrs from 7 Oct.

9 Dec.   Simpson, Robert son of William, tailor late of London
Stephens, Thomas & Elizabeth, pinmaker, 7 yrs

23 Dec.   Medway, Amity son of Abraham, bricklayer, dec'd, of Gloucester
Veysey, Nathaniel & Elizabeth, tailor, 7 yrs

3/589   1718   3 Feb.   Hale, William son of William, labourer of Gloucester
Wilton, Henry & Mary, pinmaker, 7 yrs

Elliott, Edward son of Edward, glass blower of Gloucester
Critchley, Ralph & Elizabeth, carpenter, 7 yrs

10 Feb.   Ady, Thomas son of Edward, baker of Gloucester
Lander, William & Hester, grocer, 7 yrs from 24 June 1717

17 Feb.   Gartrill, John son of John, tobacconist of Gloucester
Mowtlow, John & Elizabeth, mercer, 7 yrs from 1 Feb.

3/590   14 Mar.   Hoskins, James son of James, [—] of Barton Street, Gloucester
Draper, Richard & Grace, cordwainer, 7 yrs

[1] 18 July 1718: To receive £4 of Mrs Sarah Browne's money: William Swayne, [—] Pope alias Walker, Joseph Bond, Thomas Puxon. To receive £5 of Mr William Holliday's money or Alderman Powell's money: John Bright, John Shingler, Josiah Randle, John Tayler, Robert Phelps, Thomas Bower. GBR B3/9 f. 43v.

1718 31 Mar. Dowlas, Thomas son of William, mariner of Littleworth
            Rogers, Thomas & Hester, feltmaker, 7 yrs

  16 May Clement, John son of Gerard, clerk of Hawling
            Harris, John & Elizabeth, mercer, 7 yrs from 5 Nov. 1717

        Cull, Stephen son of Stephen, carpenter of Gloucester
            Jefferis, John & Anne, pinner, 7 yrs

  19 May Hayward, Thomas son of John, yeoman of Minsterworth
            Cox, Mary, widow, 7 yrs from 25 Mar.

3/591   Ravenell, Lawrence son of Charles, baker of Gloucester
            Tyler, John & Elinor, tailor, 7 yrs

        Maverly, John son of James, buttonmaker of Gloucester
            Tyler, Elinor, widow, 7 yrs from 24 June

  21 June Little, Walter son of William, yeoman, dec'd, of Ashleworth
            Cooper, Charles & Mary, butcher, 7 yrs from 3 May

  8 Aug. Bower, Thomas son of Samuel, pipemaker, dec'd, of Gloucester
            Stephens, William & Mary, weaver, 7 yrs

        Shingler, John son of John, pinmaker of Gloucester
            Shingler, John, his father, & Sarah, 7 yrs

3/592   Taylor, John son of Thomas, pipemaker, dec'd, of Gloucester
            Smith, Joseph & Rebecca, pipemaker, 7 yrs

        Butt, John son of [—], gentleman, dec'd, of Arlingham
            Bryan, Daniel & Mary, apothecary & surgeon, 7 yrs from 24 June

  11 Aug. Phelps, Robert son of William, tanner, dec'd, of Gloucester
            Pace, William & Hester, pinmaker, 7 yrs

  8 Aug. Swayn, William son of Swayne, Edward, innholder of Gloucester
            Wheeler, John & Margaret, joiner, 7 yrs

  11 Aug. Bright, John son of Thomas, innholder of Gloucester
            Jefferies, Samuel & Katharine, joiner, 7 yrs from 4 Aug.

3/593 22 Aug. Graffstock, George son of John, butcher, dec'd, of Gloucester
            Roberts, William & Mary, carpenter, 7 yrs from 24 June

        Lewin, Joseph son of Joseph, brazier of Littleworth
            Motlow, James & Margaret, glover, 7 yrs

  29 Aug. Parker, John son of Thomas, carpenter, dec'd, of Barnwood
            Mason, William & Mary, tailor, 7 yrs from 10 Oct.

  2 Sept. Harris, Benjamin son of William, yeoman of Painswick
            Engly, John, tailor, 7 yrs

  12 Sept. Canning, John son of John, labourer, dec'd, of Tibberton
            Young, Walter & Margaret, cordwainer, 7 yrs

  25 Sept. Pope, Richard son of John, yeoman, dec'd, of Beverstone
            Engly, Richard & Flinor, bricklayer, 7 yrs

3/594 22 Sept. Kemble, William son of John, weaver, dec'd, of Bristol
            Hale, John & Anne, barber surgeon, 7 yrs from 12 Aug.

        Puxon, Thomas son of John, labourer of Gloucester
            Baker, John & Anne, carpenter, 7 yrs from 1 Sept.

	1718	22 Sept.	Bond, John son of Joseph, cordwainer of Gloucester Baker, James & Elizabeth, cordwainer, 7 yrs
		6 Oct.	Cox, John son of Henry, labourer of Gloucester Hutchins, Francis & Elizabeth, tailor, 7 yrs from 25 Mar.
3/595			Warnford, Walter son of Walter, cordwainer of Gloucester Warnford, Walter, his father, 7 yrs

James Furney, mayor 1718–9[1]

3/595	1718	17 Oct.	Bidwell, Charles son of William, cutler of Gloucester Land, Thomas & Susannah, butcher, 7 yrs from 1 Aug. 1717
			Hampton, Peter son of John Woodward, John & Mary, pinmaker, 7 yrs from 24 Sept.
		27 Oct.	Grimmett, John son of Thomas, labourer of Tewkesbury Billings, William & Isabella, cordwainer, 7 yrs from 29 Sept.
		3 Nov.	Barnes, Edward son of Edward, brazier of Gloucester Collericke, Anne, barber surgeon [deleted] widow, 7 yrs from 1 Nov.
3/596		7 Nov.	Hyett, Robert son of William, mariner of Gloucester Nott, George & Mary, cooper, 7 yrs from 29 Sept.
		21 Nov.	Fluck, William son of Giles, yeoman of Lower Norton Green, Joan, widow, cordwainer, 7 yrs from 5 Nov.
		1 Dec.	Rogers, William son of Samuel, clerk, dec'd, of Painswick Bennett, Edward & Hester, apothecary, 7 yrs
3/597		15 Dec.	Playdell, John son of John, yeoman of Westbury Pawlin, Samuel & Mary, baker, 7 yrs from 12 Dec.
			James, Edward son of [—], yeoman of Twigworth Wintle, Henry sr & Elizabeth, distiller & maltster, 7 yrs from 29 Sept.
	1719	19 Jan.	Cooke, John son of Thomas, labourer of Coleford Rooke, Thomas & Alice, joiner, 7 yrs from 8 Dec. 1718
		6 Mar.	Weston, Edward son of John, dyer of Bedlam, Swindon Iremonger, John & Elizabeth, apothecary, 7 yrs from 25 Dec. 1718
			Ashwood, John son of Abraham, clothier of Gloucester Tomlins, William of St Catherine's parish & Anne, 7 yrs
		6 May	Harris, William son of John, yeoman, dec'd, of Hempsted Evenis, William & Mary, cordwainer, 7 yrs from 30 Mar.
3/598		4 May	Cooke, George son of Thomas, tailor, dec'd, of Gloucester Wells, Mary, cordwainer, 7 yrs
		8 May	Heene, Henry son of James, blacksmith of Ruardean Hayward, Samuel & Hannah, barber surgeon, 7 yrs from 1 May
			Mayer, John son of Peter, yeoman of [—], Glos Perris, John & Margaret, butcher, 7 yrs from 25 Mar.

---

[1] 21 Aug. 1719: To receive £4 of Mrs Sarah Browne's money: John Ashworth, George Bennett, Luke Severne, Charles Smith. To receive £5 of Mr William Holliday's money: William Stephens, John Holder, William Hancks, Edward Normand, Henry Fewtrell, Thomas Adams, Walter Wanford. GBR B3/9 ff. 61, 61v.

3/599	1719	4 May	Fuller, Henry son of John, yeoman, dec'd, of Whitchurch, Oxon. Benson, John & [—], plasterer, 7 yrs from 26 Mar.
		25 May	Wats, John son of John, brazier, dec'd, of Gloucester Webly, Thomas, brazier, 7 yrs from 2 Feb.
		22 June	Harris, Samuel son of John, baker, dec'd, of Gloucester Harris, John, barber surgeon, 7 yrs from 25 Dec. 1718
		10 July	Ford, William son of John, tailor, dec'd, of Gloucester Watts, Giles & Hester, tailor, 7 yrs
3/600		17 July	Barnes, Edward son of Thomas, gentleman of Queenhill, parish of Ripple [MS Ripill], Worcs. Barnes, Nicholas & Elizabeth, mercer, 7 yrs from 25 June
		17 Aug.	Butter, Richard son of Edward, tailor, dec'd, of Gloucester Prinn, William & Mary, tailor, 7 yrs from 17 Aug.
		7 Sept.	Robinson, Giles son of Philip, nailer, dec'd, of Littledean Smith, Abraham & Susannah, cooper, 7 yrs from 7 Sept.
		14 Sept.	Jones, Henry son of Henry, labourer, dec'd, of Barton Street, Gloucester Church, Richard & Elizabeth, glover, 7 yrs from 29 Sept.
			Martshall, Job son of Job, tailor of Longhope Richards, Samuel & [—], carpenter, 7 yrs from 12 Aug.
3/601		28 Sept.	Ellis, John son of Richard, serge weaver of Taunton Dean, Som. Hale, Thomas & Mary, tailor, 7 yrs
			Norman, Edward son of Edward, butcher, dec'd, of Gloucester Way, John, butcher, 7 yrs
		16 Oct.	Seaverne, Lucas son of Samuel, carpenter of Gloucester Sparks, William & Hester, cordwainer, 7 yrs from 17 Sept.
		20 Oct.	Holder, John son of John, pinmaker of Gloucester Holder, John, his father, & Sarah, pinmaker, 7 yrs

Richard Cossley, mayor 1719–20[1]

3/602	1719	20 Oct.	Stephens, William son of William, pinmaker of Gloucester Stephens, William, his father, & Hannah, 7 yrs from 29 Sept.
		2 Nov.	Fewterell, Henry son of George, labourer of Gloucester Davis, Moses & Hannah, 7 yrs
		6 Nov.	Randle, Samuel son of Thomas, yeoman of Hartpury Weale, Thomas & Margery, baker, 7 yrs from 29 Sept.
		26 Nov.	Bonnett, George son of George, bricklayer of Gloucester Engley, Henry, 7 yrs from 26 Nov.

---

[1] 22 July 1720: To receive £4 of Mrs Sarah Browne's money: Ralph Critchley, Andrew King, Robert Bubb, [—] Lapington, William Blanch. GBR B3/9 f. 84.

10 Aug. 1720: To receive £5 of Mr William Holliday's money: Robert Freeman, William Axon, Aaron Cowdall, John Cooppy, Virgil Cryps, Ellis Tayler. To receive £5 of Alderman Powell's money: John Williams. GBR B3/9 f. 86v.

28 Sept. 1720: To leave Sir Thomas Rich's hospital and receive £10: Thomas Lucas, Samuel Hill, Robert Longdon, John Wright, Humphrey Smith, John Hobson. GBR B3/9 f. 91.

3/603	1719	8 Dec.	Carpenter, Francis son of James, ironmonger of Gloucester Bishop, Daniel & Mary, barber, 7 yrs from 6 Nov.
		4 Nov.	Havard, John son of William, tanner of Hereford Hill, Thomas, apothecary, 7 yrs
			Hawkins, Thomas son of Samuel, yeoman of Huntley Brabant, Francis & Margaret, cooper, 7 yrs from 5 Nov.
		21 Dec.	Prestbury, Edward son of [—], dec'd, of Churcham Perkins, George & Martha, baker, 7 yrs
	1720	18 Jan.	Carpenter, George son of James, ironmonger of Gloucester Longden, Robert, gentleman, & Lucy?, 7 yrs
3/604		1 Feb.	Wheeler, William son of Thomas, millwright of Gloucester Wheeler, Thomas, millwright, 7 yrs
		22 Apr.	Sheppard, Samuel son of William, maltster of Pershore, Worcs. Ball, Samuel & Hannah, baker, 7 yrs from 25 Mar.
		25 Apr.	Yates, William son of John, innholder of Chipping Campden Pegler, Andrew & Hannah, saddler, 7 yrs from 25 Mar.
		27 May	Tayler, John son of John, yeoman of [—], Herefs. Arnold, Robert & Margaret, pinmaker, 7 yrs from 30 May
		3 June	Fletcher, Thomas son of Richard, yeoman, dec'd, of Eldersfield, Worcs. Fletcher, Thomas & Hannah, baker, 7 yrs from 25 Jan.

3/605		11 June	Broadstock, William son of John, of Northleach
			    Bonner, John, grocer, 7 yrs
			    12 Nov. 1723: the master and apprentice did agree to vacate these
			    indentures and to part by consent and therefore the apprentice is
			    not to be free at the end of the term. [entry crossed through]

		8 July	Box, John son of Stephen, saddlemaker of Gloucester Shipton, Cowcher & Martha, pinmaker, 7 yrs
		18 July	Harrison, Thomas son of Thomas, dec'd, of Gloucester Oatley, Sarah, widow, 7 yrs from 20 May

		8 Aug.	Smith, Charles son of John, clothworker of Gloucester
			    King, John, gentleman & alderman, & Susannah, 7 yrs from 1 Aug.
			      £4 boy

		25 July	Critchley, Ralph son of Ralph, carpenter of Gloucester Bicke, Robert & Elizabeth, joiner, 7 yrs from 25 Mar. *£5 boy*
3/606		15 Aug.	Adams, Thomas son of John, weaver of Gloucester Evans, William, tailor of Rudford, 7 yrs from 25 Mar. *£5 boy*
		16 Sept.	Freeman, Robert son of Robert, joiner of Gloucester Freeman, Robert, his father, & Frances, 7 yrs from 25 Sept. 1719 *£5 boy*
		15 Aug.	Williams, John son of John, cordwainer of Gloucester Williams, John, his father, & Anne, 7 yrs
		25 Sept.	Axon, William son of Samuel, cutler of Gloucester Axon, Samuel, his father, & Mary, 7 yrs *£5 boy*
		24 Sept.	Webb, Jonathan son of John, butcher, dec'd, of Newnham Cowles, John & Bridget, butcher, 7 yrs from 25 Mar.
		8 Aug.	Swaine, Edward son of Edward, labourer of Gloucester Freame, William & Elizabeth, feltmaker, 7 yrs from 1 Aug.

3/607	1720	29 Sept.	Coopey, John son of John, cooper of Churchdown Coopey, John, his father, & Anne, 7 yrs

John King, mayor 1720–1[1]

3/607	1720	19 Oct.	Lewin, George son of Joseph, tinker of Littleworth Ricketts, Dinah, widow, 7 yrs
		28 Oct.	Reading, Philip son of Samuel, yeoman of Powick, Worcs. Spencer, Samuel & Grace, cooper, 7 yrs from 12 Sept.
		31 Oct.	Harding, Richard son of Richard, gardener of St Catherine's, Kingsholm, Gloucester Wilton, Henry & Mary, pinmaker, 7 yrs
		7 Nov.	Bubb, Robert son of John, yeoman, dec'd, of Maisemore Kirby, Jacob & Sarah, serge weaver, 7 yrs
		9 Nov.	Lewis, William son of Richard, yeoman, dec'd, of Littleworth Kirby, Jacob & Sarah, weaver, 7 yrs
3/608		14 Nov.	Mayo, William son of William, yeoman of Westbury-on-Severn Harris, John, barber surgeon, 7 yrs
		25 Nov.	Hartland *alias* Jones, William Davis, Joan, widow, 7 yrs from 9 Aug.
			Cowdall, Charles son of Robert, labourer of Gloucester Way, John & Anne, butcher, 7 yrs
		5 Dec.	Tayler, Ellis son of William, baker of Gloucester Tayler, William, his father, & Anne, 7 yrs
		19 Dec.	Arnold, Richard son of Richard, clothier of Stroud Stock, Samuel & Hannah, baker, 7 yrs from 28 Aug.
3/609	1721	9 Feb.	Hobson, John son of Joseph, bodicemaker of Gloucester Rathbund, John & Susannah, farrier, 7 yrs from 6 Jan.
		16 Jan.	Preece, Timothy son of John, bricklayer, dec'd, of Acton Beauchamp, Worcs. Pegler, Joseph, tanner, 7 yrs
	1720	20 Mar.	Ashmead, John son of John, mercer of Gloucester Ashmead, John, his father, & Sarah, 7 yrs from 29 Sept.
	1721	21 Apr.	Sheppard, George son of Joshua, gentleman, dec'd, of Calne, Wilts. Longden, Capel, ironmonger, 7 yrs from 10 Jan.
		4 Apr.	Mills, William son of William, innholder of Gloucester Longden, Thomas & Mary, mercer, 7 yrs from 3 Oct.

---

[1] 11 Aug. 1721: To receive £4 of Mrs Sarah Browne's money: Thomas Bennett, Samuel Johnson, William Drinkwater, Thomas Maverley, Joseph Smith. To receive £5 of Mr William Holliday's money: Daniel Carter, John Hayes, George Jones, Thomas Fryer, John Lane, Daniel Jackson, John Greenway. GBR B3/9 ff. 110, 110v.

11 Sept. 1721: To leave Sir Thomas Rich's hospital and receive £10: John Mayor, William Collett, Benjamin Baker, Isaac Gyles, Thomas Merrett, Philip Greene. GBR B3/9 f. 112.

6 Nov. 1721: Philip Greene to stay in the hospital and Rupert Lugg to leave. GBR B3/9 f. 116.

3/610	1721	24 Apr.	Rowley, Francis son of John, dyer of Stroud Cooke, Sarah, widow, 7 yrs from 4 Oct.

			Bond, Thomas son of Anthony, yeoman, dec'd, of Eldersfield, Glos.
			        [*recte* Worcs.]
			    Edwards, James & Mary, baker, 7 yrs from 25 Mar.

		5 May	Hornidge, Thomas son of John, pinmaker, dec'd, of St Mary de Lode,
			        Gloucester
			    Winnett, Thomas & Arabella, pinmaker, 7 yrs

			Underwood, Samuel son of Samuel, carpenter of Barton Street, Gloucester Cother, Joseph & Mary, cordwainer, 7 yrs
		15 May	Brudges, Thomas son of Richard, cooper of Stroud Mills, William & Mary, glover, 7 yrs from 29 Sept. next
3/611		19 May	Wright, John son of John, tailor of Gloucester Lye, Thomas & Elizabeth, buttonmaker, 7 yrs from 19 May
		22 May	Smith, Humphrey son of John, currier of Gloucester Fletcher, John & Mary, currier, 7 yrs
		26 May	Vyner, William son of Giles, yeoman, dec'd, of Churchdown Stocke, John & Susannah, grocer, 7 yrs from 1 May
		9 June	Selwyn, Thomas son of Anne, of Frampton on Severn Edwards, George & Anne, heelmaker, 7 yrs
		5 June	Innell, John son of John, weaver, dec'd, of Maisemore Lumbard, Jacob & Sarah, weaver, 7 yrs from 25 July
3/612		16 June	Gears, Thomas son of [—], yeoman of Hucclecote, Churchdown Roberts, William & Mary, carpenter, 7 yrs [*entry crossed through*]
			Cheston, Joseph son of Richard, tallowchandler of Hereford Cowcher, John & Anne, apothecary, 7 yrs
		[—] June	Bradley, Thomas son of Samuel, yeoman of Longney Lea, Daniel & Elizabeth, cordwainer, 7 yrs from 1 June
		7 July	Spillman, Richard son of Thomas, yeoman of Brookthorpe Pawling, Samuel & Mary, baker, 7 yrs from 20 June
		10 July	Woore, John son of John, feltmaker of Monmouth Oatley, Sarah, widow, 7 yrs
		21 July	Fisher, Clement son of Clement, yeoman, dec'd, of Brockworth Browne, Thomas jr & Dorothy, cordwainer, 7 yrs from 20 June
3/613		25 Aug.	Fryer, Thomas son of William, pargeter, dec'd, of Gloucester Window, Richard & Joyce, cordwainer, 7 yrs

			Evenis, Robert son of Thomas, yeoman, dec'd, of Brookthorpe
			    Evenis, William & Mary, cordwainer, 7 yrs
			    The apprentice is discharged by consent of the master and the
			    indenture cancelled within a year [*entry crossed through*]

		28 Aug.	Drinkwater, William son of William, labourer of Gloucester
			    Hale, Joseph & Margaret, cordwainer, 7 yrs
			    10 Feb. 1726: William Drinkwater was in due form of law and by
			    the consent of all parties turned over to serve the residue of his time
			    to and with Joseph Cother of the city of Gloucester, cordwainer.
			    Before Thomas Ludlow, mayor, and Capel Payne, alderman.

	1721	28 Aug.	Bonnett, Thomas son of William, bricklayer of Gloucester Goodwin, Francis & Anne, butcher, 7 yrs
			Johnson, Samuel son of James, labourer of Gloucester Hayes, William & Sarah, cordwainer, 7 yrs
3/614		4 Sept.	Underhill, Posthumus son of James, silkweaver, dec'd, of Gloucester Archer, Thomas & Mary, bricklayer, 7 yrs from 24 June
		25 Aug.	Wilse, Samuel son of Samuel, gentleman of Barton Street, Gloucester Haynes, William, gentleman, & Frances, 7 yrs from 1 May
		4 Sept.	Jones, George son of Thomas, glover of Gloucester Jones, Thomas, his father, 7 yrs
		25 Sept.	Greenway, John son of Walter, cordwainer of Gloucester Jenkins, Jonathan, of Cheltenham, cordwainer, 7 yrs

Gabriel Harris, mayor 1721–2[1]

3/614	1721	16 Oct.	Hayes, John son of Josiah, cordwainer of Gloucester Merry, Thomas & [—], cordwainer, 7 yrs
3/615		27 Oct.	Lane, John son of John, cordwainer of Gloucester Savory, Robert & Elizabeth, farrier, 7 yrs
		3 Nov.	Jackson, Daniel son of Daniel, tiler & plasterer of Gloucester Jackson, Daniel, his father, 7 yrs
		10 Nov.	Barker, John son of John, gentleman of Berkeley Hendy, Samuel & Sarah, mercer, 7 yrs
		24 Nov.	Hope, Holman son of William, clothier of English Bicknor Gardner, Anthony & Sarah, baker, 7 yrs
		27 Oct.	Smith, Joseph son of Thomas, flax dresser of Gloucester Hale, Thomas & Mary, tailor, 7 yrs
3/616		15 Dec.	Cripps, Virgil son of William, butcher of Gloucester Sparks, William & Hester, cordwainer, 7 yrs
		28 Dec.	Garne, Matthew son of William, weaver of Gloucester Garne, William, his father, & Elizabeth, 7 yrs from 29 Sept.
	1722	19 Jan.	Mayer, John son of John, pinner of Gloucester Hickman, John, cordwainer, 7 yrs from 25 Dec. 1721
			Clarke, Moses son of John, yeoman, dec'd, of Newent Hall, John, baker, 7 yrs from 21 Dec. 1721
		26 Jan.	Hipsley, John son of John, yeoman of Highnam Fletcher, Edward & Sarah, barber surgeon, 7 yrs
3/617		29 Jan.	Meighen, James son of Ferdinand, yeoman, dec'd, of Gloucester Pegler, Joseph jr, tanner, 7 yrs from 29 Sept. 1721

---

[1] 7 Sept. 1722. To receive £4 of Mrs Sarah Browne's money: William Hampton, John Woolly, Thomas Symonds, George Cowle, William Garne. To receive £5 of Mr William Holliday's money: Thomas Shipton, Thomas Long, Richard Cox, John Barnfield, Daniel Winniatt, Thomas Swayne. To receive £5 of Alderman Powell's money: William King. GBR B3/9 f. 128.

27 Sept. 1722: To leave Sir Thomas Rich's hospital and receive £10: John Beal, Thomas Pace, William Taynton, Paul Stephens, Isaac Brotherton, Henry Cleevly. GBR B3/9 f. 129.

	1722	8 Jan.	Gyles, Isaac son of Isaac, tailor of Gloucester Bullocke, John & Elizabeth, cordwainer, 7 yrs
		2 Feb.	Collett, William son of William, grocer, dec'd, of Gloucester Tranter, John & Anne, barber surgeon, 7 yrs
			Brock, Daniel son of Daniel, dec'd, of London Brian, Daniel & Mary, apothecary, 7 yrs from 5 Nov.
		16 Feb.	Rudge, John son of Henry, yeoman, dec'd, of Newent Shatford, John & Mary, joiner, 7 yrs
3/617 bis		2 Mar.	Kent, Joseph son of Samuel, joiner, dec'd, of Gloucester Ricketts, John, sculptor, 7 yrs
			Rickets, William son of John, sculptor of Gloucester Rickets, John, his father, 7 yrs from 29 Sept.
		9 Apr.	Taylor, Thomas son of Francis, mouldmaker of Cheltenham Rudhall, Abraham jr & Eleanor, bellfounder, 7 yrs from 25 Mar.
		20 Apr.	Oldaker, James son of James, miller, dec'd, of Campden Blackwell, John & Mary, baker, 7 yrs
		27 Apr.	Parker, James son of Edward, yeoman of Sapperton Jones, Anne, widow, 7 yrs
3/618		7 May	Carter, Daniel son of John, cordwainer of Gloucester Carter, John, his father, & [—], 7 yrs
		11 May	Faucks, Thomas son of William, yeoman of Bisley Ady, Ralph & Dorothy, butcher, 7 yrs
		25 May	Beach, Thomas son of [—], baker of Dymock Carter, John & Sarah, baker, 7 yrs
		2 July	Hewett, Peter son of Thomas, cordwainer of Gloucester Baker, John & Anne, carpenter, 7 yrs from 29 June
		13 July	Quarrington, Daniel son of Edward, distiller of Gloucester Quarrington, Edward, his father, & Margaret, 7 yrs from 25 Dec. 1721
3/619		20 July	Carter, Henry son of Henry, maltster, dec'd, of Cirencester Wyman, Ambrose & Elizabeth, baker, 7 yrs *10 Mar. 1728: Ran away several times & left his master's service & so ordered to be crossed out by the mayor & aldermen & not have his freedom thereof*
		3 July	Lawrence, George son of George, clothier, dec'd, of Brimpsfield Hawkins, Jeremiah, barber surgeon, 7 yrs from 1 June
		3 Aug.	Merrett, Thomas son of William, innholder, dec'd, of Gloucester Brotherton, James, cordwainer, 7 yrs from 24 June
		13 Aug.	Simons, William son of Thomas, yeoman of Minsterworth Sparrowhawke, William & Hannah, 7 yrs
			Wilson, James son of James, dec'd, of [—] Hutchings, Francis & Elizabeth, tailor, 7 yrs from 1 Nov. 1721
3/620		27 Aug.	Selwyn, Charles son of John, yeoman, dec'd, of Dymock Heaven, John & Deborah, barber surgeon, 7 yrs
			Griffetts, Edward son of Owen, feltmaker of Southwark Heath, Samuel & Mary, joiner, 7 yrs from 3 Oct. 1721

1722   24 Sept.   Beard, Joseph son of James, woolcomber of Gloucester
                    Hayward, Thomas & Anne, weaver, 7 yrs

                    Cowles, George son of George, innholder of Gloucester
                    Draper, Richard & Grace, cordwainer, 7 yrs from 25 July

                    Garne, William son of William, weaver of Gloucester
                    Garne, William, his father, & [—], 7 yrs

                    Woolly, John son of Henry, carrier, dec'd, of Gloucester
                    Stephens, William & Hannah, pinmaker, 7 yrs from 29 Sept. inst.

3/621   28 Sept.   Lewis, Richard son of Richard, gardener of Gloucester
                    Arnold, Robert & Margaret, pinmaker, 7 yrs

                    Barnfield, John son of Richard, blacksmith of Gloucester
                    Barnfield, Richard, his father, & Anne, 7 yrs

                    Cooke, Thomas son of John, plasterer of Gloucester
                    Bird, Joseph & Anne, cordwainer, 7 yrs from 25 July

        13 Sept.   Hamlin, Francis son of Francis, haulier of Gloucester
                    Stephens, William & Mary, weaver, 7 yrs from 1 Oct.

Daniel Washbourne, mayor 1722–3[1]

3/621 1722   12 Oct.   Gough, Richard son of William, yeoman of Hartpury
                    Cowles, John & Anne, tailor, 7 yrs

        12 Oct.   Swaine, Thomas son of Thomas, tiler & plasterer of Gloucester
                    Hooke, Jonathan & Rebecca, joiner, 7 yrs from 29 Sept.

3/622   Hampton, William son of John, innholder of Gloucester
                    Stephens, John & Anne, glazier, 7 yrs

        15 Oct.   Hall, Thomas son of Samuel, yeoman of Gloucester
                    Window, Richard & Joyce, cordwainer, 7 yrs from 29 Sept.

                    Long, Thomas son of William, cordwainer of Gloucester
                    Long, William, his father, & Mary, 7 yrs from 29 Sept.

        16 Nov.   Coxe, Richard son of Richard, labourer of Gloucester
                    Smart, William & Mary, cordwainer, 7 yrs

        17 Dec.   Symonds, Thomas son of Thomas, yeoman, dec'd, of Gloucester
                    Thomas, Abraham, buttonmaker, 7 yrs from 23 Nov.

3/623 1723   4 Feb.   Evenis, Robert son of Thomas, yeoman, dec'd, of Brookthorpe
                    Brimyard, Henry & Anne, cordwainer, 7 yrs

        8 Feb.   Cleevely, Henry son of Henry, tailor of Gloucester
                    Cleevely, Henry & Anne, tailor, 7 yrs from 1 Jan.

        19 Feb.   Compton, Thomas son of William, chandler of Winchcombe
                    Mowtlow, John & Elizabeth, mercer, 7 yrs from 21 Dec. 1722

---

[1] 27 Aug. 1723: To receive £4 of Mrs Sarah Browne's money: Thomas Wilton, John Church, William Chamberlayne, Thomas Kaise. To receive £5 of Mr William Holliday's money: Samuel Merrett, Samuel Sayer, Henry Harris, Lawrence Price, Thomas Lewis, [—] Saunders. To receive £5 of Alderman Powell's money: Richard Dix. GBR B3/9 f. 150.
    26 Sept. 1723: To leave Sir Thomas Rich's hospital and receive £10: John Benson, Philip Greene, Ephraim Higgins, John Holford, Edward Bradshaw, Richard Walker. GBR B3/9 f. 152.

	1723	25 Feb.	Haynes, Peter son of Peter, grocer of Gloucester Haynes, Peter, his father, & Susannah, 7 yrs from 25 Mar. 1722
			Bright, Thomas son of Thomas, innholder of Gloucester Beard, Richard & Mary, barber, 7 yrs
3/624		4 Mar.	Haynes, Henry son of Henry, tailor of Barton Street, Gloucester Weaver, Henry jr & Mary, tailor, 7 yrs
		15 Mar.	Dugmore, Jonathan son of William, yeoman of Ledbury, Herefs. Gooding, Joseph & Elizabeth, butcher, 7 yrs from 1 Mar.
			Stevens, Paul son of Francis, feltmaker of Gloucester Gregory, John & Elizabeth, barber surgeon, 7 yrs
		18 Mar.	Darke, John son of John, victualler of Gloucester Cooke, Sarah, widow, 7 yrs from 6 Oct.
		22 Mar.	Milton, Peter son of Peter, woolcomber of Gloucester Ricketts, William & Elizabeth, pinmaker, 7 yrs
3/625		25 Mar.	Webb, Richard son of Walter, mason, dec'd, of Linton, Herefs. Collins, Sarah, widow, 7 yrs from 25 June
		3 May	Wells, John son of John, innholder of Littleworth Holder, John & [—], pinmaker, 7 yrs
		7 May	Swayne, Richard son of Richard, tailor of Barton Street, Gloucester Luter, John & Elizabeth, butcher, 7 yrs
		25 May	Barnes, John son of John, innholder of Newent Baker, James & Elizabeth, cordwainer, 7 yrs
		27 May	Powell, Richard son of Thomas, innholder of Littleworth Shingler, John & Sarah, pinmaker, 7 yrs from 1 May
3/626			Coopey, William son of Richard, yeoman late of Hartpury Stephens, Zachariah & Margaret, tailor, 7 yrs from 1 May
			Beard, Thomas son of John, yeoman of Hasfield Price, John & Sarah, cordwainer, 7 yrs
		10 June	Tayler, James son of Jasper, dec'd, of Gloucester Evenis, William & Mary, cordwainer, 7 yrs from 30 May
		17 June	Griffitts, Thomas son of Matthew, cordwainer, dec'd, of Gloucester Weaver, Thomas, pinmaker, 7 yrs
		28 June	Chester, Joseph son of Anthony, chandler of London Wood, James & Dorothy, mercer, 7 yrs
		27 May	Jeens, Thomas son of Jeans, Thomas, feltmaker of Gloucester Jeens, Thomas, his father, & Martha, 7 yrs
3/627		8 July	Lloyd, Martin son of Martin, clothier of Gloucester Lloyd, Martin, his father, & Martha, clothier, 7 yrs
			Paul, John son of Nathaniel, mercer of King's Stanley Lane, Nicholas jr & Jane, apothecary, 7 yrs from 31 May
		22 July	Powell, William son of John, pipemaker of Gloucester Ellis, Thomas & Hester, blacksmith, 7 yrs
		15 July	Bingley, James son of Giles, yeoman late of Barnwood Pegler, Andrew & Anne, saddler, 7 yrs from 1 May

	1723	19 Aug.	Herbert, James son of John, yeoman of Llanfihangel Crucorney, Mon. Wadley, John & Sarah, baker, 7 yrs from 1 Aug.
3/628		16 Sept.	Caise, Thomas son of Richard, carpenter of Gloucester Lumbard, Jacob & Sarah, weaver, 7 yrs
		9 Sept.	Gardner, Thomas son of Thomas, glover of Gloucester Gardner, Thomas, his father, & Sarah, 7 yrs

John Rodway, mayor 1723–4[1]

3/628	1723	4 Oct.	Merret, Samuel son of Merrett, Samuel, glover, dec'd, of Gloucester Window, James & Anne, cordwainer, 7 yrs
		21 Oct.	Keyse, John son of William, barber surgeon of Gloucester Weaver, Thomas, pinmaker, 7 yrs
			Saunders, John son of Thomas, tanner of Gloucester Pace, William & Mary, pinmaker, 7 yrs
3/629			Wilton, Thomas son of Henry, woolcomber of Gloucester Shingler, John & Sarah, pinmaker, 7 yrs
		28 Oct.	Child, John son of Richard, carpenter of Hempsted Weaver, Richard & Mary, blacksmith, 7 yrs
		15 Nov.	Evans, Thomas son of John, labourer of Upton St Leonards Jones, Thomas & Anne, glover, 7 yrs from 29 Sept.
			Chamberlayne, William son of William, weaver, dec'd, of Gloucester Brotherton, James, cordwainer, 7 yrs from 5 Nov.
3/630		25 Nov.	Church, John son of Richard, labourer of Gloucester Swaine, Thomas & Rejoice, turner & plasterer, 7 yrs
		7 Dec.	Selwyn *alias* Blainsh, Thomas son of Selwyn, Anne late of Frampton on Severn Edwards, George & Anne, heelmaker, 7 yrs
		9 Dec.	Dickes, Richard son of William, bricklayer of Gloucester Archer, Abraham & Abigail, bricklayer, 7 yrs
	1724	1 Jan.	Whitfield, Richard son of Thomas, innholder, dec'd, of Gloucester Longden, Capel & Elizabeth, ironmonger, 7 yrs
		27 Jan.	Harris, William Henry son of Henry, waterman of Gloucester Harris, Henry, his father, & Anne, 7 yrs
3/631		10 Feb.	Bonner, Thomas son of George, yeoman of Walford, Herefs. Lane, Richard & Anne, grocer, 7 yrs from 21 Jan.
			Lewis, Thomas jr son of Thomas, gardener of Gloucester Lewis, Thomas, his father, & Dorothea, 7 yrs from 21 Dec. 1723

---

[1]8 Sept. 1724: To leave Sir Thomas Rich's hospital and receive £10: Eleazar Dawe, Richard Darke, James Ricketts, Richard Barton, Daniel Remington, Thomas Randle. GBR B3/9 f. 167.

18 Sept. 1724: To receive £4 of Mrs Sarah Browne's money: Thomas Child, John Weston, George White, James Maverly. To receive £5: William Swayne, Charles Wilton, Henry Beard, James Randle, Samuel Millard, Joseph Holder. GBR B3/9 f. 168.

	1724	14 Feb.	Benson, John son of John, plasterer of Gloucester Wooding, William, buttonmaker, 7 yrs from 1 Jan.
		17 Feb.	Holford, John son of John, cordwainer of Gloucester Holford, John, his father, & Margaret, 7 yrs
		21 Feb.	Bradshaw, Edward son of William, joiner of Gloucester Jefferys, John & Anne, pinmaker, 7 yrs from 7 Jan.
3/632		28 Feb.	Hooper, William son of William, yeoman of Wallhill, Ledbury, Herefs. Brabant, Francis & Margaret, cooper, 7 yrs from 24 Nov. 1723
		23 Mar.	Higgins, Ephraim son of Ephraim, bricklayer of Gloucester Bonner, John, grocer, 7 yrs from 4 Mar.
		30 Mar.	Drake, Henry son of Henry, labourer, dec'd, of Gloucester Wilton, Henry & Mary, pinmaker, 7 yrs from 29 Sept. 1723
			Weal, Thomas son of John, yeoman, dec'd, of Dymock Weal, Thomas & Margery, baker, 7 yrs
			Jones, John son of Henry, labourer, dec'd, of Gloucester Woodward, John & Mary, pinmaker, 7 yrs
3/633		20 Apr.	Beal, Richard son of Richard, yeoman, dec'd, of Flaxley Baker, James jr & Elizabeth, cordwainer, 7 yrs from 25 Mar.
		24 Apr.	Cheesman, John son of Paul, tailor, dec'd, of Gloucester Perry, William & Elizabeth, tailor, 7 yrs from 17 Apr.
		1 May	Bowley, Joseph son of Joseph, tiler & plasterer, dec'd, of Gloucester Engley, Henry, bricklayer, 7 yrs from 23 Apr.
		11 May	Bloxam, Samuel son of Joseph, labourer of Gloucester Lodge, William, cooper, 7 yrs
			Williams, Jeremiah son of Charles, labourer of Churchdown Merry, Thomas & Elizabeth, cordwainer, 7 yrs from 25 Mar.
3/634			Bridges, William son of Richard, cooper of Stroud Cooke, William & Anne, barber surgeon, 7 yrs from 1 May
		1 June	Talbott, Samuel son of Thomas, mercer of Shrewsbury, Salop Griffitts, Alexander & Avice, mercer, 7 yrs
		15 May	Sayer, Samuel son of Daniel, ropemaker, dec'd, of Gloucester Gibbons, Samuel, of Barton Street, tailor, 7 yrs
		1 June	Witchell, John son of Jonathan, clothier, dec'd, of North Nibley Smith, James & Sarah, distiller & maltster, 7 yrs
		20 July	Spencer, Benjamin son of Lewis, clothworker of Cirencester Draper, Richard & Grace, cordwainer, 7 yrs from 29 Sept.
		7 Sept.	Gardner, Samuel son of Thomas, skinner of Gloucester Gardner, Thomas, his father, 7 yrs
3/635		28 Sept.	Pembruge, Thomas son of Anthony, yeoman of Elmore Hawkins, John & Mary, cordwainer, 7 yrs

Richard Greene, mayor 1724–5[1]

3/635	1724	2 Oct.	Humphris, Thomas son of Thomas, soapmaker, dec'd, of Gloucester Ricketts, John & [—], pinmaker, 7 yrs
			Millard, Samuel son of Samuel, gardener of Gloucester Millard, Samuel, his father, 7 yrs
		9 Oct.	Wilton, Charles son of Henry, pinmaker, dec'd, of Gloucester Wilton, Mary, widow, 7 yrs
			Weston, John son of John, baker of Gloucester Hickman, John & [—], cordwainer, 7 yrs
3/636		19 Oct.	Swayne, William son of Thomas, tiler & plasterer of Gloucester Cother, Joseph & Mary, cordwainer, 7 yrs from 17 Oct.
		2 Nov.	Randall, James son of John, tiler & plasterer of Gloucester Randall, John, his father, 7 yrs
		19 Oct.	Holder, Joseph son of John, pinmaker of Gloucester Wiltshire, John & Mary, tailor, 7 yrs
		23 Oct.	Jelfe, Thomas son of Thomas, labourer of Gloucester Holder, John & Sarah, pinmaker, 7 yrs
			Cooke, John son of John, yeoman of Gloucester Kirby, Jacob & Sarah, serge weaver, 7 yrs
		16 Nov.	Grove, John son of Samuel, cordwainer of Gloucester Grove, Samuel, his father, 7 yrs
3/637		17 Nov.	Rudge, Thomas son of William, fisherman late of Westbury Ricketts, Samuel & Mary, carpenter, 7 yrs
	1725	25 Jan.	Broadwell, Isaac son of Isaac, yeoman of Gloucester Mason, William & Mary, tailor, 7 yrs
			Daws, Eleazer son of Eleazar, carpenter of Gloucester Dowdy, George & Rebecca, carpenter, 7 yrs from 6 Jan.
		29 Jan.	Pace, Solomon son of Robert, labourer of Gloucester Sparks, William & Hester, cordwainer, 7 yrs
3/638		1 Mar.	Nash, Benjamin son of Benjamin, woolcomber of Gloucester How, Thomas & Elizabeth, innholder, 7 yrs
			Edwards, Thomas son of [—], yeoman, dec'd, of Churchdown Draper, Richard & Grace, cordwainer, 7 yrs from 14 Feb.
			Price, John son of John, gentleman of Urishay, Herefs. Bennett, Edward & Hester, apothecary, 7 yrs from 2 Feb.
		12 Mar.	Drake, William son of Henry, coachman, dec'd, of Gloucester Cowcher, Richard & Elizabeth, pinmaker, 7 yrs
		12 Mar.	Randle, Thomas son of Thomas, plastercr, dec'd, of Gloucester Pace, William & Mary, pinmaker, 7 yrs from 21 Dec. 1724

---

[1] 20 Aug. 1725: To receive £4 of Mrs Sarah Browne's money: Henry Window, Robert Mathews, John Latham, Jacob Brotherton. To receive £5: Ambrose Wright, Abraham Howell, William Coopy, John Powell, James Nott, Adam Gyles, William Welch. GBR B3/9 f. 181.

22 Sept. 1725: To leave Sir Thomas Rich's hospital and receive £10: Luke Hooke, Edmund Ady, Edward Nott, George Deane, Robert Stephens, Philip Philipps. GBR B3/9 f. 184.

3/639	1725	15 Mar.	Macocke, Benjamin son of John, currier of Cheltenham Charleton, Meshach & Margaret, feltmaker, 7 yrs from 30 Jan.
		22 Mar.	Ricketts, James son of John, pinmaker, dec'd, of Gloucester Ricketts, Dinah, his mother, pinmaker, 7 yrs
			Price, Richard son of John, bricklayer of Gloucester Davis, John, pinmaker, 7 yrs from 25 Dec. 1724
		12 Apr.	Purton, Thomas son of Thomas, yeoman of Minsterworth Cother, Joseph & Mary, cordwainer, 7 yrs
		16 Apr.	Darke, Richard son of Richard, gunsmith of Gloucester Darke, Richard, his father, & Mary, 7 yrs
3/640			Cooke, James son of James, joiner of Gloucester Weal, Richard & Sarah, baker, 7 yrs from 2 Feb.
		12 May	Browne, Thomas son of Thomas, sawyer of Gloucester Pegler, Joseph & Mary, tanner, 7 yrs from 25 Mar.
		14 May	Wright, Ambrose son of John, glover of Gloucester White, Thomas & Elizabeth, glover, 7 yrs from 1 May
			Barton, Richard son of John, bricklayer of Gloucester Payne, Thomas & Sarah, plumber, 7 yrs from 25 Mar.
3/641		24 May	Muskett, Henry son of Thomas, labourer of Gloucester Worrall, George, pinmaker, 7 yrs
		4 June	Buckle, Robert son of William, yeoman of Haresfield Puckeridge, Thomas & Mary, tailor, 7 yrs from 25 Apr.
		11 June	Spillman, Benjamin son of Thomas, yeoman of Brookthorpe Smith, Abraham & Susannah, cooper, 7 yrs from 21 May
		25 June	Child, Thomas son of Richard, yeoman of Hempsted Rickards, Samuel & Martha, carpenter, 7 yrs from 25 Mar.
3/642		2 July	Maverly, Samuel son of James, buttonmaker of Gloucester Maverly, William & Mary, tailor, 7 yrs from 25 Dec. 1724
		5 July	Weal, Thomas son of John, yeoman, dec'd, of Dymock Hale, John & Sarah, barber surgeon, 7 yrs from 26 June
		9 July	Millington, Jonathan son of James, victualler of Cirencester Spencer, Samuel & Grace, cooper, 7 yrs
		25 June	Chandler, Thomas son of Mary, widow of Gloucester Steel, Thomas, grocer & tallowchandler, 7 yrs
		20 Aug.	Tranter, John son of John, labourer of Horsley Smith, Humphrey & Elizabeth, glover, 7 yrs
3/643		23 Aug.	Turner, Samuel son of John, yeoman of Painswick Pruin, William, tailor, 7 yrs
		3 Sept.	Matthews, Robert son of [—], blacksmith of Gloucester Arnold, Robert & Margaret, pinmaker, 7 yrs from 25 Mar.

Samuel Brown, mayor 1725–6[1]

3/643	1725	8 Oct.	Hicks, Samuel son of Samuel, gardener of Gloucester Davis, Henry & Mary, pinmaker, 7 [*deleted*] 8 yrs from 25 Mar.
3/644		11 Oct.	Prosser, Daniel son of John, yeoman of Gloucester Brotherton, Jeremiah jr & Mary, tailor, 7 yrs
		25 Oct.	Powell, John son of John, pipemaker of Gloucester Smith, Joseph & Rebecca, pipemaker, 7 yrs
		1 Nov.	Mynett, Thomas son of Thomas, yeoman of Painswick Bullock, John & Elizabeth, cordwainer, 7 yrs
		7 Nov.	Latham, John son of John, dyer of Gloucester Best, John & Mary, tailor, 7 yrs
3/645		12 Nov.	Window, Henry son of Richard, yeoman of Gloucester Coucher, Richard & Elizabeth, pinmaker, 7 yrs
			Stratford, Valentine son of John, yeoman of Barnwood Jeffereys, John & Anne, pinmaker, 7 yrs
		15 Nov.	Coopy, William son of John, yeoman of Churcham Coopy, John, his father, & Elizabeth, 7 yrs

		22 Nov.	Furley, Henry son of Clement, gentleman, dec'd, of Bruern Grange
			    [MS 'Brewing Grange'], Oxon.
			    Dimocke, Charles & Mary, mercer, 7 yrs from 22 May [*see 3/664*]

3/646		10 Dec.	Nott, James son of Laurence, [—] of Gloucester Kemis, Samuel & Joan, woolcomber, 7 yrs
			Bradley, James son of Henry, butcher of Gloucester Bradley, Henry, his father, & Jane, 7 yrs
		17 Dec.	Cullurne, James son of John, gardener of Barton Street, Gloucester Heaven, John & Deborah, barber surgeon, 7 yrs
	1726	14 Jan.	Howell, Abraham son of Abraham, cordwainer of Gloucester Howell, Abraham, his father, & Mary, 7 yrs
3/647		17 Jan.	Hayward, William son of Edward, weaver of Gloucester Cowles, John & Bridget, butcher, 7 yrs
		24 Jan.	Reeve, Richard son of Richard, innholder of Gloucester Reeve, Richard, his father, & Ann, 7 yrs
		7 Mar.	Weyman, Daniel son of Thomas, yeoman of Ashleworth Wadley, John & Elizabeth, baker, 7 yrs
		18 Feb.	Philipps, Philip son of John, tailor of Gloucester Window, William & Sarah, buttonmaker, 7 yrs

---

[1] 5 Aug. 1726: To receive £4 of Mrs Sarah Browne's money: William Bennett, Francis Brotherton, Charles Wheeler, Giles Browne. GBR B3/9 f. 197v.

22 Aug. 1726: To receive £5: John Davis, Henry Brimyard, Richard Sanders, Walter Mason, Thomas Best, William Bishopp. To receive £5 of Alderman Powell's money by Mr Snell's nomination: James Gunn. GBR B3/9 f. 199.

23 Sept. 1726: To leave Sir Thomas Rich's hospital and receive £10: Samuel Wellavise, William Haynes, John Wheeler, Thomas Sparks, Thomas Partridge, William Reeve. GBR B3/9 f. 200.

	1726 11 Feb.	Farr, Roger son of Roger, gentleman of Evesham, Worcs. Webley, Thomas, brazier, 7 yrs
		[There is no page 648]
3/649	11 Feb.	Walford, Thomas son of Gardner, yeoman of Icomb Phipps, Joseph & Sarah, cooper, 7 yrs
	7 Mar.	Deane, George son of Thomas, baker, dec'd, of Gloucester Freeman, Robert & Frances, joiner, 7 yrs
	18 Mar.	Welch, William son of William, yeoman of Barnwood Drinkwater, Richard & Sarah, cordwainer, 7 yrs
	22 Apr.	Rickards, George son of Samuel, yeoman of Bredon, Worcs. Palling, Samuel & Mary, baker, 7 yrs
3/650	15 Apr.	Hyett, William son of William, yeoman of Minsterworth Brotherton, James & Winifred, cordwainer, 7 yrs
	20 May	Graffstocke, Daniel son of Daniel, yeoman, dec'd, of Hempsted Harris, Nathaniel & Hannah, woolcomber, 7 yrs
	6 June	Mayoe, Thomas son of Robert, yeoman of Hartpury Jennings, Michael sr & Abigail, butcher, 7 yrs from 3 May
	13 June	Ady, Edmund son of Edmund, baker of Gloucester Townsend, Richard jr & Mary, tailor, 7 yrs
3/651	20 June	Hayle, Richard son of Robert, tanner, dec'd, of Blaisdon Pegler, Joseph & Mary, tanner, 7 yrs from 25 Mar.
	1 July	Hooke, Luke son of Jonathan, joiner of Gloucester Hooke, Jonathan, his father, & Rebecca, 7 yrs from 25 Mar.
	15 July	Harris, Wintour son of Henry, sailor of Gloucester Harris, John & Sarah, barber surgeon, 7 yrs from 1 May
		Darby, Samuel son of Joseph, butcher of Upton upon Severn, Worcs. Cooke, William & Margaret, butcher, 7 yrs from 25 Dec. 1725
3/652		Rawlings, Richard son of [—], dec'd, of Gloucester Graffstocke, George, carpenter, 7 yrs from 25 June
	8 Aug.	Pace, Richard son of Robert, yeoman of Barton Street, Gloucester Ward, Thomas & Margaret, pinmaker, 7 yrs from 1 Aug.
		Swayne, Thomas son of Richard, tailor of Barton Street, Gloucester Holder, John & Sarah, pinmaker, 7 yrs from 11 Apr.
	12 Sept.	Gunn, Samuel son of James, glazier of Gloucester Gunn, James, his father, & Margaret, 7 yrs
3/653		Davis, John son of Henry, pinmaker of Gloucester Davis, Henry, his father, & Mary, pinmaker, 7 yrs
	19 Sept.	Sanders, Richard son of Thomas, tanner of Gloucester Browne, Thomas & Dorothy, cordwainer, 7 yrs
	23 Sept.	Bonnett, William son of William, bricklayer of Gloucester Hickman, John & Elizabeth, cordwainer, 7 yrs
		Wheeler, Charles son of Charles, labourer of Gloucester Shingler, John jr & Elizabeth, pinmaker, 7 yrs

Thomas Ludlow, mayor 1726–7[1]

3/654	1726	17 Oct.	Brocke, John son of Joseph, mercer late of Cheltenham 　　Charleton, Meshach & Margaret, feltmaker, 7 yrs
			Bishopp, William son of John, labourer of Gloucester 　　Cooke, Thomas, cordwainer, 7 yrs
			Bretherton, Francis son of Solomon, bricklayer late of Gloucester 　　Rogers, James & Susannah, bricklayer, 7 yrs
		11 Nov.	Browne, Giles son of Thomas, labourer of Gloucester 　　Bicke, Robert & Elizabeth, joiner, 7 yrs
3/655		23 Dec.	Greene, William son of John, labourer, dec'd, of Ely, Cambs. 　　Taylor, Richard & Hester, barber surgeon, 7 yrs from 2 Feb.
			Wells, Caleb son of Isaac, yeoman of Brookthorpe 　　Bryan, Daniel, apothecary, 7 yrs
	1727	16 Jan.	Wagstaffe, Miles son of Henry, gentleman, dec'd, of Gloucester 　　Lane, Richard, grocer & chandler, 7 yrs
		23 Jan.	Merrick, William son of John, carpenter of Ross-on-Wye, Herefs. 　　Stephens, Zachariah & Margaret, tailor, 7 yrs[2]
3/656		27 Jan.	Wells, Thomas son of John, victualler, dec'd, of Lower Southgate 　　Street, Gloucester 　　Edwards, George & Anne, heelmaker, 7 yrs
		2 Feb.	Davis, John son of Henry, pinmaker of Gloucester 　　Davis, Henry, his father, & Mary, 7 yrs
			Harmer, John son of Richard, dyer of Chalford 　　Fownes, Joseph & Sarah, distiller, 7 yrs
3/657		10 Feb.	Hill, Thomas son of Richard, tailor, dec'd, of Ledbury, Herefs. 　　Lovett, James & Martha, barber, 7 yrs
		13 Feb.	Wellavise, Samuel son of Samuel, glazier of Gloucester 　　Wellavise, Samuel, his father, & Sarah, 7 yrs
		10 Feb.	Smith, Joseph son of Edward, labourer, dec'd, of Guiting 　　Parker, Thomas, barber surgeon, 7 yrs
			Mayo, Peter son of Peter, labourer, dec'd, of Placketts Farm 　　Hale, Jesse & Mary, pinmaker, 7 yrs
3/658		10 Mar.	Freeman, Benjamin son of [—], labourer, dec'd, of Gloucester 　　Price, John, blacksmith, 7 yrs
		24 Mar.	Webb, Timothy son of Nathaniel, yeoman, dec'd, of Baunton 　　Perkins, Martha, widow, baker, 7 yrs
		21 Apr.	Turner, John son of John, yeoman of Painswick 　　Ellis, Guy & [—], grocer, 7 yrs

---

[1] 30 June 1727: To receive £4 of Mrs Sarah Browne's money: Richard Armitage, Richard Ashworth, Thomas Dicks, Anthony Brotherton. GBR B3/9 f. 213.

22 Sept. 1727: To leave Sir Thomas Rich's hospital and receive £10: John Nelme, John Haynes, Gregory Nicholls, Nathaniel Castle, Thomas Barrett, Samuel Brimyard. To receive £5 [of Mr William Holliday's money] or Alderman Powell's money: John Cleevly, Samuel Best, Adam Fletcher, John Garne, Henry Harris, Thomas Williams, Thomas Remington. GBR B3/9 f. 225.

[2] Entry repeated at the top of p. 656.

	1727	1 May	Bannaster, Willoughby son of Willoughby, yeoman of Puckstoole Ricketts, John & Hannah, pinmaker, 7 yrs
3/659			Swaine, Thomas son of Edward, innholder of Gloucester Fitchew, Josiah & Eleanor, feltmaker, 7 yrs
		19 May	Garnor, Cornelius son of Sarah, widow of Painswick Taylor, Richard & Hester, barber & perukemaker, 7 yrs
		9 June	Rider, Benjamin son of Samuel, yeoman of Maisemore Rathbone, John & Susannah, blacksmith, 7 yrs
		23 June	Hicks, James son of Samuel, gardener of Gloucester Rickards, William & Elizabeth, pinmaker, 7 yrs
3/660		1 July	Best, Thomas son of Thomas, gardener, dec'd, of Gloucester Halford, Philip, cordwainer of Maisemore, 7 yrs
		7 July	Reeve, William son of Richard, innholder of Gloucester Hale, Thomas & Mary, tailor, 7 yrs from 9 May
		10 July	Sparks, Thomas son of Thomas, cordwainer, dec'd, of Gloucester Roberts, John, of St Mary Magdalen, & Elizabeth, weaver, 7 yrs
		7 Aug.	Brotherton, Anthony son of Thomas, tiler & plasterer of Gloucester Brotherton, Thomas, his father, & Anne, 7 yrs
3/661		14 Aug.	Brimyard, Henry son of John, cordwainer of Gloucester Brimyard, John, his father, & Hester, 7 yrs
		22 Sept.	Dicks, Thomas son of Thomas, bricklayer of Gloucester Dancy, William & Anne, bricklayer, 7 yrs

James Selwyn, mayor 1727–8[1]

	1727	20 Oct.	Bloxom, Charles son of Joseph, labourer of Gloucester Lumbard, Jacob & Sarah, shagmaker, 7 yrs
3/661		[—]	Ashworth, Richard son of Abraham, weaver, dec'd, of Gloucester Colwell, James & Mary, cordwainer, 7 yrs from 24 June
3/662		3 Nov.	Fletcher, Adam son of John, currier of Gloucester Fletcher, John, his father, & Mary, 7 yrs
			Tomlins, Thomas son of Philip, barber of Hereford Freeman, Robert sr & Frances, joiner, 7 yrs from 1 Nov.
			Andrews, Richard son of Richard, yeoman of Hill Shatford, John & Mary, joiner, 7 yrs
		10 Nov.	[—], Richard son of [—], weaver of Bisley Jones, Anne, widow, 7 yrs
3/663			Wheeler, John son of John, joiner of Gloucester Heath, Samuel & Mary, joiner, 7 yrs

[1] 22 Aug. 1728: To receive £4 of Mrs Sarah Browne's money: William Hatton, Joseph Darke, Thomas Herbert, Edmund Gotheridge. To receive £5 [of Mr William Holliday's money] or Alderman Powell's money: William Draper, James Engly, Michael Arnold, George Phillips, William Hayes, Giles King, Thomas Mills. GBR B3/9 f. 238.

26 Sept. 1728: To leave Sir Thomas Rich's hospital and receive £10: William Bicknell, John King, Daniel Randle, Thomas Pace, Henry Grevile, John Hathaway. GBR B3/9 f. 225.

	1727	20 Nov.	Gibbs, Picke Nathaniel son of William, yeoman of Mitcheldean Mutlow, Robert & Elizabeth, cordwainer, 7 yrs
	1728	22 Jan.	Garn, John son of William, weaver of Gloucester Garn, William, his father, & Elizabeth, 7 yrs from 25 Mar. 1727
		22 Jan.	Williams, Elisha son of Thomas, gardener of Gloucester Williams, Thomas, his father, & Margaret, 7 yrs
3/664		9 Feb.	Brotherton, James son of Moses, bricklayer, dec'd, of Gloucester Woolford, Thomas & Beata, basketmaker, 7 yrs from 2 Nov. 1727
		19 Feb.	Furley, Henry son of Clement, gentleman, dec'd, of Bruern Grange [MS 'Brewing Grange'], Oxon. Dimocke, Charles & Mary, mercer, 7 yrs from 17 May 1725 [*see 3/645*]
		26 Feb.	Fownes, Gabriel son of Godfrey, tobacconist of Gloucester Fownes, Godfrey, his father, & Mary, 7 yrs
		1 Mar.	Best, Samuel son of Samuel, gardener of Gloucester Holford, John, cordwainer, of Maisemore, 7 yrs
3/665		4 Mar.	Millington, Thomas son of James, woolcomber of Cirencester Prestbury, Edward & Hester, baker, 7 yrs
			Macock, Ebenezer son of John, carrier of Cheltenham Stock, Samuel & Hannah, baker, 7 yrs
		15 Mar.	King, Samuel son of Samuel, maltster, dec'd, of Cheltenham Parker, John & Anne, tailor, 7 yrs from 1 Mar.
		29 Mar.	Harmitage, Richard son of Edward, cordwainer of Gloucester Reeve, James & Jane, combmaker, 7 yrs
3/666		27 May	Alford, Thomas son of Thomas, victualler of Gloucester Pace, William & Mary, pinmaker, 7 yrs
		3 June	Wood, William son of Thomas, yeoman of Eldersfield, Worcs. Robinson, Giles & Elizabeth, cooper, 7 yrs
			Browne, John son of William, labourer of St Mary, Wotton Weaver, Thomas & Elizabeth, pinmaker, 7 yrs
3/667		1 July	Warton, William son of William, yeoman, dec'd, of Hasfield Norman, Edward & Elizabeth, butcher, 7 yrs from 1 July 1726
		2 Aug.	Gun, James son of James, glazier of Gloucester Price, Joseph, cordwainer, 7 yrs from 18 July
		9 Aug.	Harris, Richard son of John, clerk, dec'd, of Easton Grey, Wilts. Stocke, John & Susannah, grocer, 7 yrs from 9 May
		26 Aug.	Herbert, Thomas son of Thomas, tailor of Gloucester Smith, Joseph & Rebecca, pipemaker, 7 yrs
		30 Aug.	Hatton, William son of John, labourer, dec'd, of Uckington Church, Richard & Elizabeth, glover, 7 yrs from 29 Sept.
3/668			Engly, James son of Thomas, butcher of Gloucester Engly, Thomas, his father, & Mary, 7 yrs
		2 Sept.	Draper, William son of Richard, cordwainer of Gloucester Draper, Richard & Grace, cordwainer, 7 yrs
		9 Sept.	Byard, William son of Samuel, maltster of Gloucester Hawkins, Jeremiah, barber surgeon, 7 yrs from 1 July

| | 1728 | 13 Sept. | Simmonds, Benjamin son of Samuel, soapboiler of Mitcheldean
    Ades, Thomas & Grace, cordwainer, 7 yrs from 24 Aug. |
| 3/669 | | 16 Sept. | Trigg, Thomas son of Thomas, yeoman of Churcham
    Pawling, Samuel & Mary, baker, 7 yrs from 24 Aug. |

John King, mayor 1728–9[1]

3/669	1728	14 Oct.	Mills, Thomas son of Thomas, pinmaker of Gloucester Stephens, William & Hannah, pinmaker, 7 yrs
			Hayes, William son of Josiah, cordwainer of Gloucester Hayes, Josiah, his father, & Elizabeth, 7 yrs from 29 Sept.
			Gutheridge, Edward son of William, gardener of Gloucester Gutheridge, William & Elizabeth, gardener, 7 yrs
3/670		18 Oct.	Arnold, Michael son of Michael, [—] of Gloucester Grymett, John & Elizabeth, cordwainer, 7 yrs
			King, Giles son of John, bricklayer of Gloucester King, John, his father, & Elizabeth, 7 yrs
		28 Oct.	Wagstaffe, Thomas son of Henry, armiger late of Gloucester Taylor, Ellis & Alice, baker, 7 yrs from 6 Aug.
		8 Nov.	Darke, Joseph son of William, fisherman of Gloucester Harrison, Thomas & Martha, carpenter, 7 yrs
3/671		15 Nov.	Mayoe, Robert son of William, yeoman, dec'd, of Westbury Mayoe, William & Anne, barber surgeon, 7 yrs
		25 Nov.	Phillips, George son of George, pinmaker of Gloucester Phillips, George, his father, & Mary, 7 yrs
		6 Dec.	Haynes, John son of Thomas, tailor of Gloucester Bishopp, Samuel & Alice, barber surgeon, 7 yrs from 9 Nov.
		9 Dec.	Partridge, Richard son of Joseph, clothier, dec'd, of Cowley Weaver, Matthew & Susannah, baker, 7 yrs
3/672	1729	12 Jan.	Prinn, William son of William, tailor of Gloucester Cowcher, John & Anne, apothecary, 7 yrs from 1 Nov.
		31 Jan.	Niccolls, Gregory son of Thomas, saddler of Hucclecote in Churchdown Carpenter, Francis, barber surgeon, 7 yrs
		14 Feb.	Bonner, John son of George, yeoman of Ruardean Bond, Thomas & Elizabeth, baker, 7 yrs from 1 Jan.
		17 Feb.	Randall, Daniel son of John, tiler & plasterer of Gloucester Acock, John & Jane, painter, 7 yrs from 2 Feb.

---

[1] 5 Aug. 1729: To leave Sir Thomas Rich's hospital and receive £10: Benjamin Long, John Greene, William Staight, Thomas Millard, Joshua Brotherton, Joseph Mayoe. GBR B3/9 f. 256.

28 Aug. 1729: To receive £4 of Mrs Sarah Browne's money: William Hare, Joseph Hockley, Humphrey Moore, Thomas Garrett. To receive £5 [of Mr William Holliday's money] or Alderman Powell's money: William Long, John Bradshaw, [—] Annis, [—] Keylock, [—] Griggs, [—] Ravenhill, [—] Yeend. GBR B3/9 f. 257.

3/673	1729	3 Mar.	Mathews, Humphrey Scutt son of Thomas, glover of Malmesbury, Wilts. Shatford, John & Mary, joiner, 7 yrs
		17 Mar.	Hathaway, John son of Richard, innholder of Gloucester Wadley, Sarah, widow, baker, 7 yrs
			Wadley, Thomas son of John, baker, dec'd, of Gloucester Wadley, Sarah, his mother, widow, baker, 7 yrs
		20 Apr.	Weston, Thomas son of John, dyer of Swindon, Glos. Bryan, Daniel, surgeon & apothecary, 7 yrs from 25 Mar.
3/674		28 Apr.	Reane, Richard son of Richard, chairmaker of Gloucester Kirby, Jacob & Sarah, weaver, 7 yrs from 23 Apr.
		9 May	Garne, John son of John, weaver, dec'd, of Barton Street, Gloucester Cother, Joseph & Mary, cordwainer, 7 yrs from 1 May
		19 May	Engley, Richard son of Richard, bricklayer, dec'd, of Gloucester Price, Thomas, silversmith, 7 yrs
			Baker, James son of John, carpenter of Gloucester Baker, James & Elizabeth, cordwainer, 7 yrs from 25 Dec.
3/675		9 June	Bicknell, William son of William, barber surgeon, dec'd, of Gloucester Axon, William & Elizabeth, cutler, 7 yrs
		7 July	Eden, Robert son of Robert, gentleman, dec'd, of London Vernon, Henry, apothecary, 7 yrs from 1 May
		14 July	Hardwick, John son of [—], baker of Gloucester Perry, William & Elizabeth, tailor, 7 yrs
		28 July	Clarke, John son of Joseph, gentleman of Taynton Webb, John, baker, 7 yrs from 2 June
3/676			Vickers, James son of James, labourer of Gretton Cowles, John & Anne, tailor, 7 yrs from 20 July
		1 Aug.	Pace, Thomas son of Thomas, cordwainer of Gloucester Wheeler, William & Elizabeth, bricklayer, 7 yrs from 25 July
		8 Aug.	King, John son of Samuel, innholder of Gloucester Cooke, Thomas & Sarah, barber surgeon, 7 yrs
		29 Aug.	Grevill, Henry son of Henry, barber of London Webb, Nicholas & Susannah, mercer, 7 yrs
3/677		15 Aug.	Hicks, William son of Samuel, gardener of Gloucester Prinn, William, tailor, 7 yrs
		1 Sept.	Hunman, William son of [—], yeoman, dec'd, of Elmore Weaver, Richard & Elizabeth, blacksmith, 7 yrs from 9 Apr.
		12 Sept.	Shatford, William son of Daniel, gentleman of Stroud Rogers, William, apothecary, 7 yrs
		15 Sept.	Moore, John son of John, yeoman of Sandhurst Weale, Richard, tailor, 7 yrs
3/678		19 Sept.	Ravener, George son of Thomas, gardener of Gloucester Ravener, Thomas, his father, & Elizabeth, 7 yrs

			Still, William son of Edward, yeoman, dec'd, of Alstone
			        [MS 'Arlestone']
			    Still, Francis & Mary, cornchandler, 7 yrs from 25 Oct. 1728

Thomas Carrill, mayor 1729–30[1]

3/678	1729	10 Oct.	Long, William son of William, cordwainer of Gloucester Long, William, his father, & Mary, 7 yrs
		16 Oct.	Hockley, Joseph son of Joseph, gardener of Gloucester Meadway, Amity & [—], staymaker, 7 yrs
3/679			Griggs, James son of Henry, pinmaker of Gloucester Dowdy, George, carpenter, 7 yrs
		20 Oct.	Hannis, Thomas son of Thomas, pinmaker of Gloucester Hannis, Thomas, his father, & Honour, 7 yrs
		27 Oct.	Keylock, Thomas son of Jasper, cordwainer of Gloucester Keylock, Jasper, his father, & Dinah, 7 yrs
		31 Oct.	Yeend, James son of William, barber surgeon of Gloucester Yeend, William, his father, & Sarah, 7 yrs [*entry deleted; repeated at 3/681 with a different date*]
3/680			Pritchard, Richard son of Robert, labourer of Cromhall Bowler, George & Elizabeth, tailor, 7 yrs
		10 Nov.	Hathaway, John son of John, cordwainer, dec'd, of London Parker, John & Anne, tailor, 7 yrs from 1 Nov.
		14 Nov.	Niblett, Samuel son of Daniel, baker of Haresfield Viner, William & Deborah, grocer, 7 yrs from 5 Nov.
		21 Nov.	Garrett, Thomas son of Thomas, labourer, dec'd, of Gloucester Jackson, Daniel & Margaret, plasterer, 7 yrs
3/681		1 Dec.	Hare, William son of John, labourer of Gloucester Ricketts, William & Elizabeth, pinmaker, 7 yrs
			Moore, Humphrey son of John, bricklayer of Gloucester Moore, John, his father, & Margaret, 7 yrs
		8 Dec.	Yeend, James son of William, barber surgeon of Gloucester Yeend, William, his father, & Sarah, 7 yrs [*repeat of entry at 3/679 with a different date*]
		22 Dec.	Trotman, Daniel son of William, tailor of Gloucester Trotman, William & Sarah, tailor, 7 yrs
3/682	1730	26 Jan.	Pennell, John son of John, cordwainer, dec'd, of Sandhurst Hornedge, Thomas & Mary, pinmaker, 7 yrs
		6 Feb.	Overthrow, Thomas son of William, carpenter of Minsterworth Church, Richard & [—], glover, 7 yrs [*entry crossed through*]
		13 Feb.	Greene, John son of [—], weaver of Gloucester Harris, Samuel, barber surgeon, 7 yrs
		16 Feb.	Robinson, Henry son of Edward, ironmonger of Gloucester Playdell, John & Sarah, baker, 7 yrs from 5 Jan.

---

[1] 2 Sept. 1730: To leave Sir Thomas Rich's hospital and receive £10: Jacob Kirby, Jesse Nash, Robert Wheeler, James Mann, William Attwood, Capel Scudamore. GBR B3/9 f. 280v.

8 Sept. 1730: To receive £4 of Mrs Sarah Browne's money: Thomas Wilke, John Locksley, Thomas Lewis, Jonathan Keeble. To receive £5 [of Mr William Holliday's money] or Alderman Powell's money: Thomas Gardner, William Bicke, John Phipps, Jonathan Hooke, James Long, Samuel Pitts, [—] Lightfoot. GBR B3/9 f. 282.

	1731	20 Sept.	Clarke, John son of John, labourer of Gloucester Cowcher, Richard & Elizabeth, pinmaker, 7 yrs
3/693		24 Sept.	Pitman, Zacharias son of Richard, blacksmith of Longhope Smith, Humphrey & Elizabeth, 7 yrs
		27 Sept.	Clarke, Charles son of Nicholas, wiredrawer of Gloucester Clarke, Robert, of Arlingham, & Anne, blacksmith, 7 yrs

William Bell, mayor 1731–2[1]

3/693	1731	22 Oct.	Boon, Isaac son of Abraham, gardener of Gloucester Jew, Samuel, of 'le Chappell House',[2] Glos. & Elizabeth, staymaker, 7 yrs
3/694		25 Oct.	Hill, William son of John, yeoman of Hempsted Ricketts, Hannah, pinmaker, 7 yrs
			Cheeslett, Thomas son of Abraham, wiredrawer of Gloucester Holder, John & Sarah, pinmaker, 7 yrs from 21 Dec.
		29 Oct.	Jones, William son of Nathaniel, plasterer of Gloucester Andrews, Philip & Sarah, pipemaker, 7 yrs
3/695		19 Nov.	Cowles, William son of Edward, yeoman of Thrupp, Faringdon, Berks. Pytt, Roland & Hannah, ironmonger, 7 yrs from 29 Sept.
		3 Dec.	King, Samuel son of John, [—] of Gloucester Hornedge, Thomas & Mary, pinmaker, 7 yrs
	1732	7 Jan.	Hutchins, Denis son of Denis, baker of Gloucester Broughton, William & Elizabeth, farrier, 7 yrs from 21 Dec. 1731
		24 Jan.	Rathborne, Richard son of John, farrier of Gloucester Rathborne, John, his father, & Susannah, 7 yrs
3/696		11 Feb.	Stephens, Thomas son of William, weaver of Gloucester Barnes, John & Bridget, cordwainer, 7 yrs from 24 Jan.
			Lane, John son of Richard, cordwainer of Gloucester Weaver, Richard & Elizabeth, farrier, 7 yrs
		14 Feb.	Barrett, Thomas son of John, yeoman, dec'd, of Elmore Pleydell, John & Sarah, baker, 7 yrs from 24 Mar. *The said apprentice refused to be bound* [*entry deleted*]
		15 Feb.	Cripps, Samuel son of Edward, butcher, dec'd, of Gloucester Cripps, Virgil & Mary, cordwainer, 7 yrs
		24 Feb.	Okey, John son of William, butcher of Littledean Workman, Anthony & Jane, butcher, 7 yrs from 29 Sept. 1731
3/697		28 Feb.	Marshfield, Thomas son of James, fisherman of Gloucester Jeffs, John & Mary, blacksmith, 7 yrs

[1] 29 Aug. 1732: To leave Sir Thomas Rich's hospital and receive £10: Ralph Ady, Thomas Phipps, Thomas Hale, Robert Gregory, George Deane, John Ireland. GBR B3/9 f. 321v.

27 Sept. 1732: To receive £4 of Mrs Sarah Browne's money: Thomas Jones, John Hill, Abel Pryde, Thomas Halford, John Jennings. To receive £5 of Mr William Holliday's money or Alderman Powell's money: Henry Clayton, Anthony Williams, William Powell, Robert Greene, William Badger, Samuel Bullocke, William Salcomb. GBR B3/9 f. 324v.

[2] Not further identified; places of this name are found in at least five parishes in the county.

	1732	20 Mar.	Mills, John son of Thomas, tiler & plasterer of Gloucester Burroughs, Samuel, linendraper, 7 yrs
		27 Mar.	Smith, Charles son of Charles, cordwainer of Gloucester Evenis, William & Mary, cordwainer, 7 yrs
			Smith, Edward son of Francis, yeoman of Newent Washborne, John, clockmaker, 7 yrs [entry deleted; replaced by an identical one dated 27 July]
3/698		1 May	Bishopp, Hugh son of George, barber, dec'd, of Gloucester Bishopp, Samuel, barber, 7 yrs
		5 May	Barrett, John son of John, yeoman of Minsterworth Jennings, Michael jr & Mary, butcher, 7 yrs from 25 Mar.
		2 June	Crump, John son of John, maltster of Gloucester Cooke, William & Anne, barber, 7 yrs from 29 May
		9 June	Turner, William son of William, yeoman of Tirley Weal, Richard & Mary, baker, 7 yrs from 1 May
3/699		16 June	Phillips, George son of Richard, yeoman of Enstone, Oxon. Spencer, Samuel & Grace, cooper, 7 yrs from 24 Oct.
			Bassett, Isaac son of Thomas, mason, dec'd, of Ashchurch Collett, John & Mary, joiner, 7 yrs from date of these presents
		7 July	Cocks, Seth son of Peter, gentleman late of Bishop's Cleeve Dymocke, Charles & Mary, gentleman, 7 yrs from 24 June
		31 July	Ready, John son of John, gentleman, dec'd, of Bulley Hill, Thomas, apothecary, 7 yrs from 12 Oct. 1731
3/700		11 Aug.	Ball, Samuel son of Samuel, baker, dec'd, of Gloucester Fownes, Joseph & Susannah, distiller, 7 yrs from 26 July
		22 Sept.	Randolph, Charles son of James, gentleman of Tetbury Bennett, Edward & [—], apothecary, 7 yrs from date of these presents
		28 Sept.	Clayton, Henry son of Henry, tailor of Wormington Clayton, Henry, his father, & Anne, tailor, 7 yrs from date of these presents

Gabriel Harris, mayor 1732–3[1]

3/700	1732	5 Oct.	Fletcher, William son of William, gentleman of Maisemore Draper, Richard & Grace, cordwainer, 7 yrs from 29 Sept.
3/701		9 Oct.	Bonnor, Benjamin son of George, yeoman of Walford, Herefs. Webley, Thomas, brazier, 7 yrs
		16 Oct.	Field, John son of John, yeoman of Oxford Wilcocks, Thomas & Mary, upholsterer, 7 yrs from 20 May

[1] 14 Aug. 1733: To leave Sir Thomas Rich's hospital and receive £10: John Baldwin, John Hickman, Thomas Davis, Thomas Stephens, James Waverly, John Baker. GBR B3/9 f. 340.

21 Sept. 1733: To receive £4 of Mrs Sarah Browne's money: William Bonnet, Edward Lindsay, William Timbrell, William Nelme. To receive £5: Edward Man, Henry Lye, William Dancey, John Bevan, Samuel Mathews, George Reeve, Hugh Bishop. GBR B3/9 f. 342.

	1732	20 Oct.	Bubb, Thomas son of Daniel, yeoman of Churcham
			  Pleydell, John & Sarah, baker, 7 yrs from 29 Sept.
			  The boy refused to be bound [*deleted and replaced by:*] *Is since bound*

		23 Oct.	Hill, John son of John, labourer, dec'd, of Gloucester Lee, Thomas & Anne, tailor, 7 yrs from date of these presents
3/702			Greene, Robert son of Robert, pipemaker of Gloucester Smith, Joseph & Rebecca, pipemaker, 7 yrs from date of these presents
		30 Oct.	Jones, Thomas son of Thomas, gardener of Gloucester Cole, George & Elizabeth, tailor, 7 yrs from date of these presents
			Bullocke, Samuel son of John, cordwainer of Gloucester Bullock, John, his father, & Elizabeth, 7 yrs from date of these presents
		3 Nov.	Salcomb, William son of Salcombe, William, cordwainer of Gloucester Salcomb, William, his father, & Hannah, 7 yrs
		17 Nov.	Holford, Thomas son of Joseph, yeoman of Bromsberrow Ricketts, William & Elizabeth, pinmaker, 7 yrs from date of these presents
		1 Dec.	Pride, Abel son of Abel, wiredrawer, dec'd, of Gloucester Shingler, John jr, pinmaker, 7 yrs from date of these presents

3/703		18 Dec.	Cowcher, William son of William, yeoman, dec'd, of Kingsholm,
			    Gloucester
			  Lindsey, John, pinmaker, 7 yrs from date of these presents

	1733	15 Jan.	Long, Newton son of Benjamin, sailor, dec'd, of Gloucester Kirby, Jacob & Sarah, weaver, 7 yrs from date of these presents
		26 Jan.	Powell, William son of William, plumber of Gloucester Powell, William, his father, & Anne, 7 yrs from 26 Jan. 1731
		5 Feb.	Ireland, John son of Cornelius, gentleman, dec'd, of Gloucester Hayes, William & Sarah, cordwainer, 7 yrs
		26 Feb.	Cowley, Job son of Job, glazier of Gloucester Maverley, John, plumber, 7 yrs from date of these presents
			Law proceedings to be in English
3/704		25 May	Fifield, Cornelius son of William, clerk of Minety [*now* Wilts.] Weaver, Matthew & Susannah, baker, 7 yrs from 25 Mar.
			Clarke, John son of John, tailor of Cheltenham Cowles, George & Mary, cordwainer, 7 yrs from 25 Mar.
			Gregory, Robert son of William, tailor of Gloucester Perks, John, cork cutter, 7 yrs from date of these presents
3/705		1 June	Merrett, Thomas son of Thomas, clothier, dec'd, of Painswick Smith, Abraham & Anne, cooper, 7 yrs from 16 Apr.
			Shurmer, Richard son of William, clothier of Rodborough Perkins, Martha, widow, baker, 7 yrs from date of these presents
		4 June	Jennings, John son of John, gardener, dec'd, of Gloucester Lumbard, Jacob, weaver, 7 yrs from 29 May
			Hall, George son of William, gentleman of Bourton-on-the-Water Bower, Thomas & Hannah, tanner, 7 yrs from 4 May
			Guest, Jacob son of John, glass seller, dec'd, of Gloucester Cowdall, Charles & Mary, butcher, 7 yrs from 29 Sept. 1732

3/706	1733	25 May	Marchant, John son of John, maltster of Cirencester Branch, Thomas & Margaret, tinman, 7 yrs from 25 Mar.
		3 Aug.	Wilks, Samuel son of John, weaver of Gloucester Estcott, Samuel & Mary, pinmaker, 7 yrs from 1 Jan.
		3 Aug.	Deane, George son of William, carpenter of Gloucester Deane, William, his father, & [—], 7 yrs from [—]
		6 Aug.	Badger, William son of Jonathan, labourer of Gloucester Freeman, Benjamin & [—], whitesmith, 7 yrs
3/707		27 Aug.	Worgan, Thomas son of Thomas, gentleman, dec'd, of Newland Dimocke, Charles & Mary, mercer, 7 yrs from 31 July

		31 Aug.	Newcombe, William son of William, weaver, dec'd, of Alstone, Cheltenham
			    Lloyd, Martin & Martha, woolstapler, 7 yrs from 28 May
			    The indenture not yet signed [*entry deleted*]

		7 Sept.	Lane, William son of William, yeoman of Chaceley, Worcs. Drew, Thomas & Sarah, baker, 7 yrs from 7 Aug.
3/708		21 Sept.	Clift, Gameliel son of John, labourer of Gloucester Weaver, Thomas & Elizabeth, pinmaker, 7 yrs
			Cleever, Daniel son of John, haberdasher of London Brock, Nathaniel & Sarah, fellmonger, 7 yrs from 29 Sept.
		28 Sept.	Man, Edward son of John, glover of Gloucester Man, John, his father, & Hester, 7 yrs from 24 Feb.
		8 Oct.	Perrin, Richard son of Richard, woolcomber of Gloucester Cowles, John & Bridget, butcher, 7 yrs

John Selwyn, mayor 1733–4[1]

3/709	1733	15 Oct.	Lindsey, Thomas son of Edward, labourer of Gloucester Lindsey, John & Hester, pinmaker, 7 yrs
		26 Oct.	Crowther, John son of John, yeoman of Leonard Stanley Porter, Thomas & Elizabeth, apothecary, 7 yrs
			Bonnor, James son of William, bricklayer of Gloucester Grimmett, John & Elizabeth, cordwainer, 7 yrs
		29 Oct.	Hale, Thomas son of Joseph, cordwainer of Gloucester Hale, Thomas, his father, & Margaret, 7 yrs
3/710		12 Nov.	Bishop, Hugh son of George, barber, dec'd, of Gloucester Keyse, John & Elizabeth, pinmaker, 7 yrs
		19 Nov.	Mathews, Samuel son of John, pinmaker of Gloucester Mathews, Samuel, his father, & Elizabeth, 7 yrs

---

[1] 9 Aug. 1734: To receive £4 of Mrs Sarah Browne's money: Daniel Fereby, Abraham Ashworth, John Wansy, George Brotherton. GBR B3/9 f. 353v.

23 Aug. 1734: To receive £5: John Roff, Josiah Fitchew, Richard Mathews, John Ward, William Trotman, Henry Holder, Thomas Parker. GBR B3/9 f. 355v

19 Sept. 1734: To leave Sir Thomas Rich's hospital and receive £10: John Fletcher, Zachariah Stephens, John Smith, Roger Horsman, John Cocks, Abel Welladvize. GBR B3/9 f. 356v

	1733	3 Dec.	Lye, Henry son of Francis, cooper, dec'd, of Gloucester Price, Joseph & Elizabeth, cordwainer, 7 yrs
	1734	22 Feb.	Baker, John son of Richard, joiner of Gloucester Bright, John & Elizabeth, joiner, 7 yrs
		22 Mar.	Stephens, Thomas son of William, pinmaker of Gloucester Stephens, Thomas, his father, & Hannah, pinmaker, 7 yrs
3/711		29 Apr.	Dancy, Joseph son of William, bricklayer of Gloucester Dancy, William, his father, & Anne, 7 yrs
		27 May	Spiller, Joseph son of [—], yeoman, dec'd, of Minsterworth Bowler, George & Elizabeth, tailor, 7 yrs from 10 May [*entry deleted*]
			Sayer, Jarvis son of Joseph, yeoman, dec'd, of Lower Duntisbourne Cother, Joseph & Mary, cordwainer, 7 yrs
		17 June	Jones, William son of Thomas, yeoman, dec'd, of Hartpury Evenis, Robert, cordwainer, 7 yrs
		21 June	Bevan, John son of Thomas, victualler, dec'd, of Gloucester Cooke, James, baker, 7 yrs from 14 Apr.
3/712		22 July	Bayliss, Benjamin son of Edward, woolcomber of Gloucester Wadley, Sarah, baker, 7 yrs from 24 June
		26 July	Day, Robert son of Henry, yeoman, dec'd, of Dorchester, Dorset Ricketts, William & Elizabeth, pinmaker, 7 yrs
		2 Aug.	Mathews, William son of Richard, butcher, dec'd, of Gloucester Swayne, James & Margaret, butcher, 7 yrs from 24 June
		12 Aug.	Palmer, Thomas son of William, yeoman of Moreton Valence Robinson, Giles, cooper, 7 yrs
		23 Aug.	Terrett, Joseph son of William, yeoman of Owlpen Cooke, Sarah, saddler, 7 yrs from 20 July
3/713		6 Sept.	Trotman, William son of William, tailor of Gloucester Smith, Humphrey & Elizabeth, cutler, 7 yrs
		20 Sept.	Fereby, Daniel son of John, tailor of Uley Fereby, John, his father, & Elizabeth, 7 yrs
			Ward, John son of Thomas, pinmaker of Gloucester Branch, John, of Hatherley, & Anne, cordwainer, 7 yrs
		23 Sept.	Reeve, George son of Richard, innholder of Gloucester Edwards, James & Mary, baker, 7 yrs from 29 Sept.
			Parker, Thomas son of John, hatter of Gloucester Perin, Richard & Elizabeth, woolcomber, 7 yrs
3/714			Holder, Henry son of John, pinmaker of Gloucester Holder, John, his father, & Sarah, 7 yrs
		4 Oct.	Fitchew, Thomas son of Josiah, feltmaker of Gloucester Fitchew, Josiah, his father, & Eleanor, 7 yrs

John Hayward, mayor 1734–5[1]

3/714	1734	11 Oct.	James, John son of Jasper, yeoman, dec'd, of Newent Cother, Joseph & Mary, cordwainer, 7 yrs
		18 Oct.	Peachy, Richard son of Obadiah, tailor of Elmore Playdell, John & Sarah, baker, 7 yrs from 30 Sept.
		21 Oct.	Stocke, Benjamin son of John, maltster, dec'd, of Tewkesbury Hippisley, John & Frances, barber, 7 yrs from 30 Sept.
3/715			Stratford, William son of Joshua, cooper of Coaley Smith, Abraham & Anne, cooper, 7 yrs
		25 Oct.	Rosse, Jasper son of John, tailor of Gloucester Rosse, John, his father, & Margaret, 7 yrs

		8 Nov.	Gotheridge, Joseph son of Thomas, gardener, dec'd, of Gloucester
			    Field, Samuel & Anne, joiner, 7 yrs
			    Not bound [*entry deleted*]

		25 Nov.	Jauncey, Benjamin son of Benjamin, chandler, dec'd, of Hereford Cowcher, John & Anne, apothecary, 7 yrs
		12 Dec.	Fowler, Giles son of [—], yeoman of Longford Harris, Samuel & Elizabeth, barber surgeon, 7 yrs from 30 Sept.
3/716	1735	10 Jan.	Wood, William son of Thomas, yeoman, dec'd, of Flaxley Luter, Elizabeth, widow, 7 yrs from [—]
			Fletcher, Joseph, labourer of Barton Street, Gloucester Jefferys, John & Anne, pinmaker, 7 yrs
		24 Jan.	Wantsy, John son of Nathaniel, metalman, dec'd, of Gloucester Andrews, Peter & Sarah, pipemaker, 7 yrs
			Jaines, William son of Matthew, butcher, dec'd, of Tewkesbury Bond, Thomas & Anne, baker, 7 yrs
		27 Jan.	Ashworth, Abraham son of Abraham, cordwainer, dec'd, of Gloucester Colwell, James & Mary, cordwainer, 7 yrs
3/717		5 Feb.	Hamlett, Malachiah son of Thomas, stonecutter, dec'd, of Painswick Taylor, Richard & Hester, barber surgeon, 7 yrs
		10 Feb.	Parsons, Thomas son of Andrew, yeoman of Lydney Nest, William & Mary, joiner, 7 yrs
			Jocham, James son of James, joiner of Bristol Brabant, Francis & Elizabeth, cooper, 7 yrs
		16 Feb.	Fletcher, John son of John, currier of Gloucester Steel, Thomas & Sarah, grocer, 7 yrs

---

[1] 12 Sept. 1735: To leave Sir Thomas Rich's hospital and receive £10: Henry Remington, Peter Lugg, Winston John Bishop, Rowles Scudamore, William Dunne, Charles Watson. GBR B3/9 f. 367v.

19 Sept. 1735: To receive £5: Philip Hewett, Robert Savory, John Gulliver, James King, Daniel Greening, Robert Gorton, John Pace. GBR B3/9 f. 369.

3 Oct. 1735: To receive £4 of Mrs Sarah Browne's money: William Gardner, Samuel Hornsby, John Twining, Ferdinand Meighen. GBR B3/9 f370v.

	1735	20 Feb.	Mills, Thomas son of Thomas, tiler & plasterer of Gloucester
			    Mills, Thomas, his father, & Elizabeth, tiler & plasterer, 7 yrs
			      from 29 Sept. 1734 [*see also 3/720*]

3/718		28 Feb.	Smith, John son of John, yeoman, dec'd, of Gloucester Smith, Humphrey & Elizabeth, cutler, 7 yrs
		18 Apr.	Curtis, William son of George, apothecary, dec'd, of Stow on the Wold Rogers, William & Mary, apothecary, 7 yrs
			Reeve, William son of James, yeoman, dec'd, of Southam Baker, James & Elizabeth, cordwainer, 7 yrs from 25 Mar.
		21 Apr.	Phelps, William son of Nicholas, yeoman, dec'd, of Minsterworth Moor, Winstone, butcher, 7 yrs
		23 May	Welladvise, Abel son of Samuel, glazier of Gloucester Perry, William & Elizabeth, tailor, 7 yrs
3/719		2 June	Etheridge, Giles son of Giles, weaver of Painswick Parker, John & Anne, tailor, 7 yrs
		6 June	Horsman, Roger son of John, gentleman, dec'd, of Gloucester Wadley, Sarah, widow, 7 yrs
		23 June	Woodward, John son of Richard, wiredrawer, dec'd, of Gloucester Woodward, John & Mary, pinmaker, 7 yrs from 1 May
		21 July	Powell, William, yeoman of Gloucester Box, John & Martha, pinmaker, 7 yrs
		18 Aug.	Browning, Samuel son of Samuel, cordwainer of Painswick Cripps, Virgil & Mary, cordwainer, 7 yrs from 24 June
3/720		5 Sept.	Hodskis, Thomas son of Thomas, waterman, dec'd, of Bewdley, Salop. Knott, George & Mary, cooper, 7 yrs from 1 Aug.
			Smith, Thomas son of William, yeoman, dec'd, of Guiting Jennings, Michael & Mary, butcher, 7 yrs from 25 July

Richard Lewis, mayor 1735–6[1]

3/720	1735	13 Oct.	Hewlett, Philip son of Thomas, flaxdresser dec'd, of Gloucester Kingman, James & Elizabeth, wiredrawer, 7 yrs from 29 Sept.
		20 Oct.	Kesey, Thomas son of Thomas, gardener, dec'd, of Gloucester Ward, Thomas & Elizabeth, pinmaker, 7 yrs from 3 Oct.
			Mills, Thomas son of Thomas, tiler & plasterer of Gloucester Webb, Timothy & Sarah, baker, 7 yrs [*see also 3/ 717*]
3/721			Twinning, John son of John, yeoman of Gloucester Browne, Thomas & Dorothy, cordwainer, 7 yrs from 24 June
			Stephens, John son of William, pinmaker of Gloucester Stephens, William, his father, & Hannah, pinmaker, 7 yrs

---

[1] [?Sept.] 1736: To receive £4 of Mrs Sarah Browne's money: Edward Smart, William Bird, John Ratcliff, John Hutchins. To receive £5: John Adams, William Motlow, James Pitt, Henry Wilton, John Wilton, William Lane, Abel Weladvise. GBR B3/9 f. 385.

1 Oct. 1736: To leave Sir Thomas Rich's hospital and receive £10: John Cox, Edward Long, Richard Sims, Thomas Cole, William Humphris, William Jeffs. GBR B3/9 f. 385v.

	1735	27 Oct.	Holford, John son of Joseph, labourer of Gloucester Price, Thomas & Elizabeth, blacksmith, 7 yrs from 29 Sept.
			Meighen, Ferdinand son of Ferdinand, gardener of Gloucester Meighen, James & Elizabeth, gardener, 7 yrs
		3 Nov.	Hornsby, Samuel son of Samuel, pinmaker of Gloucester Haynes, John & Christian, pinmaker, 7 yrs from 17 Sept.

3/722		7 Nov.	King, James son of Samuel, tiler & plasterer of Gloucester
			    Rogers, James & Susannah, bricklayer, 7 yrs from 29 Sept.
			      [*see also 3/689*]

		14 Nov.	Savery, Robert son of William, blacksmith, dec'd, of Gloucester Simpson, Robert & Sarah, pinmaker, 7 yrs from date of indenture
	1736	12 Jan.	Phillips, John son of John, tailor of Gloucester Haynes, John & Christian, pinmaker, 7 yrs from 1 Dec. 1735
		16 Jan.	Barrett, Thomas son of John, yeoman, dec'd, of Minsterworth Taylor, Ellis & Alice, baker, 7 yrs from 6 Dec. 1735
		23 Jan.	Winstone, Peter son of John, glazier of Gloucester Barnes, John & Bridget, cordwainer, 7 yrs from date of indenture
3/723		2 Feb.	Moor, John son of John, bricklayer of Gloucester Baker, Benjamin & Martha, cordwainer, 7 yrs from 1 Jan.
		5 Mar.	South, John son of William, yeoman of Eastnor, Herefs. Fletcher, Thomas & Mary, baker, 7 yrs

		8 Mar.	Stratford, Walter son of Walter, esquire of Farmcote, Lower Guiting
			    Lawrence, William & Elizabeth, baker, 7 yrs from 2 Feb.
			    Note: He is not bound

		22 Mar.	Gorton, Robert son of William, cordwainer of Gloucester Merry, Thomas & Elizabeth, cordwainer, 7 yrs
		12 Apr.	Baylis, Benjamin son of Edward, woolcomber of Gloucester Webb, John, baker, 7 yrs from 1 Mar.
3/724		10 May	Innell, James son of James, woolcomber of Gloucester Mason, William & Mary, tailor, 7 yrs
		28 May	Bennett, Richard son of John, clothier, dec'd, of Stroud Shatford, John & Mary, joiner, 7 yrs from 15 Apr.
			Cowcher, Richard son of Richard, pinmaker, of Gloucester Cowcher, Richard, his father, & Elizabeth, pinmaker, 7 yrs
		31 May	Done, William son of William, tiler & plasterer of Gloucester Hewett, William & Sarah, whitesmith, 7 yrs from 6 Feb.
		11 June	Wood, Robert son of Thomas, yeoman of Flaxley Ellis, John & Anne, ironmonger, 7 yrs from 29 Sept. 1735

3/725		21 June	Edwards, John son of John, yeoman, dec'd, of Over
			    Randle, John & Elizabeth, tiler & plasterer, 7 yrs from 29 Sept.
			    [*entry deleted*]

		2 July	Taylor, John son of John, perukemaker of Cirencester Axon, William & Elizabeth, cutler, 7 yrs from 24 Feb.
		1 Oct.	Peace, John son of Thomas, cordwainer of Gloucester Peace, Thomas, his father, cordwainer, 7 yrs from 29 Sept.

Charles Selwyn, mayor 1736–7[1]

3/726 1736 18 Oct. Wilton, Henry son of Henry, pinmaker, dec'd, of Gloucester
                          Hale, William & Mary, pinmaker, 7 yrs from 24 June

          1 Nov.   Brabant, William son of William, cooper, dec'd, of Gloucester
                          Gardner, John & Elizabeth, tailor, 7 yrs

          12 Nov. Ratcliff, John son of Abraham, joiner of Gloucester
                          Kingman, James & Elizabeth, wiredrawer, 7 yrs

                   Adams, John son of John, gardener of Gloucester
                          Williams, Jeremiah & Fortunata, cordwainer, 7 yrs

3/727   Hutchins, John son of Dennis, fisherman of Gloucester
                          Robinson, Giles & Mary, cooper, 7 yrs

                   Fletcher, Charles son of John, writing master of Gloucester
                          Evenis, Robert & Mary, cordwainer, 7 yrs from 1 Nov.

          22 Nov. Rudge, John son of John, yeoman of Ruardean
                          Perks, John & Elizabeth, cork cutter, 7 yrs [entry deleted]

          26 Nov. Smart, Edward son of Edward, tailor of Gloucester
                          Ward, Thomas & Elizabeth, pinmaker, 7 yrs from 25 Oct.

3/728   3 Dec.   Motley, William son of Robert, cordwainer of Gloucester
                          Merrett, Thomas & Sarah, cordwainer, 7 yrs

       1737 15 Jan.   Wilton, John son of John, pinmaker of Gloucester
                          Wilton, John, his father, & Sarah, pinmaker, 7 yrs

          21 Jan.   Jones, William son of Edward, [—] of Thornbury
                          Cooke, George, grocer & chandler, 7 yrs

          7 Feb.   Hammond, Robert son of Thomas, innholder of Stroud
                          Jones, John & Elizabeth, innholder, 7 yrs from 17 Jan.

3/729   Merrett, Richard son of Thomas, clothier, dec'd, of Painswick
                          Weaver, Richard & Elizabeth, farrier, 7 yrs from 10 Jan.

                   Jeffs, William son of John, blacksmith of Gloucester
                          Jeffs, John, his father, blacksmith, 7 yrs

          11 Feb.   Gardner, Anthony son of John, clothworker, dec'd, of Painswick
                          Gardiner, Cornelius, barber surgeon, 7 yrs

          25 Feb.   Bird, William son of Thomas, labourer of Gloucester
                          Lane, John & Mary, blacksmith & farrier, 7 yrs from 26 Jan.

3/730   14 Mar.   Pitt, James son of Roger, carpenter of Gloucester
                          Barnes, John & Bridget, cordwainer, 7 yrs from 15 Feb.

          [—]   Harris, Thomas son of Samuel, waterman, dec'd, of Gloucester
                          Wood, William & Sarah, cooper, 7 yrs from 10 Mar.

          25 Apr.   Shatford, William son of William, glover, dec'd, of Gloucester
                          Weaver, Kirkham & Katherine, collarmaker, 7 yrs

---

[1] 5 Sept. 1737: To receive £4 of Mrs Sarah Browne's money: William Felton, William Moore, Richard Harding, Thomas Bromley. To receive £5: John Rosse, Charles Williams, Samuel Remington, Samuel Williams, James Gardiner, Thomas Ireland, Thomas Badger. GBR B3/9 f. 401.

16 Sept. 1737: To leave Sir Thomas Rich's hospital and receive £10: John Stock, Thomas Pace, Lawrence Crump, John Engley, Daniel Greening, John Lugg. GBR B3/9 f. 403.

	1737	2 May	Swettman, John son of George, weaver of Barton Street, Gloucester Weaver, Thomas & Elizabeth, pinmaker, 7 yrs
3/731		20 May	Cooke, George son of William, butcher, dec'd, of Gloucester Rene, John & Elizabeth, weaver, 7 yrs
			Jenkins, William son of Robert, yeoman, dec'd, of Lydney Cowles, John, butcher, 7 yrs
		30 Sept.	Cox, John son of John, barber surgeon, dec'd, of Gloucester Cox, Elizabeth, widow, his mother, 7 yrs
			Welladvise, William son of Samuel, glazier of Gloucester Price, Joseph, cordwainer, 7 yrs

Thomas Hill, mayor 1737–8[1]

	1737	17 Oct.	Felton, William son of Richard, innholder of Gloucester Nurse, Richard, barber surgeon, 7 yrs
3/732			Bromley, Thomas son of William, labourer, dec'd, of Gloucester Hyett, Robert & Anne, cooper, 7 yrs from 31 Oct.
		24 Oct.	Williams, Job son of Job, yeoman of Eldersfield, Worcs. Brabant, Francis & Elizabeth, cooper, 7 yrs from 1 Sept.
			Ireland, Thomas son of John, woolcomber, dec'd, of Gloucester Barrett, William & Elizabeth, joiner & carpenter, 7 yrs from 29 Sept. [*entry deleted*]
			Williams, Samuel son of Thomas, gardener of Gloucester Smith, John & [—], dyer, 7 yrs from 29 Sept. [*entry deleted*]
3/733		31 Oct.	Gardner, James son of Andrew, tailor of Gloucester Gardner, Andrew, his father, & Hannah, 7 yrs
		4 Nov.	Gardner, Joseph son of Anthony, baker, dec'd, of Gloucester Clark, Moses & Anne, baker, 7 yrs from 2 Feb.
		7 Nov.	Curtis, Henry son of Richard, innholder, dec'd, of Gloucester Curtis, [—], grocer, 7 yrs from 11 July
		16 Dec.	Gurner, James son of John, yeoman, dec'd, of Hempsted Beale, Benjamin & Sarah, blacksmith, 7 yrs
	1738	20 Jan.	Pace, Thomas son of Thomas, cordwainer of Gloucester Pace, Thomas, his father, & Anne, 7 yrs from date of indenture
3/734		23 Jan.	Remington, Samuel son of Daniel, mercer of Gloucester Cripps, Virgil, cordwainer, 7 yrs
		3 Feb.	Stoner, Antioch son of John, clothier of Chalford Weaver, Matthew & Susannah, baker, 7 yrs

[1] 25 Aug. 1738: To receive £4 of Mrs Sarah Browne's money: William Field, John Doggett, Benjamin Hare, Francis Church. To receive £5 of Mr William Holliday's money: Richard Weston, James Fitche, John Philipps, William Phipps, William Hale, Thomas Harris, William Rudge. GBR B3/9 f. 418.

25 Sept. 1738: To leave Sir Thomas Rich's hospital and receive £10: William Bayley, Charles Deane, Thomas Pembruge, John Kemys, John Charles. GBR B3/9 f. 420.

1738	3 Feb.	Rodway, William son of Thomas, yeoman of Upton St Leonards Clarke, Moses & Anne, baker, 7 yrs from 1 Jan.
	10 Feb.	Humphris, William son of John, butcher, dec'd, of Gloucester Moore, George & Jane, butcher, 7 yrs
3/735	3 Mar.	Freeman, Thomas son of Thomas, saddler, dec'd, of Cirencester Weaver, William & Anne, saddler, 7 yrs
	21 Apr.	Niccolls, Thomas son of Thomas, yeoman of Cheltenham Bennett, Edward & Hester, apothecary, 7 yrs from 1 Mar.
		Engly, John son of Arthur, bricklayer of Gloucester Bright, Thomas & Hannah, barber surgeon, 7 yrs
		Greening, Daniel son of Daniel, butcher of Gloucester Cother, Joseph & Mary, cordwainer, 7 yrs from 2 Mar.
	9 June	Herbert, Richard son of Thomas, tailor of Gloucester Grimmett, John & Elizabeth, cordwainer, 7 yrs from 1 May
	10 July	Cole, Thomas son of George, tailor, dec'd, of Gloucester Davis, John & Elizabeth, pinmaker, 7 yrs from 21 Dec. 1737
3/736	31 July	Badger, Thomas son of Nathaniel, tiler & plasterer of Gloucester Badger, Thomas, his father, & Elizabeth, 7 yrs
		Smith, Thomas son of Richard, yeoman, dec'd, of Frampton on Severn Heath, Samuel & Mary, joiner, 7 yrs from this day
	28 Aug.	Bradley, James son of James, labourer, dec'd, of Newent Baker, James & Elizabeth, cordwainer, 7 yrs
	8 Sept.	Woodward, William son of John, weaver of Gloucester Kirby, Jacob & Sarah, weaver, 7 yrs from 29 Mar.
	11 Sept.	Sadler, James son of John, yeoman of Cranham Spillman, Richard & Joyce, baker, 7 yrs from 1 Sept.
3/737	15 Sept.	Head, Samuel son of Samuel, collier of Broseley, Salop. Shatford, John & Mary, joiner, 7 yrs
	22 Sept.	Harris, Thomas son of Richard, smith & farrier of Gloucester Broughton, William & Elizabeth, smith & farrier, 7 yrs from 29 Sept.
	25 Sept.	Rudge, William son of Thomas, carpenter of Gloucester Simpson, Robert & Sarah, pinmaker, 7 yrs
	29 Sept.	Hale, William son of Joseph, cordwainer of Gloucester Hale, Joseph, his father, & Margaret, 7 yrs
	6 Oct.	Philips, John son of Thomas, pinmaker of Gloucester Philips, Thomas & Elizabeth, pinmaker, 7 yrs
		Dew, Thomas son of Thomas, yeoman, dec'd, of Braunton, Herefs. Drew, Thomas & Sarah, baker, 7 yrs

---

[1] 20 Aug. 1739: To receive £4 of Mrs Sarah Browne's money: William Barrett, William Robins, Timothy Dicks, Thomas Ellis. To receive £5 of Mr William Holliday's money: George Barrett, Henry Wintle, [—] Humphris, William Freame, Jonathan Badger, James Smart, William Mason. GBR B3/9 f. 424.
    28 Sept. 1739: To leave Sir Thomas Rich's hospital and receive £10: Edward Addis, William Maverly, Elton Wantner, Moses Randall, William Webley, Richard Rayer. GBR B3/9 f. 430.

William Niccolls, mayor 1738–9[1]

3/738	1738	10 Nov.	May, John son of James, saddler of Gloucester Wheeler, James & Elizabeth, joiner, 7 yrs from 29 Sept.
		20 Nov.	Hare, Benjamin son of John, labourer of Gloucester Lindsey, John & Hester, pinmaker, 7 yrs from 17 Sept.
			Church, Francis son of Francis, labourer of Gloucester Davis, John & Elizabeth, pinmaker, 7 yrs from 1 Oct.
			Weston, Richard son of John, fisherman of Gloucester Garne, John & Sarah, cordwainer, 7 yrs
			Beard, James son of Thomas, woolcomber, dec'd, of Gloucester Beard, Joseph & Frances, woolcomber, 7 yrs from 5 Nov.
		24 Nov.	Field, William son of Thomas, labourer of Gloucester Cother, Joseph & [—], cordwainer, 7 yrs
3/739		8 Dec.	Wadley, Ambrose son of John, baker, dec'd, of Gloucester Wadley, Thomas, baker, 7 yrs
		18 Dec.	Platt, Thomas son of Thomas, pinmaker of Nuneaton, Warws. Barrett, Anthony & Hester, pinmaker, 7 yrs
			Peyton, Mainard son of Henry, gentleman of Gloucester Barrett, Anthony & Hester, pinmaker, 7 yrs
	1739	19 Jan.	Jelfe, Joseph son of William, yeoman, dec'd, of Tirley Higgins, Ephraim, grocer, 7 yrs from 6 Jan.

		5 Feb.	Elmes, William son of Thomas, gentleman, dec'd, of Barton Street,
			        Gloucester
			    Webb, Nicholas & Susannah, mercer, 7 yrs from 20 Jan.

		12 Feb.	Lewis, Charles son of John, pinmaker of Gloucester Draper, Richard & Grace, cordwainer, 7 yrs
3/740		9 Mar.	Goodrich, Edward son of Walter, glover, dec'd, of Cheltenham Harris, Samuel & Elizabeth, barber surgeon, 7 yrs from 25 Dec.
		25 May	Kemis, John son of John, tailor of Gloucester Haynes, William & Sarah, joiner, 7 yrs
			Sparrow, James son of Noah, clothier of Chalford Robinson, Giles & Mary, cooper, 7 yrs
			Townsend, Samuel son of Richard, tailor, dec'd, of Gloucester Bright, John & Elizabeth, joiner, 7 yrs
		28 May	Moy, Richard son of Thomas, yeoman of Highnam Bower, Edward & Elizabeth, currier, 7 yrs
		1 June	Boulton, John son of [—], yeoman, dec'd, of Tirley Playdell, John & Sarah, baker, 7 yrs from 24 Feb.
3/741		4 June	Fitchew, James son of Josiah, hatmaker, dec'd, of Gloucester Hook, Jonathan & Rebecca, joiner, 7 yrs
		22 June	Coxe, Richard son of Daniel, yeoman of How Capel, Herefs. Weaver, Matthew & Susannah, baker, 7 yrs
			Bird, Thomas son of Thomas, labourer of Gloucester Ward, Thomas & Elizabeth, pinmaker, 7 yrs from 14 May

	1739	2 July	Farmer, Samuel son of John, mercer, dec'd, of Gloucester Farmer, Samuel, apothecary, 7 yrs from 24 June
		3 Aug.	Wools, Jonathan son of Abraham, carpenter of Cirencester Ellis, John & Martha, tailor, 7 yrs from 24 June 1738
		13 Aug.	Jennings, Harry son of Robert, barber surgeon of Worcester Tyler, Francis & Sarah, plumber & glazier, 7 yrs from 25 Dec. 1738
3/742		24 Aug.	Barrett, William son of Abraham, sawyer of Gloucester Box, John & Martha, pinmaker, 7 yrs
		27 Aug.	Pembruge, Thomas son of Thomas, woolcomber of Gloucester Cooke, William & Anne, barber surgeon, 7 yrs
		28 Aug.	Smart, Giles son of Richard, miller, dec'd, of Churchdown Barrett, Anthony & Hester, pinmaker, 7 yrs
		21 Sept.	Wintle, Henry jr son of Henry sr, cordwainer of Gloucester Wintle, Henry, his father, & Grissell, 7 yrs
		24 Sept.	Mason, William son of John, tailor of Gloucester Mason, John, his father, & Anne, 7 yrs
			Barrett, George son of William, pinmaker of Gloucester Barrett, William, his father, & Mary, 7 yrs

Edward Machen, mayor 1739–40[1]

3/742	1739	15 Oct.	Ellis, Richard son of David, yeoman of Charlton Kings Price, Thomas & Anne, goldsmith, 7 yrs
3/743		23 Nov.	Smart, James son of William, cordwainer of Gloucester Kirby, Jacob & Sarah, weaver, 7 yrs from 29 Sept.
		10 Dec.	Ellis, Thomas son of Richard, weaver of Gloucester Davis, Henry, pinmaker, 7 yrs
		14 Dec.	Baldwyn, Robert son of Edward, labourer of Gloucester Weaver, Richard & Elizabeth, farrier, 7 yrs from 26 July
	1740	11 Jan.	Wantner, Elton son of Charles, barber surgeon, dec'd, of Gloucester Smith, Joseph & Anne, barber surgeon, 7 yrs
		28 Jan.	Webley, William son of William, yeoman of Gloucester Parker, Thomas, barber surgeon, 7 yrs
		15 Feb.	Addis, Edward son of Edward, tailor, dec'd, of Gloucester Gibbs, George Gwinnett of Barton Street, & Mary, joiner, 7 yrs
		18 Feb.	Mantle, William son of Thomas, clerk of Longhope Hayle, Richard, [—], 7 yrs from 25 Dec. 1739
3/744		29 Feb.	Badger, Jonathan son of Jonathan, labourer of Gloucester Holder, John & Sarah, pinmaker, 7 yrs

---

[1] 10 Sept. 1740: To receive £4 of Mrs Sarah Browne's money: Thomas Morse, Benjamin Halford, Joseph Boucher, John May. To receive £5 of Mr William Holliday's money: Richard Bryan, John Fords, Samuel Spiller, Joseph Morris, John Hawkins, John Chewet, James Philips. GBR B3/9 f. 446.
　19 Sept. 1740: To leave Sir Thomas Rich's hospital and receive £10: Daniel Bond, Samuel Salcomb, John Clarke, William Leighton, Benjamin Cooke, Joseph Fownes. GBR B3/9 f. 447.

	1740	28 Mar.	Yate, Thomas son of Henry, yeoman of Brockworth Yate, Daniel, grocer, 7 yrs from 29 Sept. 1739

1740   28 Mar.   Yate, Thomas son of Henry, yeoman of Brockworth
                   Yate, Daniel, grocer, 7 yrs from 29 Sept. 1739

           Maverly, William son of William, tailor of Gloucester
           Maverly, John & Anne, plumber & glazier, 7 yrs

           Sexty, George son of William, yeoman of Winchcombe
           Hayward, William & Sarah, cordwainer, 7 yrs

28 Apr.   Hartland, John son of Thomas, yeoman of Newent
           Clarke, John & Elizabeth, baker, 7 yrs from 25 Mar.

5 May   Barton, George son of John, bricklayer of Gloucester
           Barton, Richard & Martha, plumber & glazier, 7 yrs from 25 Dec.

12 May   Smart, William son of Richard, miller, dec'd, of Hucclecote
           Barrett, Anthony & Hester, pinmaker, 7 yrs

3/745   13 June   Mills, Thomas son of William, yeoman of Frampton on Severn
                      Ward, Thomas & Elizabeth, pinmaker, 7 yrs from 29 May

4 July   Yeend, John son of Thomas, butcher of Ashchurch
           Jennings, Michael & Mary, butcher, 7 yrs from 29 May

1 Aug.   Randall, William son of Josiah, baker, dec'd, of Gloucester
           Rogers, William & Sarah, apothecary, 7 yrs

4 Aug.   Hawkes, Joseph son of Joseph, miller, dec'd, of Barton Street, St
             Mary de Lode, Gloucester
           Browne, Thomas & Dorothy, cordwainer, 7 yrs from 24 June

8 Sept.   Bullocke, John son of John, cordwainer of Gloucester
           Holder, John & Sarah, pinmaker, 7 yrs from 29 Aug.

15 Sept.   Freame, William son of John, feltmaker of Gloucester
           Freame, John, his father, & Hannah, 7 yrs

Samuel Worral, mayor 1740–1[1]

3/746   1740   20 Oct.   Spiller, Samuel son of John, pinmaker, dec'd, of Gloucester
                             Keyse, John & Elizabeth, pinmaker, 7 yrs

31 Oct.   Fords, John son of William, tailor of Gloucester
           Fords, William, his father, & Anne, 7 yrs

7 Nov.   Philipps, William son of George, pinmaker of Gloucester
           Phillips, George jr & Mary, pinmaker, 7 yrs

10 Nov.   Webb, John son of Richard, grocer of Gloucester
           Webb, Richard, his father, & Mary, 7 yrs

           Bryan, James son of Richard, brazier of Gloucester
           Bryan, Richard, his father, 7 yrs

21 Nov.   Hawkins, John son of John, cordwainer of Gloucester
           Hawkins, John, his father, 7 yrs

           Hewett, John son of William, blacksmith of Gloucester
           Hewett, William, his father, & Sarah, 7 yrs

---

[1] 10 Aug. 1741: To leave Sir Thomas Rich's hospital and receive £10: William Dix, Edward Elliott, Thomas Glendall, William Puxon, John Cole, John Ellis. GBR B3/9 f. 463.

3/747	1740	24 Nov.	Porter, Thomas son of Thomas, apothecary of Gloucester Porter, Thomas, his father, & Elizabeth, 7 yrs from 11 July
		19 Dec.	Morse, John son of Thomas, labourer of Gloucester Cowdall, Mary, widow, 7 yrs
	1741	13 Jan.	Davis, John son of John, yeoman of Cam Davis, Robert & Sarah, grocer, 7 yrs
		19 Jan.	Whithorne, Samuel son of Samuel, gentleman, dec'd, of Charlton Kings Cooke, James & Anne, baker, 7 yrs
		6 Feb.	James, Matthew son of Matthew, yeoman, dec'd, of Eldersfield, Worcs. Perris, John & Anne, butcher, 7 yrs from 2 Feb.
		9 Feb.	Salcomb, Samuel son of William, cordwainer of Gloucester Salcomb, William, his father, & Anne, 7 yrs
		2 Mar.	Webb, John son of Anthony, yeoman of Bishops Cleeve Swayne, James & Elizabeth, butcher, 7 yrs from 2 Feb.
3/748		10 Apr.	Wilson, Samuel son of John, baker, dec'd, of Tewkesbury Wood, James & Dorothy, mercer, 7 yrs from 3 Feb.
		15 June	Clarke, John son of John, pinmaker, dec'd, of Gloucester Worrall, George & Mary, pinmaker, 7 yrs from 1 Mar.
			Gravesmore, Robert son of Edward, weaver of Painswick Workman, Anthony & Jane, butcher, 7 yrs from 25 Mar.
		19 June	Mills, John son of William, glover of Gloucester Mills, William, his father, & Mary, 7 yrs
		27 July	Counsell, Joshua son of Joshua, gentleman, dec'd, of Bristol Rogers, William, apothecary, 7 yrs
		11 Sept.	Dew, Daniel son of Thomas, yeoman, dec'd, of Brampton, Herefs. Bonner, Thomas & Sarah, grocer & chandler, 7 yrs from 25 Mar.
3/749		18 Sept.	Rayer, Richard son of George, barber & periwigmaker of Gloucester Rayer, Richard, his father, 7 yrs

Thomas Hayward, mayor 1741–2[1]

3/749	1741	23 Oct.	Shipton, Thomas jr son of Thomas sr, pinmaker of Gloucester Shipton, Thomas, his father, & Martha, 7 yrs
		2 Nov.	Harris, John son of John, victualler, dec'd, of Gloucester Draper, William & Mary, cordwainer, 7 yrs from 29 Sept.
			Fownes, Joseph son of Joseph, distiller, dec'd, of Gloucester Washbourne, George & Hannah, clockmaker, 7 yrs from 29 Sept.
			Payne, Anthony son of Anthony, clothier, dec'd, of Stroud Lodge, William jr & Martha, cooper & tobacconist, 7 yrs from 25 July

		9 Nov.	Woodiate, George son of [—], yeoman, dec'd, of Redmarley
			    D'Abitot, Worcs.
			    Barnfield, John, blacksmith, 7 yrs

---

[1] 27 Sept. 1742: To receive £4 of Mrs Sarah Browne's money: John Ireland, Thomas Stroud, Richard Pegler, Joseph Nash. To leave Sir Thomas Rich's hospital and receive £10: John Pennington, Benjamin Randall, Daniel West, Samuel Hale, James Motloe, Thomas Hartland. GBR B3/10 f. 11.

3/750	1741	13 Nov.	Laighton, William son of Anthony, weaver of Gloucester Laighton, Anthony, his father, 7 yrs
		23 Nov.	Gardiner, John son of Andrew, tailor of Gloucester Ward, Thomas & Elizabeth, pinmaker, 7 yrs
			Machin, William son of William, cordwainer of Barton Street, Gloucester Draper, Richard & Grace, cordwainer, 7 yrs from 17 Nov.
			Hunt, George son of Edward, gentleman, dec'd, of London Heath, Samuel & Mary, joiner, 7 yrs from 29 Sept.
		27 Nov.	Holford, Benjamin son of Joseph, labourer of Gloucester Holford, Thomas, cordwainer, 7 yrs
		11 Dec.	Baker, Samuel son of John, carpenter of Gloucester Baker, John, his father, & Anne, 7 yrs
3/751			Oakey, Samuel son of William, butcher of Littledean Workman, Anthony, butcher, 7 yrs from 17 Nov.
		14 Dec.	Boulton, Anthony son of John, yeoman of Rodley Playdell, John & Sarah, baker, 7 yrs from 10 Nov.
	1742	25 Jan.	Pool, George son of Sampson, yeoman of Halesowen, Salop. [*recte* Worcs.] Colles, William & Hannah, ironmonger, 7 yrs
		12 Feb.	Dicks, William son of William, bricklayer, dec'd, of Gloucester Lane, John & Mary, farrier, 7 yrs from 12 Jan.
		19 Feb.	Ross, George son of John, tailor of Gloucester Ross, John, his father, & Margaret, 7 yrs
		14 May	May, John son of James, saddler of Gloucester Guest, Jacob & Jane, butcher, 7 yrs
		3 May	Window, William son of William, buttonmaker of Gloucester Haynes, William & Sarah, joiner, 7 yrs from 1 May

[As noted in the Introduction, the volume covering the years 1742–65 has been lost. The names of Gloucester apprentices whose masters paid tax during this period have been abstracted from TNA IR/1 and appear in the Appendix.]

GBR C10/4: 1765–1834[1]

Thomas Branch, mayor 1764–5[2]

4/1	1765	[—]	Draper, William, sum given £10 charity Barton, Martha, widow, plumber & glazier
		8 July	Hook, James, sum given £16 Maddocks, Cartwright, baker
		[2 Aug.]	Lawrence, Henry, sum given £30 Taylor, Ellis, baker [*see 55/161 below*]

George Augustus Selwyn, mayor 1765–6[3]

4/1	1765	28 Oct.	Jones, Thomas jr, sum given £4 charity Braban, Newton, pinmaker, from 7 Oct.
		15 Nov.	Hopkins, Richard, sum given £10 Wood, Benjamin, tailor *Discharged Trinity Sessions 1766*
		18 Nov.	Court, John, sum given £10 Ireland, William, cooper, from 2 Feb. 1766
		13 Dec.	Palmer, Thomas, sum given £7 17s. 6d. charity Watts, John, tailor, from 21 Dec.
	1766	24 Jan.	Beard, Ben, sum given £6 charity Adams, John, cordwainer
		3 Feb.	Jones, John, sum given £4 country charity Washbourne, Nathaniel, baker, from 4 Feb. 1765
			Woodward, Thomas, sum given £10 Woodward, John, pinmaker
4/1		3 Mar.	Rudge, John, sum given £15 Wheatstone, William, saddler, cap & coach harnessmaker, from 2 Feb.

[1] GBR C10/4 does not give the length of apprenticeship, presumably because indentures were normally for seven years; neither does it give mayors' names or dates; these are here supplied editorially.

[2] 16 Sept. 1765: To receive £5 of Mr William Holliday's money: Charles King, James Bourn, John Phillipps. To receive £4 of Mrs Sarah Browne's money: Thomas Keele, Thomas Jones, Benjamin Beard, William Thompson. GBR B3/11 f. 59v.
26 Sept. 1765: To leave Sir Thomas Rich's hospital and receive £10: Thomas Walker, Charles Hutchings, Thomas Woodward, Elton Wantner, Richard Taylor, John Perris. GBR B3/11 f. 62.

[3] 19 Sept. 1766: To receive £4 of Mrs Sarah Browne's money: John Jewell, James King, Jasper Selwyn, James Harper. GBR B3/11 f. 70.
3 Oct. 1766: To leave Sir Thomas Rich's hospital and receive £10: John Philips, William Holton, Thomas Nest, William Lane, William Davis, Thomas Moye. To receive £5 of Mr William Holliday's money: William Hatton, Richard Gardiner, William Badger, William Mann, Charles Fletcher, William Walker. GBR B3/11 ff. 73v–74v.

	1766	7 Mar.	Milton, Samuel, sum given £10 10s. Workman, Anthony jr, butcher, from 26 Apr. 1765
		14 Apr.	Gardiner, Peter, sum given £12 Garner, Thomas, butcher, from 14 Mar.
			Bourne, James, sum given £5 charity Bourne, James, cordwainer
		28 Apr.	Hawkes, Robert, sum given £10 charity Hickman, Benjamin, cordwainer
		30 June	Williams, George, sum given £10 charity Ireland, William, cooper
		21 July	Hopkins, Richard, sum given £10 Baldwin, William, tailor, from 14 July
		18 Aug.	Jeynes, Edwin, sum given £150 Wilson, Samuel, mercer, from 5 July [*edge of page damaged, year illegible*]
		29 Aug.	Rodway, Thomas, sum given £10 charity Price, William, cordwainer
		15 Sept.	Friend, Thomas, sum given £10 Lewis, James, collarmaker
			Keele, James, sum given £4 + £4 charity Cripps, Virgil, cordwainer, from 15 Aug. [*year illegible*]
		22 Sept.	Tompson, William, sum given £4 charity Elton, Edward, grocer

Joseph Cheston, mayor 1766–7[1]

4/1	1766	17 Oct.	Welles, Henry, sum given £50 Stephens, William, upholder, from 1 June 1765
		3 Nov.	Jewell, John, sum given £4 charity Elliott, Benjamin, cordwainer, from 17 Oct.
		1 Dec.	Belcher, John, sum given £10 Rodway, William, baker, from 3 Nov.
4/2	1767	4 May	Perris, Joseph, sum given £20 Bushell, William, saddler, from 25 Mar.
		8 May	Harper, James, sum given £3 charity + £4 charity Roberts, Samuel, brushmaker
		2 Feb.	Phillips, John, sum given £10 charity Wintle, Henry, brushmaker

[1] 15 Sept. 1767: To leave Sir Thomas Rich's hospital and receive £10: John Dix, James Workman, Charles Elliot, Henry Lander, Henry Fords, Robert Coleman, Charles Crump. GBR B3/11 f. 85.

25 Sept. 1767: To receive £5 of Mr William Holliday's money: Isaac Bennett Webley, Jesse Hale, Charles Maverley, Samuel Best, Henry Price, Thomas Ellis, James Collericke. To receive £4 of Mrs Sarah Browne's money: Robert Hazell, James Starling, James Wingate, Joseph Broughton. GBR B3/11 f. 86v.

1767	14 Aug.	Varnham, William, sum given £10 Maverley, Samuel, cordwainer
		Ford, William, sum given £5 charity Bower, William, cordwainer
	29 June	Roston, James Davis, John, pinmaker, from 24 June
	2 Oct.	Broughton, James, sum given £4 charity Lewis, Joseph, barber

Richard Webb, mayor 1767–8[1]

4/2	1767	17 Oct.	Price, Henry, sum given £5 charity Clark, William, pinmaker
		23 Nov.	Long, James, sum given £21 Cowcher, Robert, cutler, from 11 Nov.
	1768	18 Jan.	Window, William, sum given £8 Wood, Joseph, baker
		29 Jan.	Dix, John, sum given £10 charity Webley, Richard, barber
		29 Jan.	Reade, John Wilton, Charles, pinmaker
		19 Feb.	Ford, Henry, sum given £10 charity Cheeseman, John, tailor, from 16 Jan.
			Workman, James, sum given £10 charity Workman, Anthony sr, butcher
		7 Mar.	Sadler, Elisha Farmer, sum given £120 Wood, Richard, mercer
		18 Mar.	Oakey, Thomas, sum given £8 charity Stock, Thomas, butcher
		21 Mar.	Hatton, William, sum given £5 charity Hatton, William, glover
		[—] Mar.	Ward, John Adey, Mary, widow, grocer, from 20 Feb.
		11 Apr.	Chamflower, George, sum given £30 Wintle, James, pinmaker
		17 Apr.	Haskins, John, sum given £2 charity Critchley, Ralph, pinmaker
		10 June	Bourne, Charles Bourne, James, cordwainer, from 29 Sept. 1767

---

[1] 15 Sept. 1768: To leave Sir Thomas Rich's hospital and receive £10: James Hanman, James Powell, William Woodward, James Keys, John Gardner, Hugh Middleton. GBR B3/11 f. 98v.

   27 Sept. 1768: To receive £5 of Mr William Holliday's money: William Lane, William Badger, James Mann, William Richards. To receive £4 of Mrs Sarah Browne's money: Thomas Hammond, Joseph Sharp, Charles Pert, Robert Dadd. GBR B3/11 f. 101.

	1768	20 June	Ruck, James, sum given £25 Hall, Stephen, baker & maltster, from 6 June
		27 June	Holder, Edward, sum given £105 Niblett, Samuel & John, grocers, from 25 Mar.
		15 July	Hill, James, sum given £12 Wintle, Henry, brushmaker
		2 Sept.	Hooper, William, sum given £10 Wheatstone, John, cordwainer, from 29 Sept.
4/3		5 Sept.	Martin, George, sum given £100 Webb, Richard & John, grocers, from 24 June
		12 Sept.	Hawkins, Charles, sum given £150 Wilson, Samuel, mercer, from 1 Aug.
		19 Sept.	Dunn, Richard Cox, Richard, barber
		30 Sept.	Elliots, Charles, sum given £10 charity Deane, William, carpenter
			Lane, William, sum given £5 charity Lane, William, brushmaker

Edward Baylis, mayor 1768–9[1]

4/3	1768	21 Oct.	Richards, William, sum given £5 charity Richards, John, barber
		7 Nov.	Butt, James, sum given £15 15s. Swayne, Richard, butcher, from 24 June
		25 Mar.	Fifield, Edward jr, sum given £105 Smith, Robert, mercer, from 19 Feb.
			Dorsett, William Cheston, Joseph, apothecary
		2 Dec.	Herbert, James, sum given £10 Faucks, Elizabeth, widow, butcher, from 1 Oct.
			Holt, John, sum given £10 charity Dudley, John, grocer & tallowchandler
	1769	27 Feb.	Hanman, James, sum given £10 charity Workman, John, butcher
			Johnsons, William Niblett, Samuel John, grocer, from 1 Jan.
		10 Apr.	Lane, Samuel Brabant, Newton, pinmaker

---

[1] 22 Sept. 1769: To leave Sir Thomas Rich's hospital and receive £10: John Hartland, John Adams, James Maverley, James Ward, John Archer, Richard Lane, James Butt. GBR B3/11 f. 110v.

27 Sept. 1769: To receive £5 of Mr William Holliday's money: Francis King, Benjamin Wilkes, William Kirby, Isaac Turner Glendale, Matthew Cook, William Merry, Joseph Reeve, Charles Woodward, James Hutchings, John Ridge. To receive £4 of Mrs Sarah Browne's money: James Mann, William Smart, Ferdinand Myon, John Cleaveland. GBR B3/11 f. 111v.

1769	14 Apr.	Hathaway, Richard, sum given £10 Cowcher, William, pinmaker
	17 Apr.	Binning, Thomas, sum given £10 10s. Bloxsome, Edward, cooper
	22 May	Wassell, John Saunders, Thomas, soapboiler & tallowchandler, from 22 Apr.
	26 May	Butt, William, sum given £10 Humphris, William, butcher, from 4 Apr. 1768
	2 June	Pride, William, sum given £2 charity Stock, Thomas Richard, grocer
	5 June	Gale, Thomas, sum given £4 Simpson, Thomas, baker
	9 June	Mount, Thomas, sum given £20 Charleton, Shadrach, apothecary, from 14 Mar.
	26 June	Powell, James, sum given £10 charity Mutlow, Thomas, tailor, from 1 Mar.
	31 July	Smith, Daniel, sum given £10 10s. Rea, Thomas, baker, from 24 May
	25 Aug.	Surman, John, sum given £15 15s. Bevan, Thomas, baker, from 23 Apr.

[*entered in another hand at the foot of 4/3*] *Inspected 1769 Thos James*

John Jefferis, mayor 1769–70[1]

4/4	1769	9 Oct.	Olliver, James, sum given £21 Roberts, Samuel, brushmaker, from 1 Sept.
		10 Oct.	Glendall, Samson, sum given £5 charity Glendall, Thomas, joiner
		27 Nov.	Kirby, William, sum given £5 charity Wintle, James, pinmaker
			Palmer, William, no money Cooke, John, apothecary
		15 Dec.	Bradford, Francis, sum given £50 Mayo, Francis, grocer, from 6 Dec.
	1770	22 Jan.	Reeve, Joseph, sum given £5 charity Long, Thomas, currier
		19 Feb.	Wells, William, sum given £80 Ashmead, John jr, mercer, from 6 Jan. *See another of this date at the bottom of this page* [*sic*]

[1] 18 Sept. 1770: To leave Sir Thomas Rich's hospital and receive £10: Charles Wantner, William Bishop, George Wheeler, Richard Jeynes, Nathaniel Harris, Joseph South. GBR B3/11 f. 118v.

27 Sept. 1770: To receive £5 of Mr William Holliday's money: William Williams, James Price, James Lewis, James Hawkes, John Jennings, James Hartland, Daniel Dix. To receive £4 of Mrs Sarah Browne's money: William Price, William White, Thomas Platt, George Kibble. GBR B3/11 f. 120.

1770   30 Mar.   Selwyn, William, sum given £6
                   Wells, William, cordwainer, from 2 Feb.

        6 Apr.   Moore, Richard
                   Green, Richard, grocer

        27 Apr.   Martin, James, sum given £47 5s.
                   Dunn, Thomas, bookseller & bookbinder, from 1 Apr.

        18 May   Allen, Richard, sum given £10
                   Cripps, Virgil, cordwainer, from 28 Sept. 1769

        29 June   Merry, William, sum given £5 charity
                   Wells, William, cordwainer, from 8 June

                   Butt, James, sum given £10 charity
                   Washbourn, William, apothecary, from 26 Feb.

        30 July   Wells, John, sum given £30
                   Washbourn, George, goldsmith, from 11 July

        17 Aug.   Adams, John, sum given £5
                   Gardiner, Pettat, brushmaker, from 3 Aug.

        10 Sept.   Heaven, Thomas, sum given £15 15s.
                   Crump, Lawrence, upholder

        14 Sept.   Holt, Gabriel
                   Stephen, Merrott, mercer

John Webb, mayor 1770–1[1]

4/4   1770   2 Nov.   Perris, Thomas, sum given £18
                          Adey, John, pinmaker

                10 Dec.   Hartland, James, sum given £5 charity
                          Hartland, Thomas, pinmaker

        1771   28 Jan.   Dobles, James, sum given £84
                          Turner, William, grocer, from 1 Jan.

                11 Feb.   Harris, Nathaniel, sum given £10 charity
                          Wadley, Ambrose, baker

                          Wantner, Charles, sum given £10 charity
                          Lovet, James, barber

        1770   19 Feb.   Smart, William, sum given £4 charity
                          Adams, John, cordwainer

4/5   5 Mar.   Giles, [—], sum given £105
                          [—], mercer, from 20 Feb.

                26 Apr.   South, Joseph, sum given £10 charity
                          Murcutt, William, cabinetmaker

[1] 13 Sept. 1771: To leave Sir Thomas Rich's hospital and receive £10: William Lewis, Thomas Wilton, Henry Mutlow, Thomas Glendall, William Salcomb, William Jones. GBR B3/11 f. 129v.
   27 Sept. 1771: To receive £5 of Mr William Holliday's money: Thomas Merrett, Thomas Jeffs, William Dix, Thomas Harris, John Keys, Septimus Stroud. To receive £4 of Mrs Sarah Browne's money: Richard Collier, Richard Netherwood, John Sharp, Thomas Hall. GBR B3/11 f. 132v.

	1771	26 Apr.	Smith, James, sum given £10 Spillman, John, baker, from 18 Mar.
		21 June	Matthews, John, sum given £10 10s. Wood, Joseph, baker, from 21 June
		2 Aug.	Greatwood, Robert, sum given £31 10s. Dudley, John, grocer, soapboiler & tallowchandler
		19 Aug.	Platt, Thomas, sum given £4 charity Cowcher, William, pinmaker
		30 Aug.	Buckle, William, sum given £105 Elton, Edward, grocer
		[—]	Price, Bower, [entry incomplete]
		9 Sept.	Dobson, Thomas Boughton, Edmund, currier
		4 Oct.	Lea, Charles, sum given £20 Stephens, William, upholder

John Baylis, mayor 1771

4/5	1771	4 Nov.	Morgan, Washbourn, [entry incomplete]
		8 Nov.	Smith Bartlett, William, sum given £10 Wintle, James, pinmaker, from 23 Mar.
		15 Nov.	Hale, Ephraim, sum given £10 charity Bennett, Joseph, collarmaker, from 14 Oct.
			Truman, Thomas, sum given £9 9s Greening, William, barber
			Freeman, William, sum given £9 Peace, William, cordwainer
			Evans, William, sum given £20 Fletcher, Ralph, baker, from 16 Oct.

Thomas Branch, mayor 1772[1,2]

4/5	1772	27 Jan.	Jones, William, sum given £10 charity Lewis, Joseph, barber
		31 Jan.	Wilton, Thomas Wellavize, Abel, tailor

[1] Elected 6 Jan. 1772 after the death of John Baylis.

[2] 25 Sept. 1772: To leave Sir Thomas Rich's hospital and receive £10: Richard Bubb, Richard Crump, Francis Richards, Daniel Ellis, Charles Elliott, Henry Dunn. GBR B3/11 f. 143v.

2 Oct. 1772: To receive £5 of Mr William Holliday's money: Joseph Best, Thomas Adams, John Ricketts, Benjamin Collericke, Benjamin Hare, Robert Heath, John Davis. To receive £4 of Mrs Sarah Browne's money: John Hinton, Ansel Hanman, John Kock, James Dadd. GBR B3/11 f. 144v.

	1772	29 Feb.	Lewis, William Packer, sum given £10 charity Hyett, John, cooper, from 1 Jan.
		8 May	Harris, Thomas, sum given £5 charity Bevan, Mary, baker, from 1 Jan.
		5 June	Taylor, Samuel, sum given £21 Fletcher, Ralph, baker, from 30 May
		3 July	Page, James, sum given £10 Jeffs, Joseph, barber
		10 July	Surman, John, sum given £140 Wood, Richard, mercer
			Jeffs, Thomas, sum given £5 charity Roberts, Samuel, brushmaker
		7 Aug.	Cooke, Thomas, sum given £20 Cole, Charles jr, mercer
4/6		25 Sept.	Fowler, Thomas, sum given £15 Cheeseman, William, brushmaker, from 15 Aug.

Benjamin Baylis, mayor 1772–3[1]

	1772	26 Oct.	Godwin, Thomas, sum given [—] Saunders, Thomas, soapboiler, from 26 Sept.
4/6		2 Nov.	Peters, William, sum given £10 10s. Roberts, Edward, tinplate worker
		23 Nov.	Best, Joseph, sum given £4 charity Peace, William, cordwainer
	1773	22 Jan.	Woolley, George, sum given £50 Mayo, Francis, grocer, from 1 Jan.
		29 Jan.	Smith, John, sum given £12 Benson, Robert, glover etc., from 1 Jan.
		19 Feb.	Bubb, Richard, sum given £10 charity Gardiner, Pettat, brushmaker, from 19 Jan.
			Richards, Joseph, sum given £10 charity Roberts, Samuel, brushmaker, from 1 Jan.
		1 Mar.	Crump, Richard, sum given £10 charity Ricketts, John, barber, from 1 Jan.
		15 Mar.	Ricketts, Samuel, sum given £5 charity Wintle, James, pinmaker
		22 Apr.	Greatwood, Robert, sum given £20 Green, Richard, grocer etc., from 2 Aug. 1771

---

[1] 24 Sept. 1773: To receive £5 of Mr William Holliday's money: Richard Matthews, Joseph Badger, Thomas Jennings. To receive £4 of Mrs Sarah Browne's money: John Thomas, John Moss. GBR B3/11 f. 158.

  1 Oct. 1773: To leave Sir Thomas Rich's hospital and receive £10: James Webley, William Smith, Richard Wintle, William Bourn, James Wingate, John Mathews. GBR B3/11 f. 159.

	1773	25 Apr.	Holt, John Webb, Richard, grocer etc., from 2 Dec. 1769
		26 Apr.	Olney, John, sum given £52 10s. Bush, John, woolstapler
		14 June	Powell, William Evans, William, carpenter & joiner, from 26 Apr.
			Fletcher, William, sum given £20 Spillman, John, baker etc., from 1 Mar.
		23 July	Coleman, William, sum given £10 Barton, William, plumber & glazier, from 19 July
		20 Aug.	Caruthers, James, sum given £12 Baldwin, William, tailor, from 7 June
		10 Sept.	Adams, Thomas, sum given £5 charity Merry, Thomas, cordwainer

Abraham Saunders, mayor 1773–4[1]

4/6	1773	29 Oct.	Griffiths, John Maddocks, Cartwright, baker
			Cooke, John, sum given £30 Taylor, Ellis & Mary, baker
		8 Nov.	Harbert, William, sum given £5 Wheatstone, John & Ann, cordwainer
			Dadd, James, sum given £6 + £4 charity Wheatstone, John & Ann, cordwainer
4/7		15 Nov.	Pagett, Thomas, sum given £105 Elton, Edward, grocer, from 29 Sept.
		17 Dec.	Roberts, John Baylis, Edward, woolstapler & woolcomber, from 10 Oct.
	1774	7 Jan.	Hough, John James, sum given £20 Dunn, Thomas, book binder & stationer, from 15 Nov. 1773
		11 Feb.	Bourne, William, sum given £10 charity Alexander, William, cooper, from 25 Jan.
			Wintle, Richard, sum given £10 charity Cheeseman, William & Mary, brushmaker
			Woolley, George, sum given £50 Mayo, Francis, grocer, from 1 Jan. 1773
			Wingate, James, sum given £10 charity Wintle, Henry & Elizabeth, brushmaker

---

[1] 19 Sept. 1774: To leave Sir Thomas Rich's hospital and receive £10: Samuel Rickets, James Crowdy, John Webb, Joseph Richards, John Bullock, Charles Price, Thomas Ridgeley. GBR B3/11 f. 171v.

30 Sept. 1774: To receive £5 of Mr William Holliday's money: William Elliott, William Hicks, John Hare, John Smart, William Mutlow, John Badger, James Estcourt, Benjamin Roberts, John Webley. To receive £4 of Mrs Sarah Browne's money: John Ricketts son of John, John Ellis, Charles Brunsden, James Wakefield. GBR B3/11 f. 173.

	1774	11 Feb.	Thomas, John, sum given £6 charity Humphris, Richard, carpenter, from 2 Feb.
		18 Feb.	Kitchen, Seth, sum given £10 Barton, Elizabeth, plumber & glazier
		15 Apr.	Friend, Edward, sum given £10 Draper, William, plumber & glazier, from 15 Feb.
		3 June	Holder, William, sum given £30 Biddle, Nathaniel, grocer, from 25 Mar.
			Dadd, Nathaniel, sum given £10 charity Taylor, Charles, tinplate worker
		6 June	Hinton, John, sum given £14 charity Lewis, Joseph, perukemaker
		29 July	Webley, James, sum given £10 charity Tyler, Charles, grocer, from 1 Mar.
		5 Aug.	Lewis, Charles, sum given £10 Bennett, James & Ann, collarmaker, from 8 July
		19 Sept.	Wintle, Richard, sum given £7 7s. 6d. charity Bowdler, John, baker

John Jefferis, mayor 1774–5[1]

4/7	1774	17 Oct.	Stroud, Stephen Keersey, James, wiredrawer
		21 Oct.	Lovell, William, sum given £4 charity Wilson, Charles, pinmaker
4/8		4 Nov.	Elliotts, William, sum given £5 charity Adey, John & Mary, pinmaker
		14 Nov.	Mutlow, William, sum given £5 charity Solloway, Robert & Ann, pinmaker
			Ellis, John, sum given £4 charity Cowcher, William, pinmaker, from 5 Nov.
		18 Nov.	Bining, William, sum given £10 10s. Ricketts, John, barber, perukemaker & hairdresser, from 1 Nov.
		3 Dec.	Phelps, William, sum given £10 10s. Workman, Anthony & Elizabeth, butcher, from 14 Nov.
		12 Dec.	Hincksman, James, sum given £80 Cooke, Christopher & Elizabeth, grocer, from 14 Nov.

---

[1] 29 Mar. 1775: John Pugh, Benjamin South, Robert Ladbrook, John Crump, Edward Heath, Benjamin Hickman, Thomas Hartland, Thomas House, Thomas Williams to receive £10 of the gift of Mrs Jane Punter who, in her will of 2 July 1767, left the residue of her estate to the City for the apprenticing of poor boys. GBR B3/11 f. 182v.

25 Sept. 1775: To leave Sir Thomas Rich's hospital and receive £10: William Harris, Thomas Dix, John South, Charles Glendale, Thomas Bretherton. GBR B3/11 f. 187.

29 Sept. 1775: To receive £5 of Mr William Holliday's money: William Jones, William Ricketts. No petitioners applied for Mrs Sarah Browne's money. GBR B3/11 f. 188v.

| | 1774 | 12 Dec. | Hincksman, William, sum given £120 |
| | | | Jeynes, Edwin & Elizabeth, mercer, from 14 Nov. |

1774 12 Dec. Hincksman, William, sum given £120
Jeynes, Edwin & Elizabeth, mercer, from 14 Nov.

1775 20 Jan. Hoddinott, William, sum given £30
Cowcher, Robert, cutler, from 18 Dec. 1774

Haviland, Richard, sum given £3 3s.
Lane, John, farrier

23 Jan. Wellington, James jr
Boughton, Edmund, currier

3 Feb. Richards, Joseph, sum given £10 charity
Deane, William & Joannah, carpenter & joiner

6 Feb. Ridgeley, Thomas, sum given £11 + £10 charity
Wintle, Henry & Elizabeth, brushmaker

17 Feb. Osborn, John jr, sum given £10 10s.
Bond, Samuel, collarmaker, coach harnessmaker, bridle cutter,
& whipmaker, from 2 Feb.

3 Mar. Smart, William
Davis, Henry & Anne, pinmaker, from 24 Feb.

13 Mar. Browning, William, sum given £10 charity
Bower, William & Jane, cordwainer, from 14 Nov. 1774

20 Mar. Reeve, James, sum given £52 10s.
Parker, Thomas, apothecary

24 Apr. Rogers, William, sum given £60
Webb, Richard, grocer, tallowchandler & soapboiler, from 14 Jan.

4/9 1775 28 Apr. Warman, John, sum given £120
Mayo, Francis, grocer

5 May Howe, Thomas, sum given £10 charity
Bubb, William, carpenter

15 May Ladbrook, Robert, sum given £10 charity
Cheeseman, William & Mary, brushmaker

22 May South, Benjamin, sum given £20 charity
Price, William & Mary, cordwainer, from 10 Apr.

26 June Wells, John, sum given £10 charity
Price, William & Mary, cordwainer

7 Aug. Rayer, William, sum given £13
Wheatstone, John & Ann, cordwainer

Boughton, John, sum given £150
Wood, Richard & Elizabeth, mercer

18 Sept. Selwyn, Richard, sum given £10 charity
Lewis, James & Martha, collarmaker

William Crump, mayor 1775–6[1]

4/9	1775	16 Oct.	Lilly, Samuel jr, sum given £10 10s. Faucks, Robert, butcher

		30 Oct.	Clarke, Richard, sum given £12 12s.
			   Swayne, Richard, butcher
			   23 Oct. 1780: assigned over by John Price and John Lovett, executors of
			   Richard Swaine, dec'd, to Mary Faukes, butcher, for the rest of his term

		24 Nov.	Andrews, William Henry, sum given £5 Brabant, Newton, pinmaker
		4 Dec.	Jordan, Josiah Jenner, sum given £50 Stock, Edmund & Holder, Edward, grocers
	1776	12 Feb.	Clutterbuck, Benjamin Critchley, Ralph & Elizabeth, pinmaker
		26 Feb.	Hill, Richard, sum given £10 10s. Boughton, Joseph, currier, from 13 Jan.
		1 Mar.	Brewer, Thomas, sum given £21 Hall, Stephen, baker & maltster
		18 Mar.	Bretherton, Thomas Clark, sum given £10 charity Jeffs, Joseph, perukemaker, from 19 Feb.
		18 Apr.	Croose, George, sum given £100 Bush, John, woolstapler, from 18 Feb.
		22 Apr.	Sizemore, John, sum given £20 Goodwin, Joseph, baker
4/10		26 Apr.	Eldridge, Charles, sum given £15 Gardiner, Pettat & Elizabeth, brushmaker, from 12 Apr. 1775
		7 June	Wingate, William, sum given £10 charity Hyett, John, cooper, from 16 Sept. 1775
		10 June	Glendall, Charles, sum given £10 charity + £10 charity Wood, William, cooper, from 1 May
			Smith, Samuel, sum given £10 charity Price, William, cordwainer
		1 July	Holder, George, sum given £100 Charleton, Shadrach, apothecary
		15 July	Cocks, Charles, sum given £20 Spillman, John, baker & maltster
			Ricketts, William, sum given £5 charity Bowes, William, cordwainer, from 30 Nov. 1775

[1] 18 Apr. 1776: To receive £10 of Mrs Jane Punter's money: William Wintle, William Best, Robert Hare, Charles Wilks, Joseph Bower, William Wingate, John Powell, Thomas Webb, William Maisey, Paul Mutlow, Charles Woodward. GBR B3/11 f. 195v.

   10 Oct. 1776: To leave Sir Thomas Rich's hospital and receive £10: Thomas Lewis, Thomas Woodward, James Ellis, Joseph Bubb, William Evans, Thomas Watts. To receive £5 of Mr William Holliday's money: William Davis, Charles Wilks, William Best. To receive £4 of Mrs Sarah Browne's money: John Cradock, William Morse, John Evans, James Kirk. GBR B3/11 f. 204.

	1776	15 July	Maisey, William, sum given £10 charity Bubb, William, carpenter, from 24 July
		26 July	Marchant, Joseph Saunders, Thomas, soapboiler, tallowchandler & grocer
			Hornsby, Thomas, sum given £10 charity Southall, John, tinplate worker
		2 Aug.	Addis, Richard, sum given £10 charity Cox, Mary, perukemaker, from 1 July
		13 Sept.	Lewis, William, sum given £2 charity Brabant, Newton, pinmaker
		23 Sept.	Floyd, William Brabant, Newton, pinmaker, from 1 Sept. 1774

John Webb, mayor 1776–7[1]

	1776	8 Nov.	Cradock, John, sum given £4 charity Baldwyn, William, tailor
4/10		2 Dec.	Webb, Thomas Webb, Thomas, cordwainer, from 2 Dec. 1775
		20 Dec.	Crump, John, sum given £10 charity Roberts, Samuel, brushmaker, from 18 Nov.
	1777	7 Feb.	Andrews, William Critchley, Ralph & Elizabeth, pinmaker, from 3 Feb.
			Charter, Thomas Charter, Thomas jr & Mary, woolstapler & weaver
4/11		7 Mar.	Woodward, Charles, sum given £10 charity Price, Thomas, cordwainer
		14 Apr.	Lewis, Thomas, sum given £10 charity Lewis, Joseph, perukemaker, from 3 Feb.
		24 Mar.	Turberville, Richard, sum given £21 Fletcher, Ralph & Sarah, baker, from 18 Jan.
		9 May	Stephens, John Marcott, William, joiner & cabinetmaker
		27 June	Forster, Thomas, sum given £15 15s. Branch, Thomas, tinplate worker, from 27 June
		11 Aug.	Bower, Joseph, sum given £10 charity Solloway, Robert, pinmaker
			James, William, sum given £100 Stephens, Merrott, mercer

---

[1] 4 July 1777: To receive £10 of Mrs Jane Punter's money: Thomas Pugh, George Stroud, William Bradley, William Dadd, Joseph Bower, Robert Hare, Spencer Thompson. GBR B3/11 f. 212.

19 Sept. 1777: To leave Sir Thomas Rich's hospital and receive £10: Nathaniel Jeynes, James Gunn, William Dowell, William Hickman, James Drinkwater, James Wellavize. B3/11 f. 215v.

3 Oct. 1777: To receive £5 of Mr William Holliday's money: Thomas Rudge. To receive £4 of Mrs Sarah Browne's money: James Jew, William McCloud, James Bartholomew, John Brooks. GBR B3/11 f. 217v.

John Box, mayor 1777–8[1]

4/11	1777	24 Oct.	Dadd, William, sum given £10 charity Gardiner, Pettat, brushmaker
		1 Dec.	Meek, Thomas Brabant, Newton, pinmaker
	1778	23 Jan.	Dowell, William, sum given £10 charity Ady, John & Mary, pinmaker
			Longford, Richard, sum given £10 charity Washbourne, Nathaniel, baker
		9 Mar.	Mitchell, Joseph Cheeseman, John, tailor, from 1 Jan.
		30 Mar.	Barnfield, William, sum given £20 Smith, Daniel, grocer, from 10 Oct. 1777
		1 June	Tomson, Spencer, sum given £10 charity Washborne, William, apothecary, from 1 Nov. 1777
		15 June	Rogers, Thomas, sum given £10 10s. Moulder, John, baker

James Sadler, mayor 1778–9[2]

4/11	1778	23 Oct.	Lewis, Thomas, sum given £10 charity Peart, Charles, cordwainer
		9 Nov.	Harper, John, sum given £4 charity Wheatstone, John, cordwainer
4/12	1779	22 Feb.	Hutchings, John, sum given £10 charity Evans, William, carpenter
		26 Mar.	Dennan, Charles, sum given £16 Hyett, John, cooper, from 20 Feb.
		31 May	Charter, John Savory Charter, Thomas jr, woolstapler
			Blomer, John, sum given £21 Greatwood, Robert, soapboiler, tallowchandler & grocer
		26 July	Herbert, Thomas, sum given £31 10s. Adey, John & Mary, pinmaker
		13 Aug.	Holt, William, sum given £10 charity Cooke, Elizabeth, grocer, from 20 Aug.

---

[1] 20 May 1778: To receive £10 of Mrs Jane Punter's money: Thomas Cradock, William Wintle, William Benson, John Cox, Benjamin Perris, Thomas Holder, William Hutchings, Thomas Lewis. GBR B3/11 f. 226.

25 Sept. 1778: To leave Sir Thomas Rich's hospital and receive £10: Charles Jeffs, Samuel Mutlow, John Boughton, Thomas Rudge, William Smith, Thomas Elliott. B3/11 f. 232v.

2 Oct. 1778: To receive £5 of Mr William Holliday's money: Benjamin Freeman. To receive £4 of Mrs Sarah Browne's money: John Harper, William Tarling. GBR B3/11 f. 236.

[2] 5 May 1779: To receive £4 of Mrs Sarah Browne's money: Nathaniel Glover

1 July 1779: To receive £10 of Mrs Jane Punter's money: William Harris, John Jeynes, Thomas Gunn, William Badnege, Thomas Peart, William Lebeter, Edward King, William Hartland. GBR B3/11 f. 248.

Abraham Saunders, mayor 1779[1]

4/12	1779	27 Aug.	Peart, Thomas, sum given £10 charity Bower, William, cordwainer
		20 Sept.	Woodward, John, sum given £10 charity Price, Thomas, cordwainer

William Lane, mayor 1779–80[2]

4/12	1779	25 Oct.	Court, Samuel, sum given £15 Benson, Robert, fellmonger & glover
		12 Nov.	Cook, William, sum given £100 Wood, Richard & James, mercers
	1780	17 Jan.	Piffe, William, sum given £15 Herbert, James, butcher, from 14 Oct.
		18 Feb.	Byard, William, sum given £12 12s. Gardiner, Pettat & Elizabeth, brushmaker, from 22 Apr.
		21 Feb.	Powell, George, sum given £4 charity Davis, Henry, pinmaker
		12 Mar.	Marshall, John Spillman, John, baker & maltster, from 1 Jan.
		12 June	Fletcher, John jr, sum given £15 Bloxsom, Edward, cooper, from 17 May
		20 June	Fletcher, Lewis, sum given £21 Draper, William, plumber & glazier
		7 July	Hinton, Richard Critchley, Ralph, pinmaker, from 29 May
		10 July	Jones, Samuel, sum given £10 Roberts, Samuel, brushmaker
		11 Aug.	Dole, Richard, sum given £5 Wheatstone, John, cordwainer
		1 Sept.	Rene, James, sum given £10 + £10 charity Solloway, Robert, pinmaker
		22 Sept.	Mountain, John, sum given £50 Mayo, Francis, grocer, from 8 Apr.
4/13	1780	26 Sept.	Lewis, John, sum given £10 Meachen, John, cordwainer
		3 Sept.	Maddock, Cartwright Maddocke, Cartwright, baker, from 24 June

---

[1] Elected 19 Aug. 1779 after Sadler's death.

[2] 17 July 1780: To receive £10 of Mrs Jane Punter's money: James Broughton, James Rene, John Ladbroke, William Wren, Richard Garn, John Williams, Thomas Fream, George King. GBR B3/11 f. 269.

22 Sept. 1780: To leave Sir Thomas Rich's hospital and receive £10: William Simpson, John Estcourt, John Mann, Charles Pleydell, James Clark, Charles Bubb. B3/11 f. 277.

29 Sept. 1780: No petitioner for Mr William Holliday's money. To receive £4 of Mrs Sarah Browne's money: Charles Selwyn, James Roberts, Samuel Woodcock, William Smart. GBR B3/11 f. 280v.

John Bush, mayor 1780–1

4/13	1780	1 Dec.	Bamford, William, sum given £30 Mills, John, apothecary, from 9 Oct.
	1781	15 Jan.	Jones, Hopeful, sum given £10 charity Pettat, Gardiner, brushmaker
	1777	7 July	Meek, Thomas, sum given £10 charity Dunn, Richard, perukemaker, from 30 June 1777
	1781	2 Apr.	Bennett, William, sum given £10 Barton, William, plumber & glazier, from 3 Mar.
		28 May	Fryer, Matthew, sum given £60 Biddle, Nathaniel, grocer, from 10 Apr.

Abraham Saunders, mayor 1781[1,2]

4/13	1781	20 July	Morgan, Robert Roberts, sum given £5 Dunn, Richard, hairdresser
		13 Aug.	Broughton, James jr, sum given £10 charity Broughton, James sr (his father), perukemaker, from 29 Sept. 1780
		27 July	Fream, Thomas, sum given £10 charity Cowcher, William & Richard, pinmakers & copartners, from 2 Feb.

Thomas Weaver, mayor 1781–2[3]

4/13	1781	9 Nov.	Cradock, William, sum given £10 Page, James, perukemaker, from 9 Aug.
			Townshend, William jr, sum given £10 10s. Derrett, John, butcher, from 25 Sept.
		16 Nov.	Chandler, George, sum given £100 Martin, George, grocer, from 27 July
		10 Dec.	Bick, John, sum given £5 Brabant, Newton, pinmaker

---

[1] Elected 5 June 1781 after Bush's death.

[2] 7 June 1781: To receive £10 of Mrs Jane Punter's money: James Cook, William Gardiner, William Bower, Charles Wheeler, Thomas Maverly, James Garner, James Barnard, Thomas Drinkwater. GBR B3/11 f. 289v. 24 Sept. 1781: To leave Sir Thomas Rich's hospital and receive £10: Daniel Cope, William Hopkins, William Andrew Hamblin, Thomas Ireland, William Okey, Joseph Gunn. B3/11 f. 302v.

27 Sept. 1781: No petitioner for Mr William Holliday's money. To receive £4 [of Mrs Sarah Browne's money]: Thomas Protherow, Henry Jones, Joseph Powell, John Addis, William Jones. To leave Sir Thomas Rich's hospital and receive £10: John Best. GBR B3/11 f 305.

21 Dec. 1781: James Tombs, a poor boy, to have £5 in the gift of the Corporation to put him out apprentice. GBR B3/11 f. 312.

[3] 29 July 1782: To receive £10 of Mrs Jane Punter's money: William Deane, John Hyett, Charles Estcourt, William Hinton, Thomas Phillipps, James Hale, John Harris, James Bishop. GBR B3/11 f. 318.

23 Sept. 1782: To leave Sir Thomas Rich's hospital and receive £10: Joseph Lewis, Samuel Arch, James Woodward, Richard Good, James Powell, Richard Evans. B3/11 f. 319v.

27 Sept. 1782: To receive £5 of Mr William Holliday's money: Samuel Badger. To receive £4 of Mrs Sarah Browne's money: William Jakes, Samuel Moss, John Hulbert, John Benton. GBR B3/11 f. 322v.

	1782	26 Nov.	Roane, Thomas, sum given £10 charity Faucks, Mary, butcher, from 14 Dec.
		27 May	Phillips, James, sum given £105 Stephens, Merrott, mercer
		27 May	George, Thomas, sum given £12 Wellavize, Abel, tailor, from 8 Apr.
		2 Aug.	Haviland, William, sum given £21 Gardiner, Pettat, brushmaker
		19 Aug.	Barry, Philip, sum given £60 Greatwood, Robert, soapboiler, tallowchandler & grocer

Richard Webb, mayor 1782–3[1]

4/13	1782	22 Nov.	Hinton, William jr, sum given £10 charity Saunders, James, pinmaker, from 5 Nov.
		6 Dec.	Phillipps, Thomas, sum given £10 Mrs Punter, £8 Lady Yates Lane, Richard, farrier, from 26 Oct.
4/14	1783	24 Jan.	Bishop, James jr, sum given £10 charity Wheatstone, John, cordwainer, from 23 Dec. 1782
		14 Feb.	Hornsby, James, sum given £10 charity Davies, Henry, pinmaker
		17 Feb.	Ward, William jr Washbourne, Nathaniel, baker & confectioner, from 12 Aug. 1782
		21 Feb.	Grafton, William jr, no money Jeynes, Edwin & Elizabeth, mercer & linendraper
			Overbury, Thomas, sum given £10 Boseley, William, breechesmaker, from 1 Dec.
			Dance, Thomas, sum given £84 Wood, Richard & James, mercer & banker
		17 Mar.	Tipetts, Josiah, sum given £21 Powell, Penelope, plumber & glazier, from 11 Nov. 1782
		5 May	Perkins, William jr, sum given £40 Boughton, Edmund, currier
		4 Aug.	Roberts, Edward Roberts, Edward, tinplate worker
		22 Aug.	Woodward, Richard jr, sum given £10 charity Cox, Charles Thomas, hairdresser & perukemaker
	1783	25 Aug.	Nicholls, James, no commission Saunders, Thomas, soapboiler

[1] 4 June 1783: To receive £10 of Mrs Jane Punter's money: John Glover, Joseph Spillman, William Hale, Richard Woodward, Thomas Bower, Charles Simpson, James Bradley, Thomas Jeynes. GBR B3/11 f. 324v.

30 Sept. 1783: To receive £5 of Mr William Holliday's money: John Hanbury Heath. To receive £4 of Mrs Sarah Browne's money: John Fryer, Thomas Church, John Roberts, James Jones, Benjamin Sollis, James Powell, George Southern. GBR B3/11 f. 343v.

3 Oct. 1783: To leave Sir Thomas Rich's hospital and receive £10: James Bonnewell, Charles Jones, John Wood, William Watts, William Window, Charles Ridgeley. B3/11 f. 346v.

Charles Howard, Earl of Surrey, mayor 1783–4[1]

4/14   1783   10 Nov.   Herbert, William, sum given £50
                          Stock, Edmund & Holder, Edward, grocers, from 25 June

         1784   26 Jan.   Roberts, William, sum given £20 charity
                          Derrett, John, butcher, from 24 June

                12 Mar.   Maisey, John, sum given £10 charity
                          Rodway, Thomas, cordwainer, from 17 Feb.

                19 July   Constant, Thomas, sum given £10 charity
                          Dunn, Richard, hairdresser & perukemaker

                13 Aug.   Tustin, Thomas, sum given £16
                          Goodwin, Joseph, baker & maltster, from 5 Apr.

                30 Aug.   Rea, William jr
                          Rea, Thomas, baker, from 12 Oct. 1781

                          Driver, Thomas, sum given £21
                          Dunn, Richard & Elizabeth, hairdresser & perukemaker

Samuel Colborne, mayor 1784–5[2]

4/14   1784   8 Nov.   Reeves, John, sum given £4 charity
                          Solloway, Robert, pinmaker, from 24 June

                12 Nov.   Pickering, John, sum given £20
                          Roberts, Samuel, brushmaker, from 21 Aug.

         1785   21 Feb.   Wilson, Edward, sum given £42
                          Greatwood, Robert, grocer, chandler & tallowchandler, from 14 Feb.

Edwin Jeynes, mayor 1785–6[3]

4/14   1785   10 Oct.   Hathaway, John, sum given £49
                          Parker, Thomas, apothecary & man midwife, from 5 Sept.

4/15   31 Oct.   Smith, Thomas, sum given £100
                          Wood, Richard & James, mercers

---

[1] 14 June 1784: To receive £10 of Mrs Jane Punter's money: William Neen, Thomas Simpson, James Bower, Charles King, John Holder, Thomas Constance, James Holbert, James Bennett. GBR B3/11 f. 359.
    24 Sept. 1784: To leave Sir Thomas Rich's hospital and receive £10: John Hunter, Robert Hickes, William Bradley, James Dowell, Samuel Lane, William Cantrell. B3/11 f. 365v.
    1 Oct. 1784: To receive £4 of Mrs Sarah Browne's money: James Constant Griggs, Charles Lewis, William Bennett, Daniel Wren. GBR B3/11 f. 367.
[2] 2 Dec. 1784: To leave Sir Thomas Rich's hospital and receive £10: William White, William Lewis, Samuel Salcomb, Thomas Clark, Warren Stephens, Charles Ireland, William Gunn. GBR B3/12 f. 5v.
    10 June 1785: To receive £10 of Mrs Jane Punter's money: Robert Davies, George Deane, William Bonnewell, John Owen Bower, James Jones, William Dix, Luke Holford, Daniel Bloxsome. GBR B3/12 f. 12v.
[3] 20 June 1786: To receive £10 of Mrs Jane Punter's money: William Knight, Charles Bradgate, Henry Barrett, Benjamin Dix, John Lilley, William Hambling, William Swain, William Bradley. GBR B3/12 f. 41v.
    22 Sept. 1786: To leave Sir Thomas Rich's hospital and receive £10: Benjamin Jennings, Benjamin Elliott, John White, Joseph Mitchell, James Davis, Edward Bloxsome. No candidate for the gift of Mr William Holliday. To have £4 of Mrs Sarah Browne's money: Joseph Bennett son of Joseph and Anne, Joseph Bennett son of Joseph and Mary, John Ingram, William Holder. GBR B3/12 ff. 51, 55v.

	1786	16 Jan.	Caudle, Walter, sum given £10
			Washbourne, Nathaniel, baker & confectioner, from 24 Oct.
		3 Feb.	Bonner, Thomas
			Colborne, Samuel, apothecary, from 24 June 1785
		17 Mar.	Baldwin, Richard, sum given £15
			Lewis, James, collarmaker, from 2 Jan.

John Webb, mayor 1786–7[1]

4/15	1786	1 Dec.	Bennett, Joseph, sum given £4
			Brabant, Newton, pinmaker
	1787	23 Feb.	Marshall, Charles, sum given £70
			Stephens, Merrott, mercer
		20 Apr.	Burgess, Lawrence, sum given £120
			Sadler, James & Elisha, mercers
		22 June	Hyett, William, sum given £15
			Hall, Stephen, baker & maltster
			Harris, William, sum given £21
			Powell, Penelope, plumber & glazier
		2 July	Stiles, Richard, sum given £11
			Wheatstone, John, cordwainer
		13 Aug.	Darke, James, sum given £10 charity
			Price, Thomas, cordwainer
		24 Aug.	Fream, John, sum given £10 charity
			Rodway, Thomas, cordwainer
		25 Sept.	Barnes, Thomas, sum given £80,
			Biddle, Nathaniel, grocer

Sir John Guise, mayor 1787–8[2]

4/15	1787	12 Oct.	Benton, Clark
			Hale, Ann, hairdresser & perukemaker
		1 Dec.	Herbert, James jr
			Herbert, James sr, butcher, from 1 June

---

[1] 17 July 1787: To receive £10 of Mrs Jane Punter's money: John Fream, Thomas Spicer, Samuel Maverley, James Dark, Richard Woodward, Benjamin Peart, John Hartland, Charles Wilton. GBR B3/12 f. 70v.

27 Sept. 1787: To leave Sir Thomas Rich's hospital and receive £10: Samuel Hicks, Moses Binning, George Philips, William Lane, Charles Bonnewell, William Stephens, Isaac Watts. To have £5 of Mr William Holliday's money: Charles Williams. To have £4 of Mrs Sarah Browne's money: Benjamin Kibble, William Roan, Thomas Ingram, Thomas Wood, George Cook. GBR B3/12 f. 77.

[2] 25 July 1788: To receive £10 of Mrs Jane Punter's money: William Price, Ellis Taylor, John Brown, William Hicks, William Window Musto, George Horwood, Thomas Pitt, Benjamin Gurney. GBR B3/12 f. 91v.

26 Sept. 1788: To leave Sir Thomas Rich's hospital and receive £10: George Jones, Thomas Lewis, James Bretherton, William Greening, William Sweyn, Benjamin Lebeter. No candidate for Mr William Holliday's money. To have £4 of Mrs Sarah Browne's money: John Jaques, William Whittington, William Cook, Richard Barber, William Price, William Briscoe. GBR B3/12 f. 98v.

	1787	24 Dec.	Walker, John Davis, sum given £19 10s. Mayo, Francis, grocer, from 22 Feb.
	1788	28 Jan.	Reece, Richard, sum given £80 Mills, John & Pace, Charles, surgeon & apothecary, from 17 Nov. 1787
		21 Jan.	Kibble, Benjamin, sum given £4 Mrs Browne's charity Bower, Joseph, pinmaker
		11 Apr.	Kilmaster, Charles, sum given £22 10s. charity Barton, William, plumber & glazier, from 10 Mar.
		30 May	Lane, Richard, sum given £40 Saunders, Elizabeth, tallowchandler & soapboiler
		6 June	Dark, Edward, sum given £20 Washbourne, George, baker & confectioner, from 19 Apr.
		9 June	George, William Chandler, Powell, tobacconist, from 1 July 1787
4/16		16 June	Parry, John, sum given £50 Greatwood, Robert, grocer, chandler & soapboiler
		8 Aug.	Price, William, sum given £10 charity Hatton, William, breechesmaker & fellmonger
		15 Aug.	Smith, John, sum given £210 Joynes, Edwin & Elizabeth, mercer
		1 Sept.	Horwood, George, sum given £10 charity Allen, Richard, cordwainer, from 1 Sept.
			Brewer, George, sum given £4 4s. Evans, William, carpenter, from 14 July 1787
		5 Sept.	Browne, John, sum given £10 charity Browne, James, cordwainer, from 1 Aug.
		3 Oct.	Vaughan, John Benson, Robert, fellmonger & leather dresser, from 29 Sept. 1787
			Ingram, Thomas, sum given £4 charity Brabant, Newton, pinmaker

Samuel Woodcock, mayor 1788–9[1]

4/16	1788	24 Oct.	Beard, William jr Spencer, Charles, bricklayer, from 26 Dec.
		14 Nov.	Briscoe, William, sum given £4 charity Broughton, James jr, hairdresser, from 1 Nov.
		5 Dec.	Lawrence, John Stock, Edmund, wine merchant to learn the trade of wine cooper

---

[1] 24 July 1789: To receive £10 of Mrs Jane Punter's money: John Baker, Samuel Bond, Thomas Waller, William Cooke, John Lewis, George Wathen, William Wathen, Charles Holder. GBR B3/12 f. 111v.

    25 Sept. 1789: To leave Sir Thomas Rich's hospital and receive £10: John Bevan, George Elliott, John Derrett, Daniel Freeman, John Lander, Joseph Arch. No eligible candidate for Mr William Holliday's money. To have £4 of Mrs Sarah Browne's money: James Smart, Charles Jaques, James Bayley, James Fream, Thomas Kibble. GBR B3/12 f. 114.

1788	15 Dec.	Snow, John, sum given £10 10s. Meachen, John, cordwainer
1789	23 Feb.	Westwood, William, sum given £10 charity Price, Thomas, cordwainer
	27 Feb.	Werrett, Richard, sum given £8 8s. Osborne, John, collarmaker
	29 June	Ward, John, sum given £15 Mutlow, Paul, tailor, from 18 May
	21 Aug.	Wathen, William, sum given £10 charity Wilton, Samuel, pinmaker
	4 Sept.	Cooke, William, sum given £4 charity Ford, William, cordwainer
	29 Sept.	Sims, Samuel, sum given £21 Washbourne, John, bookbinder, bookseller & stationer, from 23 Jan.

James Sadler, mayor 1789–90[1]

4/16	1789	2 Nov.	Drinkwater, James, sum given £31 10s. Woodward, Thomas, joiner & cabinetmaker
			Bayley, James, sum given £4 charity Walker, William, whitesmith
			Jaques, Charles, sum given £4 charity Daniell, James, carpenter
4/17		16 Nov.	Freame, James, sum given £4 charity Harris, John, cordwainer
		23 Nov.	Wathen, George, sum given £10 charity Hartland, Charles, pinmaker
	1790	22 Jan.	Freeman, Daniel, sum given £10 charity Freeman, Benjamin, whitesmith
		1 Feb.	Cooksey, John Roberts, Samuel, brushmaker, from 20 Dec. 1789
		12 Feb.	Ricketts, James Bartlett, William Smith, pinmaker
		19 Apr.	Morris, John, sum given £6 6s. Evans, William, carpenter & joiner
		14 June	Smart, James, sum given £4 charity Brown, James, tailor, from 25 Aug. 1789

[1] 6 Sept. 1790: To receive £10 of Mrs Jane Punter's money: Charles Hamblin, Moses Clark, Edward Cooke, John Gurney, Henry Fuller, James Nest, James Crowdy, Richard Evenis. GBR B3/12 f. 127v.

24 Sept. 1790: To leave Sir Thomas Rich's hospital and receive £10: John Price, Thomas Ady, Wintour Harris, Joseph Wood, James Daniell, William Stephens. GBR B3/12 f. 130

29 Sept. 1790: To have £5 of Mr William Holliday's money: James Barnard. To have £4 of Mrs Sarah Browne's money: Thomas Bennett, Joshua Wren, Samuel Jones, John Goodenough, William Price, Benjamin Blewett. GBR B3/12 f. 133v.

	1790	30 July	Chappel, William, sum given £10 Broughton, Joseph, hairdresser & perukemaker, from 2 July
		3 Sept.	Eccles, John, sum given £40 Sadler, Elisha Farmer, mercer & linendraper
			Brown, Francis, sum given £10 Gardiner, Thomas, baker

Giles Greenaway, mayor 1790–1[1]

	1790	22 Oct.	Nest, James, sum given £10 charity Rodway, Thomas, cordwainer
4/17			Price, William, sum given £4 charity Gardner, Adam, pinmaker
			Blewett, Benjamin, sum given £4 charity Stroud, Stephen, wiredrawer
		29 Oct.	Barber, William, sum given £5 5s. Hickman, William, cordwainer
			Jones, Samuel, sum given £4 charity Price, Thomas, cordwainer
			King, Samuel, sum given £30 Marshall, John, baker
		12 Nov.	Jones, William, sum given £57 15s. Cooke, Charles, apothecary, surgeon & man midwife
			Spencer, George Augustus Spencer, Daniel, bricklayer
		15 Nov.	Eveniss, James, sum given £10 charity Lamb, John, baker
4/18		21 Nov.	Wiggins, James, no commission Herbert, Thomas, pinmaker, from 21 Jan. 1791
	1791	2 Feb.	Bennett, Thomas, sum given £4 charity Ady, Thomas, perukemaker, from 7 Feb.
		11 Feb.	Smith, Thomas, sum given £30 Biddle, Nathaniel & Nancy, grocer, from 1 Jan.
		2 May	Ellis, George jr, sum given £10 Cole, James & Mary, tinplate worker, from 10 Feb.
		20 May	Spire, John, no commission Gardiner, Pettat & Elizabeth, brushmaker

[1] 19 Sept. 1791: To receive £10 of Mrs Jane Punter's money: James Gunn, John Paull, William Lander, William Bourne, Francis Lye, James Hyett, Richard Workman plus John Longney on 30 Sept. on production of a certificate of age. No petitioner for Mr William Holliday's money. To have £4 of Mrs Sarah Browne's money: Benjamin Prothero, Edward Dudley Duffield. GBR B3/12 ff. 148v, 152.

30 Sept. 1791: To leave Sir Thomas Rich's hospital and receive £10: Thomas Stephens, Edward Bretherton, John Wilse, John Hickman, Benjamin Gunn, William Dunn. GBR B3/12 f. 152.

1787	6 Mar.	Barrett, Henry, sum given £10 charity
		Hardwick, William, painter & glazier, from 6 Mar. 1787
1791	10 June	Willis, Winchcomb Hartley, sum given £100
		Parker, Thomas, apothecary & man midwife

William Middleton, mayor 1791–2[1]

4/18 1791   21 Oct.   Whitehead, Richard, no commission
              Pytt, John Selwyn & Hannah, printer & bookbinder, from 29 Sept.

             14 Oct.   Coleman, John, sum given £10
              Dole, Richard, cordwainer, from 25 Oct.

             14 Nov.   Workman, Richard, sum given £10,
              Cheeseman, John, tailor, from 26 Sept.

             21 Nov.   Longney, John, sum given £10 charity
              Addis, Richard, hairdresser & perukemaker

       1792   16 Jan.   Bretherton, Edward, sum given £10 charity
              Carter, James, hairdresser, from 30 Dec. 1791

             20 Jan.   Dunn, William, sum given £10 charity
              Cooke, William, pargeter, from 25 Dec. 1791

             27 Jan.   Workman, Thomas
              Barton, William, plumber & glazier

             16 Mar.   Bourn, William, sum given £10 charity
              Bourn, James, cordwainer, from 29 Sept.

             25 May   Oakey, James jr, sum given £10 charity
              Simpson, Charles, baker, from 21 Dec.

             25 Sept.   Baylis, Thomas, no commission
              Wadley, John, baker, from 5 Apr.

                     Winch, George, sum given £21
              Heath, Richard, saddler, from 17 Sept.

Thomas Weaver, mayor 1792–3[2]

4/18 1792   12 Oct.   Prothero, Benjamin, sum given £4 charity
              Rea, John, pinmaker

[1] 21 Sept. 1792: To receive £10 of Mrs Jane Punter's money: Thomas Wellavize Coleman, William Maverley, Richard Taylor, William Jennings, Charles Cooke, Fream Window Sparkes, James Bower, Richard Drinkwater. Mr William Holliday's money and Mrs Sarah Browne's money to be added together in future [but no names listed for either charity]. GBR B3/12 f. 168.

    27 Sept. 1792: To leave Sir Thomas Rich's hospital and receive £10: Thomas Hinton, Thomas Rowles, Robert Phillips, William Davis, Thomas Greening, Samuel Jeffes. 5 Nov.: William, son of Thomas Adey, hairdresser, to leave the hospital on his father's petition. GBR B3/12 ff. 170v, 174.

[2] 14 Aug. 1793: To receive £10 of Mrs Jane Punter's money: Thomas Wathen, Thomas Hicks, James Bloxsome, William Gurney, Charles Pitcher, Samuel Bennett, John Avery, John Dix. GBR B3/12 f. 180.

    9 Sept. 1793: To leave Sir Thomas Rich's hospital and receive £10: James Wilkes, John Stephens, Thomas Daniell, Samuel Harris, Henry Mathews, William Woodward, William Heane. GBR B3/12 f. 185.

    19 Sept. 1793: To have £5 of Mr William Holliday's money: John Barton, Richard Barrett, Charles Griffiths. To have £4 of Mrs Sarah Browne's money: Edward Player, Charles Griffith, William Dunn, John Barton, Richard Barrett. GBR B3/12 f. 188.

4/19	1792	29 Oct.	Taylor, Richard, sum given £10 charity
			Window, John, cabinetmaker
		2 Nov.	Stock, William, sum given £10
			Addis, Richard, hairdresser
		19 Nov.	Keen, James
			Pytt, John Selwyn & Hannah, printer, compositor, pressman & bookbinder
	1793	25 Jan.	Herbert, Joseph
			Herbert, Thomas, pinmaker
		15 Feb.	Hooper, John, sum given £126
			Wood, James, mercer
		1 Mar.	Maisey, James, sum given £10
			Hickman, William, cordwainer, from 27 Jan.
		3 May	Hewlett, John, sum given £31 10s.
			Woodward, Thomas, cabinetmaker
		26 Apr.	Baldwin, Joseph, sum given £5
			Barrett, Richard, painter & glazier
		5 Aug.	Johnsons, James, sum given £20
			Woodward, Thomas, cabinetmaker
		23 Aug.	Coley, Richard Warren
			Parker, Thomas, apothecary & man midwife, from 25 Mar.
		2 Sept.	Williams, Penry, sum given £210
			Sadler, Elisha Farmer, mercer, from 2 Aug.
			Bennett, Samuel, sum given £10 charity
			Clark, Thomas, tailor
		9 Sept.	Church, John Lovatt
			Church, George, flax dresser

Thomas Mee, mayor 1793–4[1]

4/19	1793	25 Oct.	Barrett, Richard, sum given £9 charity
			Hutchings, John, joiner & cabinetmaker
		1 Nov.	Player, Edward, sum given £4 charity
			Bond, Samuel, collarmaker
		8 Nov.	Beard, Thomas, sum given £50
			Jordan, Josiah Jenner, grocer, from 23 Mar.
		11 Nov.	Dicks, Thomas, sum given £10 charity
			Goodwin, Richard, tailor

---

[1] 14 Aug. 1794: To receive £10 of Mrs Jane Punter's money: James Gardner, Benjamin Wilks, Charles Mutlow, Stephen Gwilliam. GBR B3/12 f. 203v.

25 Sept. 1794: To leave Sir Thomas Rich's hospital and receive £10: William Stephens, John Watts, James Maverly, Richard Woodward, Charles Lewis, Daniel Greening, Lewis Maverley. On 30 June 1794 Sarah Browne, the mother of Charles Lewis, had petitioned that he should be voted out of the hospital. GBR B3/12 ff. 204, 202v.

4/20	1793	9 Dec.	Church, Henry Spencer, Daniel, bricklayer
		16 Dec.	Avery, John, sum given £10 charity Gunn, Joseph, cordwainer
		28 Sept.	Pinching, Samuel, sum given £31 10s. Heath, Richard, saddler, from 14 Aug.
		7 Aug.	Etheridge, William, sum given £15 Wheatstone, John, cordwainer
	1794	1 Feb.	Ellis, Joshua, sum given £70 Mountain, John, grocer
		7 Mar.	Coates, William, sum given £10 Baldwin, Richard, collarmaker
		9 May	Boughton, Samuel, sum given £20 Boughton, Edmund, currier, from 17 Feb.
		30 May	Wathen, Thomas, sum given £10 charity Wathen, John, pinner
		27 June	Bubb, Thomas, sum given £36 15s. Jones, Samuel, brushmaker, from 23 June
		4 July	Guilding, William, sum given £20 Washbourn, George, baker & confectioner
		21 July	Bullock, George Hayle, Richard, tanner
			Jenkins, John, sum given £14 14s. Goodwin, Richard, tailor
		4 Aug.	Knight, James, no money Brabant, Newton, pinmaker

John Turner, mayor 1794–5[1]

4/20	1794	3 Nov.	Lane, Thomas Clifford, sum given £10 Lane, Samuel, cordwainer
		12 Dec.	Wakeman, Henry Evans, William, carpenter
	1795	17 Apr.	Field, Joseph Davies, Henry & Anne, pin manufacturer
		14 May	Jones, Thomas, sum given £10 charity Biddle, Nathaniel, grocer, from 7 Apr.

[1] 17 Aug. 1795: To receive £10 of Mrs Jane Punter's money: Adam Holder, Anthony Hinton, George Thomas Jones, Robert Wilton, John Creed, John Hall, James Clark, Joseph Mann, William Woodward. GBR B3/12 f. 228.

21 Aug. 1795: To have £5 of Mr William Holliday's money: Edmund Gardner, Thomas Calcott, William Hayling, William Goodenough, John Prothero, William Hook. GBR B3/12 f. 229.

2 Oct. 1795: To leave Sir Thomas Rich's hospital and receive £10: John Lewis, Samuel Bonnewell, John Wilkins, William Cooke, Thomas Freeman, Giles Smart. To have £5 of Mr William Holliday's money: David Hart son of David Hart. GBR B3/12 ff. 185, 202v.

	1795	22 June	Harris, Thomas, no money Rea, John, pinmaker
4/21		14 Aug.	Powell, Thomas Bartlett, William Smith, pinmaker
		28 Aug.	Hall, John, sum given £10 charity Rodway, Thomas, cordwainer
		28 Aug.	Holder, Adam, sum given £10 charity Duns, Henry, pargeter
		25 Sept.	George, Anthony Chandler, Powell, tobacconist, from 1 Sept.
			Creed, John, sum given £10 charity Plane, Samuel, collarmaker
		2 Oct.	Woodward, William, sum given £10 charity Brown, James, tailor

John Cook, mayor 1795–6[1]

4/21	1795	19 Oct.	Knowles, Henry Benson, Robert, skinner
			Gwilliam, Stephen, sum given £20 charity Gunn, Joseph, cordwainer
		2 Nov.	Jones, George Thomas, sum given £10 charity Woodward, Thomas, pinpointer
			Wilton, Robert, sum given £10 charity Hartland, Charles, pinpointer
		17 Nov.	Meredith, William, sum given £21 Hickes, William, carpenter & joiner
		11 Dec.	Evans, Edmund, sum given £5 charity Cook, John, pargeter, from 29 May
			Merrick, Thomas, sum given faithful service Bartlett, William Smith, pinmaker
			Groutage, Joseph, sum given faithful service Pytt, John Selwyn & Hannah, printer, from 11 Nov.
		14 Dec.	Cowley, Benjamin, sum given £10 charity Nest, Thomas, baker & confectioner
			Haylings, William, sum given £5 charity Woodward, Charles, cordwainer

[1] 21 Sept. 1796: To receive £10 of Mrs Jane Punter's money: John Greening, Thomas Merrett, Charles Eveniss, John Gardiner, John Badham, John Clarke, Charles Cooke, Richard Dunne. GBR B3/12 f. 252.

30 Sept. 1796: To have £5 of Mr William Holliday's money and £4 of Mrs Sarah Browne's money: John Cole, Thomas Orpin. To leave Sir Thomas Rich's hospital and receive £10: William Lewis, Richard Jones, John Mathews, John Baker, John Buckingham, Thomas Stroud, William Elliotts. John Baker, upon the petition of his mother, to go out immediately. GBR B3/12 f. 256v.

4/22	1796	29 Jan.	Prothero, John, sum given £5 charity Powell, George, pinmaker
		26 Feb.	Dobbes, William, sum given £50 Holder, Edward & Herbert, William, grocers & copartners, from 1 Jan.
		29 Feb.	Haynes, James, sum given £20 Cole, James, tinplate worker
		17 Feb.	Wimsloe, William, sum given £10 10s. Gale, Thomas, baker
		6 May	Robins, William Brabant, Newton, pinmaker
		13 June	Thackwell, Paul, sum given £50 Cook, Thomas, mercer
		17 June	Bishop, Charles Bartlett, William Smith, pinmaker
			Boon, Samuel Bartlett, William Smith, pinmaker
		20 June	Crook, John, sum given £20 Jeffes, William, tailor

		29 July	Maddox, William
			    Maddox, Cartwright, from 24 June
			    [*added at the foot of 4/23*:] *24 Nov. 1797 Wm Maddox apprentice to Cartwright Maddocks was this day turned over to serve the remainder of his time to Cartwright Madox the younger, baker*

		9 Sept.	Sherry, Thomas, sum given £10 Bourne, James, cordwainer

John Ready, mayor 1796–7[1]

4/22	1796	21 Oct.	Hill, John, sum given £50 Brabant, Newton, pinmaker
			Badham, John, sum given £10 charity Mutlow, Paul, tailor
			Longford, John Andrews, Thomas, soapboiler, tallowchandler & grocer
		28 Oct.	Calcott, Thomas, sum given £9 charity Bloxsome, Edward, cooper

---

[1] 28 Aug. 1797: To receive £10 of Mrs Jane Punter's money: John Perris, Charles Woodward, Peter Cooke, John Pitcher, Abednego Ireland, Thomas Davis, James Hulbert, Thomas Humphris. On petition of John Orpin, his father, the £9 voted to Thomas Orpin on 30 Sept. 1796 to be given to his brother Edward. GBR B3/12 f. 271.

27 Sept. 1797: To leave Sir Thomas Rich's hospital and receive £10: Thomas Gardner, William Bourn, William Barrett, Thomas Window, Henry Jacks, John Woodward, William Lewis, Thomas Matthews. To receive £5 of Mr William Holliday's money and £4 of Mrs Sarah Browne's money: William Hulbert, Eleazar Billingham, William Daniell, William Fletcher, William Jones. GBR B3/12 f. 275v.

	1796	18 Nov.	Cole, John, sum given £5 charity + £4 charity Driver, Thomas, hairdresser
4/23	1797	16 Jan.	Gardener, John, sum given £10 charity Bretherton, Thomas, hairdresser
		20 Jan.	Buckingham, John, sum given £10 charity Wood, John, of St Pancras, Middx., carpenter & joiner
		27 Jan.	Pool, Thomas, sum given £12 Baldwin, Richard, collarmaker
		13 Feb.	Eveniss, Charles, sum given £10 charity Stephens, John, baker
		10 Mar.	Sessions, James, sum given £50 Woodward, Thomas, cabinetmaker
		12 May	Davis, John, sum given £10 charity Smart, James, pinmaker
		26 May	Pagett, William, sum given £42 Heath, Richard, saddler, to learn the trade of saddler & capmaker
		14 Aug.	Church, Thomas, sum given £10 charity Mutlow, Paul, tailor
		15 Sept.	Davis, Thomas, sum given £10 charity Smart, James, pinmaker

Samuel Colborne, mayor 1797–8[1]

	1797	20 Oct.	Humphris, Thomas, sum given £10 charity Rodway, Thomas, cordwainer
4/23	1797	20 Oct.	Humphris, Thomas, sum given £10 charity Rodway, Thomas, cordwainer
		27 Oct.	Vick, William, sum given £20 Washbourne, George, baker, confectioner & maltster
		13 Nov.	Lea, William, sum given £15 Jeffs, Charles, tailor
		17 Nov.	Elliott, Cartwright, sum given service Maddocks, Cartwright, baker
		20 Nov.	Hulbert, William, sum given £9 charity Hickman, William, cordwainer
		1 Dec.	Billingham, Eliazor, sum given £9 charity Long, James, painter [*entry deleted*]
4/24	1798	9 Mar.	Taylor, Samuel, sum given service Jones, Samuel, brushmaker

[1] 20 Aug. 1798: To receive £10 of Mrs Jane Punter's money: Adam King, Robert Hawkes, Charles Wilks, Samuel Jennings, William Wathan, John Craddock, James Rudge, Thomas Price. GBR B3/12 f. 288.

27 Sept. 1798: To leave Sir Thomas Rich's hospital and receive £10: Benjamin Watts, John Maverley, Charles Reynolds Wilks, James Walker, Edwin Dunn. To receive £5 of Mr William Holliday's money and £4 of Mrs Sarah Browne's money: John Calcott, Edward Orpin. GBR B3/12 f. 289v.

29 Oct. 1798: On petition of his father, Thomas, Thomas Woodward to leave Sir Thomas Rich's hospital on St Thomas's Day. GBR B3/12 f. 293.

	1798	16 Apr.	Tombs, Thomas, sum given £10 charity Powell, William, carpenter

1798   16 Apr.   Tombs, Thomas, sum given £10 charity
                    Powell, William, carpenter

           20 Apr.   Townsend, Thomas, sum given service
                    Herbert, Thomas, pinmaker

           4 May   Edwards, George, sum given £50,
                    Holt, William, tea dealer & grocer

           16 July   Evans, John, sum given £10 charity Gloucestershire Society,
                    Bullock, John, cordwainer

           10 Sept.   Craddock, John, sum given £10 charity
                    Gunn, Thomas, hairdresser

                           Ballinger, John, sum given £50,
                    Washbourne, John, bookseller, stationer & bookbinder

           7 Aug.   Brimmall, Thomas, sum given £10
                    Bullock, John, cordwainer, from 7 Aug.

           5 Oct.   Rudge, James, sum given £10 charity
                    Holder, Geoffrey, of Mitcheldean, apothecary

Charles Howard, Duke of Norfolk, mayor 1798–9[1]

4/24   1798   19 Oct.   Butt, Richard, sum given £60
                    Charlton, Shadrach, grocer

           17 Dec.   Walker, Paul, sum given £150
                    Sadler, Elisha Farmer, mercer

      1799   28 Jan.   Heath, John, sum given £150
                    Sadler, Elisha Farmer, mercer

           1 Mar.   Rodway, Thomas, sum given service
                    Cole, Charles, tinplate worker

           8 Mar.   Orpin, Edward, sum given £5 charity + £4 charity
                    Hatton, William, breechesmaker

           3 June   Chandler, John Mayo, sum given £30
                    Wheatstone, William, cordwainer

           9 Aug.   Workman, George, sum given service
                    Herbert, Thomas, pinmaker

Edwin Jeynes, mayor 1799–1800[2]

4/25   1799   24 Oct.   Townley, William, sum given service
                    Spencer, Daniel, bricklayer, from 24 Oct.

[1] 23 Sept. 1799: To receive £10 of Mrs Jane Punter's money: Thomas Venn, King Edward Ursell, John Mann, Thomas Trickey, Joseph Owner, Benjamin Collericke, Richard Woodward, John Hartland. To leave Sir Thomas Rich's hospital and receive £10: James Duncomb Barrett, John Elliott, John Bosley, William Smart, Samuel Best, William Jeffs. GBR B3/12 f. 302v.

[2] 3 Oct. 1800: To receive £10 of Mrs Jane Punter's money: John Perris, Thomas Ravenhill, William Mann, Thomas Woodward, James Cook, John Wathen, Charles Badger, William Allen. To receive £5 of Mr William Holliday's money and £4 of Mrs Sarah Browne's money: John Kirk, John Townsend, Joseph Ellis. To leave Sir Thomas Rich's hospital and receive £10: Isaac Powell, Charles Gardner, William Floyd, John Stephens, Charles Lander, John Dunn, Samuel Matthews, Richard Bourn. GBR B3/12 f. 319v.

	1799	7 Oct.	Whitehead, William, sum given £10 charity Gloucestershire Society
			Wheatstone, William, shoemaker, from 7 Oct.
		1 Nov.	Hartland, John, sum given £10 charity
			Mutlow, Paul, tailor
		8 Nov.	Owner, Joseph, sum given £10 charity
			Broughton, James, hairdresser
		25 Nov.	Williams, Thomas, sum given £20
			Bower, Edward, currier
	1800	3 Feb.	Hervey, Octavius, sum given £100
			Stock, Edmund & Mountain, John, grocers
		30 June	Smith, Isaac, sum given £35
			Ursell, Francis & Elizabeth, plumber & glazier

John Jefferis, mayor 1800–1[1]

4/25	1800	24 Oct.	Lea, William, sum given service
			Nest, John, cordwainer, from 24 June
	1801	3 July	Jew, Joseph, sum given £40
			Wood, James, cabinetmaker & chairmaker
		31 July	Cratchley, William, sum given £40
			Hicks, William, carpenter & joiner
		18 Sept.	Bubb, Frederick, sum given service
			Jelf, James, banker

Samuel Woodcock, mayor 1801–2[2]

4/25	1801	16 Nov.	Redding, Edward, sum given £5 charity + £4 charity
			Simpson, William, carpenter & joiner
		9 Nov.	Carwardine, Joseph, sum given £30,
			Washbourne, George, baker, confectioner & maltster
4/26		18 Dec.	Holliday, Richard, sum given £20,
			Rodway, Thomas, cordwainer
	1802	29 Jan.	Marsh, John, sum given £5 + £4 charity
			Manns, Thomas, cooper

---

[1] 25 Sept. 1801: To receive £10 of Mrs Jane Punter's money: Charles Bower, Thomas Sanders, Joseph Freame, Charles Sweetland, Thomas Crooke, Thomas Mann, Edward Gardiner Jones, Samuel Woodward. To receive £5 of Mr William Holliday's money and £4 of Mrs Sarah Browne's money: James Marsh, Richard Lewis, James Whitehead, Edward Reading. GBR B3/12 f. 331.

29 Sept. 1801: To leave Sir Thomas Rich's hospital and receive £10: John Wilkes, Samuel Watts, Anthony Bretherton, James Smart, James Ireland. GBR B3/12 f. 333.

[2] 1 Oct. 1802: To receive £10 of Mrs Jane Punter's money: John Gardner, Robert Wathen, Joseph Mann, William Wilton, James Bower, Robert Barnett, William Bennett, Thomas Rose. To receive £5 of Mr William Holliday's money and £4 of Mrs Sarah Browne's money: William Jewsbury, Thomas Lewis, Robert Mitchell, Peter Bullock. To leave Sir Thomas Rich's hospital and receive £10: Samuel Wilkes, Francis Nesele, Charles Glendale, Thomas Jeffs, Decimus Best, William Hicks, Richard Dix. GBR B3/12 f. 350.

	1802	15 Feb.	Price, James, sum given £10, Lane, Samuel, cordwainer
		14 May	Jones, John, sum given £15 charity Evans, John, fellmonger, from 14 May
		30 July	Robbins, Thomas Stock, Edmund & Mountain, John [*entry incomplete*]

James Sadler, mayor 1802–3[1]

4/26	1802	18 Oct.	Jones, Edward, sum given £10 charity Woodward, Thomas, pinmaker
			Mitchell, Robert, sum given £5 & £4 charity Allen, Richard, cordwainer
		22 Oct.	Tucker, Francis, sum given £50 Woodward, Thomas, cabinetmaker
		8 Nov.	Bennett, William, sum given £10 charity Thomas, Daniel, tailor
		19 Nov.	Jewsberry, William, sum given £5 & £4 charity Allen, Richard, cordwainer
	1803	18 Feb.	Butt, John, sum given £105 Claxson, Benjamin, mercer & draper
		6 May	Wood, James, sum given £15 charity Richards, Joseph, carpenter & joiner
4/27	1801	12 Oct.	Woodward, Samuel, sum given £10 charity Jennings, Michael, tailor[2]
	1803	23 May	Cosbourne, Thomas, sum given £40 Hewlett, John, cabinetmaker[3]
		25 Apr.	Field, John Print, sum given £35 Roberts, Samuel, brushmaker
		6 June	Mann, Thomas, sum given £10 charity Wintle, James, pinmaker
		20 May	Davis, John, sum given £42 Heath, Richard, saddler & capmaker
		24 June	Roffe, Thomas, sum given £10 charity Cooke, Charles, plumber & glazier
		27 June	Bellamy, John, sum given £31 10s. Heath, Richard, saddler

[1] 22 Sept. 1803: To receive £10 of Mrs Jane Punter's money: Edward Meek, Samuel Merrett, William Wood, Richard Kirk. To receive £5 of Mr William Holliday's money and £4 of Mrs Sarah Browne's money: Abraham Mantle, George Dobbins, George Predy, William Jew. To leave Sir Thomas Rich's hospital and receive £10: Thomas Griffiths, James Wingate, Charles Woodward, James Nest, James Launder, Joseph Reeves, Job Bosley, James Estcourt. GBR B3/12 f. 370v.

[2] This entry was first written between 14 May and 30 July 1802 and was deleted.

[3] This entry was first written between 14 May and 30 July 1802 and was deleted.

	1803	11 July	Lea, Jonathan, sum given service
			Nest, James, cordwainer
		12 Aug.	Jenkins, William, sum given service
			Cook, William, plasterer & tiler
		15 Aug.	Matthews, John, sum given £50,
			Gardiner, Pettat, brushmaker

Giles Greenaway, mayor 1803–4[1]

4/27	1803	4 Nov.	Preedy, George, sum given £9 charity
			Nest, Thomas, baker & confectioner
			Wood, William, sum given £10 charity
			Mann, William, cordwainer
		18 Nov.	Kirk, Richard, sum given £10 charity
			McLaren, John, gardener
	1804	30 Jan.	Sherwood, William, sum given £42
			Hewlett, John, cabinetmaker
		6 Feb.	Butt, Thomas, sum given £150
			Tovey, John, ironmonger, from 12 Dec. 1803
4/28		13 Feb.	Jew, William, sum given £9 charity
			Trickey, Thomas, basketmaker
		24 Feb.	Chandler, George, sum given £105
			Jones, Samuel, brushmaker, from 24 Jan.
		9 July	Martin, Jonathan, sum given £20
			Wood, James, cabinetmaker
		17 Aug.	Holtham, George, sum given £12
			Wilkins, John Bell, tailor
		29 Mar.	Browning, William, sum given service
			Saunders, John Michael, soapboiler & tallowchandler, from 26 July

Thomas Mee, mayor 1804–5[2]

4/28	1804	2 Nov.	Fleming, John Reece, sum given £9 charity
			Phillips, Robert, cordwainer, from 2 Nov.
			Hudson, John, sum given service
			Jennings, Michael, tailor, from 16 Nov.

[1] 25 Sept. 1804: To receive £10 of Mrs Jane Punter's money: John Hudson, Thomas Best, William Okey, John Lewis, Richard Bower, Charles Wilkinson Barrett, James Hartland, Henry Craddock. To receive £5 of Mr William Holliday's money and £4 of Mrs Sarah Browne's money: James Meaton, John Reece Fleming, James Rock. To leave Sir Thomas Rich's hospital and receive £10: Thomas Bretherton, Ralph Lewis, Benjamin Davis, James Bourn. GBR B3/12 f. 383.

[2] 14 Aug. 1805: To leave Sir Thomas Rich's hospital and receive £10: Thomas Platt, Isaac Glendall, George Elliots, William Drinkwater, James Edwards Launder, James Woodward, John Freeman. To receive £10 of Mrs Jane Punter's money: John Jennings, Henry Wood, James Broughton, William Gardner, Charles Woodward, Joseph Bowers. To receive £5 of Mr William Holliday's money and £4 of Mrs Sarah Browne's money: George Curtis, Joseph Dykes, George Allen, Isaac Smith. GBR B3/13 f. 12.

	1804	16 Nov.	Badnedge, William Harper, sum given service Jeffs, Charles, tailor, from 16 Nov.
		19 Nov.	Hartland, James, sum given £10 charity Wilkins, John Bell, tailor, from 2 Nov.
			Craddock, Henry, sum given £10 charity Wilton, Thomas, tailor
	1805	8 Feb.	Dangerfield, Thomas, sum given £19 19s. Holt, William, grocer & tea dealer
		18 Feb.	Hanman, John, sum given £50 Biddle, Nathaniel, grocer & seedsman
		10 June	Taylor, John, sum given £10, Hewlett, John, cabinetmaker
		9 Sept.	Williams, George, sum given £10 Jennings, Michael, tailor, from 9 Sept.
		20 Sept.	Birt, Thomas, sum given service Walker, David, printer, from 20 Sept.

John Turner, mayor 1805–6[1]

4/28	1805	18 Nov.	Dike, Joseph, sum given £9 charity Manns, William, tailor, from 8 Nov.
		29 Nov.	Curtis, George, sum given £9 charity Gunn, Thomas, hairdresser & perukemaker
4/29		8 Nov.	Mayo, Thomas, sum given £10 charity Rodway, Thomas, cordwainer
	1806	3 Feb.	Cardale, Thomas, sum given service Walker, David, printer
		2 May	Cockle, John, sum given £31 10s. Cole, Charles & Prudence, tinplate worker
		7 July	Lane, James, sum given £15 charity Lane Samuel, cordwainer
		22 Aug.	Parry, Thomas, sum given service Turner, Thomas, banker
			Allen, George, sum given £9 charity Spencer, Daniel, mason & bricklayer
		15 Sept.	Holbrow, Nathaniel, sum given service + £5 Draper, Richard, plumber & glazier

[1] 2 Sept. 1806: To receive £5 of Mr William Holliday's money and £4 of Mrs Sarah Browne's money: John Venn, John Gardner, James Preedy, Edmund Parker. GBR B3/13 f. 25.

29 Sept. 1806: To leave Sir Thomas Rich's hospital and receive £10: John Woodward, Thomas Clarke, John Richards, Jacob Kirby, William Wilks, John Estcourt, John Best. To receive £10 of Mrs Jane Punter's money: William Brabant, William Merrett, William Venn, Thomas Lewis, Thomas Maverley, William Woodward, Thomas Fisher. GBR B3/13 f. 27.

Richard Nayler, mayor 1806–7[1]

4/29	1806	7 Nov.	James, Thomas, sum given £60 Butt, Richard, grocer
		24 Nov.	Preedy, James, sum given £9 charity Read, William, upholder
		22 Dec.	Rose, Charles, sum given service Washbourne, Thomas & William, druggists
	1807	20 Mar.	Haynes, William, sum given service Haynes, Thomas, pinmaker
		31 July	Maverley, Thomas jr, sum given £10 charity Wilton, Thomas, tailor
		18 Sept.	Rayer, John, sum given service Haynes, Thomas, pin manufacturer

David Willey, mayor 1807–8[2]

4/29	1807	12 Oct.	Brown, Samuel, sum given £126
			   Wood, James, banker, to learn the trade of banker & mercer,
			      from 12 Oct.

	1808	17 June	Edwards, Benjamin, sum given £25 Woodward, Thomas, cabinetmaker & upholder
		5 Sept.	Thomas, William, sum given service Stock, Edmund, Mountain, John & Mayer, Thomas, grocers
		23 Sept.	Cole, Thomas, sum given service Spencer, Charles, bricklayer

David Saunders, mayor 1808–9[3]

4/30	1808	17 Oct.	Davis, Richard, sum given £9 charity Weaver, Edward, pinmaker, from 17 Oct. 1807
		12 Dec.	Jones, Edward, sum given service Herbert, Thomas, pinmaker

---

[1] 23 Sept. 1807: To leave Sir Thomas Rich's hospital and receive £10: Amos Woodward, William Wingate, Edward Gardner, Thomas Brabant, William Rea, Thomas Manns. To receive £10 of Mrs Jane Punter's money: Robert Dunn, Thomas Day, Joseph Woodward, Samuel Jeffs, William Walker, Richard Allen. To receive £5 of Mr William Holliday's money and £4 of Mrs Sarah Browne's money: Thomas Tarling. GBR B3/13 f. 42.

[2] 19 Sept. 1808: To leave Sir Thomas Rich's hospital and receive £10: Richard Gardiner, Samuel Pitt, Walter Wood, Joseph Bennett, Thomas Powell, Daniel Bower, Henry Glendale. To receive £10 of Mrs Jane Punter's money: Jonathan Badger, Charles Lander, Adam Gardiner. To receive £5 of Mr William Holliday's money and £4 of Mrs Sarah Browne's money: Joseph Organ, John Tooth, Samuel Homan, Richard Davis. GBR B3/13 f. 60.

[3] 1 Sept. 1809: To leave Sir Thomas Rich's hospital and receive £10: Joseph Richards, Charles Griffiths, John Wingate, William Smart, William Bourn. To receive £10 of Mrs Jane Punter's money: Leonard Edwards, William Hickman, John Maysey. To receive £5 of Mr William Holliday's money and £4 of Mrs Sarah Browne's money: William Faville, John Tipping, James Simmonds, George Cooksey, Thomas Benfield, Edward Crook, William Cambridge. GBR B3/13 f. 76.

	1808	27 Dec.	Thackwell, Robert, sum given £50 Walker, David, printer
			Walker, David jr, sum given service Walker, David, his father, printer
	1809	20 Feb.	Mills, Nathaniel, sum given service Cooke, Charles, surgeon & apothecary
		17 Apr.	Organ, Joseph, sum given £9 charity Washbourne, Thomas & William, druggists
		19 June	Wilkins, Nathaniel, sum given service Weaver, Edward, pinmaker
			Rope, Michael, sum given service Weaver, Edward, pinmaker
			Green, Henry, sum given £29 19s. Washbourne, George, baker & maltster
		24 July	Millard, Joseph Bond, sum given £63 Hewlett, John, cabinetmaker
		3 Nov.	Tipping, John, sum given £9 charity Hewlett, John, cabinetmaker, from 1 Nov.
		1 Nov.	Griffiths, John, sum given £7 7s. charity Baylis, Thomas, baker
		6 Nov.	Benfield, Thomas, sum given £9 charity Trickey, Thomas, basketmaker
		30 Aug.	Humpidge, Thomas jr, sum given £199 19s. Claxson, Benjamin, mercer
		8 Sept.	Crook, Edward, sum given £9 charity Crook, John, tailor
		21 July	Mansell, Thomas, sum given £15 charity Gloucestershire Society Hicks, William, carpenter
4/31		7 July	Ingram, William, sum given service Weaver, Edward, pin manufacturer

Charles Howard, Duke of Norfolk, mayor 1809–10[1]

4/31	1809	22 Nov.	Hayle, William, sum given service Weaver, Charles, pin manufacturer, from 1 Dec.
		1 Dec.	Edwards, Leonard, sum given £10 charity Spencer, Charles, bricklayer
	1810	19 Feb.	Wingate, John, sum given £10 charity Hicks, William, carpenter

[1] 12 Sept. 1810: To leave Sir Thomas Rich's hospital and receive £10: Richard Allen, William Boughton, Joseph Freaman, William Wilkes, Richard Young. To receive £10 of Mrs Jane Punter's money: Robert Dadd, Charles Haynes, Charles Woodward, Charles Bonnewell, William Best. To receive £5 of Mr William Holliday's money and £4 of Mrs Sarah Browne's money: William Giles Maysey, Thomas Hudson, Robert Sloman, Charles Terrett, John Harris. GBR B3/13 f. 87.

	1810	2 Mar.	Diddamus, William John, sum given £84 Woodward, Thomas, cabinetmaker & upholsterer
		7 May	Alder, Benjamin, sum given £157 10s. Tovey, John, ironmonger
			Bromage, James Silvanus Fortunatus Brown, sum given service Turner, Thomas, banker
		6 June	Long, George, sum given £42 Coopey, Richard, grocer
		16 July	Warner, Robert, sum given £70 Hewlett, John, cabinetmaker
		3 Aug.	Terrett, Charles, sum given service Weaver, Edward, pinmaker, to learn the trade of pinpointer
			Clarke, Charles, sum given service Weaver, Edward, pinmaker, to learn the trade of pinpointer
		17 Aug.	Gardner, John, sum given £15 charity Taylor, John, brushmaker & turner

Sir Berkeley William Guise, mayor 1810–1[1]

4/31	1810	19 Oct.	Haines, Charles, sum given £10 charity Woodward, Richard, tailor
			Maisey, William Giles, sum given £9 charity Estcourt, John, hairdresser
		7 Nov.	Lewis, John, sum given £49 19s. Gardiner, Pettat & Elizabeth, brushmaker
4/32		7 Dec.	Harris, John, sum given £9 charity Heath, Edward, cordwainer
		17 Dec.	Hanman, Thomas, sum given service Herbert, William, grocer
	1804	25 Apr.	Holford, Elisha, sum given £10 Daniell, George, painter, from 1 May 1804
	1811	21 Feb.	Taylor, Thomas, sum given service Crook, John, tailor
		7 June	Penton, James, sum given £10 Woodward, William, tailor

---

[1] 15 Sept. 1811: To leave Sir Thomas Rich's hospital and receive £10: James Ricketts, Richard White, Thomas Simpson, William Brown. To receive £10 of Mrs Jane Punter's money: Henry Barrett, Henry Okey, Charles Crowdy, Thomas Baldwin, Edwin Reading, John Workman. To receive £5 of Mr William Holliday's money and £4 of Mrs Sarah Browne's money: William Deane, James Fletcher, William Marsh, Edwin Potter, William Joy, John Faville. GBR B3/13 f. 60.

Thomas Commeline, mayor 1811–2[1]

4/32	1811	25 Oct.	Reading, Edwin, sum given £10 charity Simpson, William, carpenter & joiner
		21 June	Tippetts, John, sum given service Tippetts, Josiah, glazier
	1812	18 Feb.	Jones, Charles, sum given service Jacques, Charles, carpenter
		30 Jan.	Taylor, Francis, sum given £30 Hudson, Thomas, tailor
		18 Jan.	Young, Richard, sum given £10 Hicks, William, carpenter
		7 Feb.	Workman, John, sum given £10 charity Workman, John, hairdresser
		16 Mar.	Hill, John, sum given service Bonnewell, Samuel, shoemaker
		15 Apr.	Calton, John, sum given service Weaver, Edward & Charles, pin manufacturers, from 1 Jan.
		13 Feb.	Field, Thomas, sum given £10 10s. Gunn, Thomas, hairdresser
		8 May	Elliott, Thomas, sum given £40 Taylor, James, brushmaker
		14 Feb.	Simpson, Thomas, sum given £10 charity Walker, David & Alexander, printers
		10 Aug.	Smith, James, sum given service Phillips, Robert, cordwainer
		28 Sept.	Darke, William, sum given £10 charity Cooke, Robert, pargeter

John Pleydell Wilton, mayor 1812–3[2]

4/32	1812	16 Oct.	Howell, Edward & James, sum given £30 Cole, Charles & Prudence, tinplate worker
	1813	4 May	Lewelling, John, sum given £10 10s. Jeff, Charles, tailor, from 8 Apr.

---

[1] 11 Sept. 1812: To leave Sir Thomas Rich's hospital and receive £10: Henry Spillman, William Greening, Henry Bradley, James Meek, John Hyett, John Bourn, John Smart. To receive £10 of Mrs Jane Punter's money: William Darke, James Bower, Benjamin Hartland. To receive £5 of Mr William Holliday's money and £4 of Mrs Sarah Browne's money: William King, William Eycott, Robert Meek, William Probert, Daniel Farley. GBR B3/13 f. 117.

[2] 20 Sept. 1813: To leave Sir Thomas Rich's hospital and receive £10: Edward Bretherton, George Gardiner, Benjamin Watts, Thomas Driver, William Maysey, William Allen, Benjamin Pitt, James Clark, John Weeks. To receive £10 of Mrs Jane Punter's money: Jeremiah Rea. To receive £5 of Mr William Holliday's money and £4 of Mrs Sarah Browne's money: William Taylor, John Wren, Thomas Walden, William Keylock, Philip Edwards. GBR B3/13 f. 134v.

4/33	1810	17 Dec.	Warner, William, sum given £78 8s. Hewlett, John, cabinetmaker
	1812	8 Oct.	King, William, sum given £9 charity Hicks, William, carpenter
	1813	25 Mar.	Hughes, Thomas Wood, James, cabinetmaker, chairmaker & carver
		7 May	Haines, George, sum given £15 Hewlett, John, cabinetmaker
		4 June	Cox, Frederick, sum given £30 Cook, George, tailor
		9 Aug.	Joy, John, sum given £20 Cole, Charles & Prudence, tinman
		8 Sept.	Evans, Robert, sum given £100 Woodward, Thomas, cabinetmaker & upholder, from 2 Aug.
		23 Sept.	Copner, Charles Spencer, sum given service Spencer, Charles, bricklayer

Edward Weaver, mayor 1813–4[1]

4/33	1813	15 Oct.	Playne, William jr, sum given £40 Taylor, Joseph, brushmaker
		11 Dec.	White, Henry, sum given £90 Roberts, Joseph, printer, bookseller, bookbinder & stationer
	1814	2 Feb.	Bartley, George, sum given £20 charity Avery, John, cordwainer
		31 Jan.	Davis, John, sum given £30 charity Phillips, Robert, shoemakcr
		28 Mar.	Lane, Richard, sum given £30 charity Jones, Samuel, brushmaker
		21 July	Parry, James, sum given love & affection Parry, John, baker & confectioner
		8 Aug.	Ingram, John, sum given service Weaver, Charles, pinmaker
	1813	29 Mar.	Hughes, William, sum given service Turner, Thomas, banker, from 29 Mar. 1813

---

[1] 17 Sept. 1814: To leave Sir Thomas Rich's hospital and receive £10: John Hyett, Charles Simpson, Charles Baldwin, William Venn. To receive £10 of Mrs Jane Punter's money: Henry Lane, John Greening, William Bennett. To receive £5 of Mr William Holliday's money and £4 of Mrs Sarah Browne's money: George Beard, Isaac Williams, Samuel Tanner, Benjamin Lock, Christopher Fisher. GBR B3/13 f. 152v.

Sir James Jelf, mayor 1814–5[1]

4/33	1814	17 Oct.	Bennett, William, sum given £10 charity Woodward, Richard, tailor
		14 Nov.	Theach, Thomas, sum given £99 Wood, James, banker, to learn the trade of banker & mercer
4/34		25 Nov.	Fewster, John, sum given £40 Washbourne, George, baker, confectioner & maltster
		12 Dec.	Fisher, Christopher, sum given £9 Wood, James, cabinetmaker & carver
	1815	30 Jan.	Sowle, Israel May, sum given £15 Maddocks, William, baker & maltster
		15 June	Mansell, John, sum given £15 Bower, Edward, currier
		2 May	Weatherstone, William, sum given £15 Heath, Edward, shoemaker

Charles Howard, Duke of Norfolk, mayor 1815

4/34	1815	13 Oct.	Meek, Thomas, sum given £9 Smart, James, tailor
			Williams, Isaac, sum given £9 Wilkes, William, hairdresser
		23 Oct.	Maddocks, Cartwright, sum given £5 Maddocks, William, baker & maltster

Richard Nayler, mayor 1815–6[2,3]

4/34	1816	3 May	Key, William, sum given service Tippetts, Josiah, plumber & glazier
		6 May	Stone, James, sum given £9 charity Estcourt, John, hairdresser
		13 May	Cox, George, sum given £28 Woodward, Richard, tailor

---

[1] 14 Sept. 1815: To leave Sir Thomas Rich's hospital and receive £10: George Wheeler, Edward Roberts, Edmund Spillman, James Brown, William Simpson, Thomas Base, James Bretherton. To receive £10 of Mrs Jane Punter's money: William Baldwin. To receive £5 of Mr William Holliday's money and £4 of Mrs Sarah Browne's money. GBR B3/13 f. 174.

[2] Elected 21 Dec. on death of Duke of Norfolk.

[3] 25 Oct. 1816: To leave Sir Thomas Rich's hospital and receive £10: William Jacques, Robert Davis, Thomas Estcourt, James Bennett, William Jennings, Richard Hudson, William Williams, James Taylor, John Brooks. To receive £10 of Mrs Jane Punter's money: Richard Driver, James Bennett. To receive £5 of Mr William Holliday's money and £4 of Mrs Sarah Browne's money: Samuel Rock, Jacob Shearman, [—] Davis, William Pear, Edward White, Robert Tarling. GBR B3/13 f. 194.

Thomas Washbourn, mayor 1816–7[1]

4/34	1816	11 Oct.	Gamblin, John, sum given service Jeffs, Thomas, hairdresser
		7 Aug.	Lewis, John, sum given £15 charity Taylor, James, brushmaker
		6 Dec.	Hewlett, William, sum given service Hewlett, John, cabinetmaker & upholsterer
			Gardiner, Robert, sum given service Turbervill, Richard, maltster & baker
		9 Dec.	Silvester, Charles Hookham, sum given £150 Washbourne, John & John jr, booksellers, stationers & printers
		30 Dec.	Gardener, Joseph, sum given £15 charity Stephens, Thomas, brushmaker
	1817	20 Jan.	Burley, William, sum given £10 Matthews, John, pipemaker
		10 Feb.	Heaven, Samuel, sum given £10 Bretherton, Anthony, hairdresser
4/35	1814	5 Sept.	Collericke, John, sum given £48 Hicks, William, carpenter
	1817	7 May	Larner, Thomas, sum given £7 10s. charity & £7 10s. charity Mann, Joseph, cordwainer
		30 May	Inkerman, Joseph, sum given £94 10s. Butt, Richard, soap & candle manufacturer & salt merchant
		20 June	Beard, George, sum given service Beard, John, coal merchant
		18 July	Mann, William, sum given £15 Craddock, Henry, tailor & habitmaker

David Walker, mayor 1817–8[2]

4/35	1817	20 Oct.	Parrott, James, sum given £7 10s. charity & £7 10s. charity Woodward, James, hairdresser
			Tarling, Robert, sum given £9 charity Taylor, John, cabinetmaker

---

[1] 11 Sept. 1817: To leave Sir Thomas Rich's hospital and receive £10: George Edwards, John Lewis, William Workman, Charles Davis. To receive £10 of Mrs Jane Punter's money: George Venn, George Clarke, James Welch, James Dark, James Wheeler, James Selby. To receive £5 of Mr William Holliday's money and £4 of Mrs Sarah Browne's money: John Edgell, Richard Halling, John Welstead, Henry Rudge, William Cowdell. GBR B3/13 f. 210.

[2] 14 Sept. 1818: To leave Sir Thomas Rich's hospital and receive £10: George Bower, Charles Jones, Henry Bourn, Joseph Wingate, William Young, John Simpson, Thomas Sparkes. To receive £10 of Mrs Jane Punter's money: John Spier, Thomas Haynes, Henry Harris, Thomas Hyett, Edwin Maverley. To receive £5 of Mr William Holliday's money and £4 of Mrs Sarah Browne's money: Charles Turner, Edwin Probert, Thomas Butler, Henry Maisey, Edward Keveren. GBR B3/13 f. 227.

1817	3 Nov.	Silvey, James, sum given £10 charity Marsh, John, cooper
	14 Nov.	Clutterbuck, Jonah, sum given £29 19s. Washbourne, George, baker, maltster & confectioner
	5 Dec.	Dadd, William, sum given £20 Craddock, Henry, tailor
1818	13 Feb.	Pritchard, William jr, sum given £20 Bevan, Benjamin, baker & confectioner
	13 Mar.	Roberts, Edward, sum given £10 Stephens, William, tinplate worker
	10 Apr.	Cromwell, John, sum given service Gransmore, Joseph, butcher
1812	16 Mar.	Taylor, John, sum given service Taylor, Hugh, grocer
1817	17 Jan.	Williams, Thomas, sum given £5 Cooke, Charles, plumber & glazier
1818	20 Apr.	Sheppard, John, sum given £45 Cooke, Charles, plumber & glazier, from 1 Apr.

4/36

	11 May	Byne, Edmund, sum given service Roberts, Joseph, printer & stationer, from 11 Apr.
	15 May	Coley, William, sum given service Turner, Thomas, banker

1811	14 June	Jollyman, William, sum given £25
		    Stephens, William & Mary & the survivor of them, tinplate
		        worker, from 14 June 1811
		    Note: This indenture is now made in consequence of a deposition
		    made & filed the day of the indenture having been a surety left with
		    the Town Clerk for such purpose on the day it bears date

1818	20 June	Smith, Henry, sum given £100 Andrews, John, grocer, tea dealer, soapboiler & tallowchandler
	29 June	Gustavus Howell, sum given £15 Gloucestershire Society Washbourn, Nathaniel, baker & confectioner
	10 July	Lewis, William, sum given £49 19s. Meadows, George, hairdresser, umbrella & parasolmaker
1818		Darke, James jr, sum given £10 charity Darke, James sr, pinner

1813	9 June	Acutt *alias* Barnard, Robert, sum given £30 charity gift of James
		        Webb, esq.
		    Bonnor, Charles & Charles jr, braziers & tinplate workers, from
		        9 June 1813, indenture enrolled 27 July 1818

1818	16 May	Kimber, Nathaniel, sum given £60
		    Bonnor, Charles sr & Charles jr, braziers & tinplate workers,
		        from 16 May 1818 to 15 Sept. 1826

Ralph Fletcher, mayor 1818–9[1]

4/36	1818	9 Oct.	Parrott, James jr, sum given £15 charity Gloucestershire [Society] in London Wheeler, Charles, carpenter
		16 Oct.	Hillier?, William, sum given £20 Woodward, Charles, painter
		17 Feb.	Smith, John, sum given £26 5s. Bining, William, cabinetmaker, from 10 May
		18 Nov.	Woodcock, Aaron, sum given £10 given by will Bonnewell of St John the Baptist, Gloucester, cordwainer
		14 Dec.	Gardiner, Samuel, sum given £15 charity Dobbins, John, cordwainer, to learn the trade of boot & shoemaker
	1819	1 Jan.	Keveren, Edward, sum given £9 charity Cooke, Robert, pargeter
		22 Jan.	Gurney, John, sum given £29 Stephens, William, tinplate worker
4/37		5 Mar.	Allaway, John jr, sum given £40 Washbourn, George & Charles, bakers, maltsters & confectioners
	1816	25 Nov.	Yeates, Edward, sum given £100 Hewlett, John, cabinetmaker & upholsterer, from 1 Nov., indenture enrolled 8 Mar. 1819
	1819	17 Feb.	Boulton, Benjamin, sum given £60 Taylor, John, cabinetmaker
		29 Mar.	Knill, John Chamberlin, sum given £20 Saunders, Thomas, tailor
		12 Aug.	Clutterbuck, Obadiah, sum given £20 Hewlett, John, cabinetmaker
		3 Sept.	Player, Thomas, sum given service Baylis, Thomas, baker
		23 Sept.	Copner, George, sum given service Spencer, Charles, bricklayer, to learn the trade of builder, indenture enrolled 14 Feb. 1820

---

[1] 18 Aug. 1819: To leave Sir Thomas Rich's hospital and receive £10: George Lewis, Thomas Woodward, William Fream, John Watts, Thomas Lewis Pool, James Base, Henry Herbert, George Henry Bower, Charles Bosley. To receive £10 [of Mrs Jane Punter's money]: Thomas Greening, Charles Best, Frederick Lane, James Drinkwater, William Monk, Joseph Base. To receive £5 of Mr William Holliday's money and £4 of Mrs Sarah Browne's money: James Hopton, Richard Morris, Thomas Price, James Crickley, Edward Probert, James Hopkins, John Kent. GBR B3/13 f. 254.

John Philpotts, mayor 1819–20[1]

4/37 1820 30 Oct. Baylis, William, sum given £9 charity
Marsh, John, cooper

22 Aug. White, James, sum given £99 15s.
Playne, William, saddler, to learn the trade of saddler & harnessmaker

11 Dec. Smith, Daniel, sum given £49 17s. 6d.
Wood, James, banker & draper

Samuel Jones, mayor 1820–1[2]

4/37 1821 12 May Phelps, Joseph, sum given £60
Taylor, John, grocer & British wine merchant

18 June Long, John, sum given £70
Andrews, John, grocer, soapboiler & tallowchandler

31 Aug. Collins, Richard, sum given £40
Stephens, William, tinplate worker & brazier

25 Sept. Taylor, William Edwin, sum given service
Birt, Thomas, printer

Henry Wilton, mayor 1821–2; David Saunders 1822[3,4]

4/37 1822 1 Mar. Niblett, Edwin, sum given £20
Taylor, John, cabinetmaker

1 May Murrell, William jr, sum given service
Wilkins, James, hairdresser

30 Aug. Jones, John, sum given £12
Bourn, John, boot & shoemaker, from 28 Aug.

28 Aug. Chandler, George jr, sum given service
Baylis, Thomas, baker

---

[1] 14 Sept. 1820: To leave Sir Thomas Rich's hospital and receive £10: James Bretherton, William Nest, Henry Spier, James Haynes. To receive £10 of Mrs Jane Punter's money: Charles Wilkes, Thomas Dix, Cornelius Taylor, Thomas Ellis. To receive £5 of Mr William Holliday's money and £4 of Mrs Sarah Browne's money: Charles Smith, William Baylis, John Oakley Packer, Stephen Workman, John Russell, Thomas Wren, George Cardell and Thomas Preece (orphans), William Stock. GBR B3/13 f. 284.

[2] 14 Sept. 1821: To leave Sir Thomas Rich's hospital and receive £10: John Maverley, William Daniell, John Ward, Charles Richards, William Cother, John Wheeler, James Drinkwater. To receive £10 of Mrs Jane Punter's money: Charles Trigge, John Harris, James Bower, Henry Best, Robert Cooke, Edmund Evans, William Holder. To receive £5 of Mr William Holliday's money and £4 of Mrs Sarah Browne's money: James Williams, Henry Rock, Robert Bryant, James Page, Edwin Harris, William Wood. GBR B3/13 f. 227.

[3] Elected 8 Feb. 1822 after Wilton's death.

[4] 22 Aug. 1822: To leave Sir Thomas Rich's hospital and receive £10: Edward Heath, Frederick Johnson, William Herbert, William Merrett, John Faville, John Boseley, Charles Okey. To receive £10 of Mrs Jane Punter's money: Thomas Daniell, Richard Dillar Jones, John Dix, William Dovey. To receive £5 of Mr William Holliday's money and £4 of Mrs Sarah Browne's money: James Gardiner, James Smith, William Harris, John Lloyd, Charles Whittick. GBR B3/13 f. 332.

William Price, mayor 1822–3[1]

4/37	1822	15 Nov.	Jackson, John, sum given £20 Ursell, Francis, plumber & glazier
		10 Dec.	Watts, John, sum given £150 Lovett, John, chemist & druggist
	1823	11 Mar.	Taylor, Thomas, sum given £20 Bevan, Benjamin, baker & confectioner
4/38		28 Apr.	Vernon, William, sum given £20 Andrews, Joseph, grocer & tallowchandler
		19 May	White, John Motley, sum given £15 Bretherton, Anthony, hairdresser

	1822	31 Jan.	Barnett, Joseph, sum given £99
			   Stanley, Thomas, cabinetmaker & upholsterer, indenture
			      enrolled 8 Aug. 1823

	1823	24 July	Beard, Edmund, sum given service Beard, John, coal merchant

Sir William Guise, mayor 1823–4[2]

4/38	1823	28 Nov.	Williams, John, sum given £20 Marsh, John, cooper
	1824	20 Jan.	Gardiner, Edward Timothy Wilshire, sum given service Gardner, John, whitesmith & bellhanger, from 20 Jan. 1820

		17 May	George, Thomas, sum given £7 10s. paid by Gloucestershire
			   Society & £7 10s. to be paid at date of indenture
			   Greening, Samuel, hairdresser, umbrella & parasolmaker

---

[1] 15 Sept. 1823: To leave Sir Thomas Rich's hospital and receive £10: John Mann, James Cull, John Stephens, Daniel Bloxsome, Thomas Bower. To receive £10 of Mrs Jane Punter's money: Charles Simpson, Edward Estcourt, Samuel Overthrow, Samuel Harris, John Wathen, Robert Church. To receive £5 of Mr William Holliday's money and £4 of Mrs Sarah Browne's money: John Morris, Shadrach Hezekiah Jones, William Chadborn Healing, George Cleveland, William Flower, Daniel Hopton, Jonah Thomas, William Cambridge. GBR B3/13 f. 359.

[2] 31 Aug. 1824: To leave Sir Thomas Rich's hospital and receive £10: Thomas Cother, Daniel Wilkins, William Maverley, William Hicks, George Baldwin, Charles Pitcher, George Spier, Henry Dix. To receive £10 of Mrs Jane Punter's money: George Evans, Isaac James Reading, John Evans, James Bonnywell. To receive £5 of Mr William Holliday's money and £4 of Mrs Sarah Browne's money: Thomas Harris, George Howell, Edwin Oakey, John Lane. GBR B3/14 f. 12v.

John Cooke, mayor 1824–5[1]

4/38	1824	25 Oct.	Rooksby, Edward jr, sum given service Perris, John, cordwainer
		1 Dec.	Whitehead, Alfred, sum given service Whitehead, William, straw hat manufacturer
		10 Dec.	Morley, George Meadows, sum given service Meadows, George, hairdresser & perukemaker
		13 Dec.	Poulton, Edward, sum given £14 10s. Taylor, John, cabinetmaker
	1823	4 Sept.	Gearing, William, sum given £45 Cooke, Charles, plumber & glazier, indenture enrolled 4 Mar. 1825
	1822	20 May	Parker, Isaac Alfred, sum given £31 10s. Daniell, George, painter & gilder, indenture enrolled 4 Mar. 1825
	1824	20 June	Neale, George William, sum given £35 Clarke, John Gilbert, butcher, indenture enrolled 24 June 1825
	1825	7 July	Segrey, Henry, sum given service Turner, Thomas, banker
		25 Mar.	Beard, William, sum given service Washbourn, George & Charles, bakers, maltsters & confectioners

Thomas Commeline, mayor 1825–6[2]

4/38	1825	22 Nov.	Phillips, Joseph, sum given £15 Marsh, John, cooper
		2 Aug.	Webb, Joseph jr, sum given service Webb, Joseph, cheese factor, indenture enrolled 27 Feb. 1826
	1826	12 Apr.	Nicholl, Robert jr, sum given £99 15s. Playne, William, saddler, to learn the trade of saddler & collarmaker

---

[1] 13 Sept. 1825: To leave Sir Thomas Rich's hospital and receive £10: James Sessions, John Heath, Charles Davis, Charles Watts, Charles Workman, John Lea, William Beard. To receive £10 of Mrs Jane Punter's money: James Sessions, William Beard, Charles Workman, Thomas Okey, Charles Hill Evans, Thomas Knight, Henry Wilkes, John Berkeley Law, James Rudge, James Cleveland, Joseph Phillips. To receive £5 of Mr William Holliday's money: Charles Watts, John Heath, Charles Davis, John Lea, Thomas Okey, Charles Hill Evans, Thomas Knight, Henry Wilkes, John Berkeley Law, James Rudge, James Cleeveland, Joseph Phillips. GBR B3/14 f. 30v.

3 Oct. 1825: There was an error in the voting at the previous meeting on 13 Sept. Charles Workman should have had Mr Holliday's £5 and John Lea Mrs Punter's £10. GBR B3/14 f. 35.

[2] 7 Sept. 1826: To leave Sir Thomas Rich's hospital and receive £10: James Bower, John Woodward, William Woodward, Henry Dark, John Bennett. GBR B3/14 f. 49v.

22 Sept. 1826: To receive £10 of Mrs Jane Punter's money: James Bower, John Woodward (Blue School), John Chandler, William James Thomas Lewis, Giles Taylor, Edmund Beard, John Woodward, James Lee, Thomas Jennings. To receive £5 of Mr William Holliday's money: William Woodward, Henry Dark, John Bennett, John Chandler, William James Thomas Lewis, Giles Taylor, Edmund Beard, John Woodward, James Lee, Thomas Jennings. GBR B3/14 f. 51.

APPENDIX

This list has been extracted from TNA IR 1/50–55. The first column gives the volume reference followed by the page number, the second two columns give the year and date of the indenture. The date on which the tax was paid to the collector is given only when it differs from the indenture date. Double duty (1s. in the £) was payable on premiums over £50, and theoretically on duty paid more than two months after the date of indenture, though this does not always seem to have been enforced.

IR 1/50

50/93 **Samuel Worrall, Gloucestershire, brought 20 indentures, 10 Aug. 1742**

1742	3 May	Window, William, son of William, premium £8 Haynes, William, joiner, 7 yrs
		Williams, Aldridge son of William, premium £10 Reading, Philip, cooper, 7 yrs
	7 May	Dymocks, William son of Francis, premium £8 Stephens, Richard, baker, 7 yrs
	18 June	Blackwell, George son of Joseph, premium £10 Gardner, Cornelius, barber etc., 7 yrs
	28 June	Blackwell, Thomas son of Mary, premium £31 10s. Niblett, Samuel, grocer, 6 yrs
	14 May	Williams, Henry son of Henry, premium £10 Washbourne, John, clockmaker, 7 yrs from 25 Mar., tax paid 28 June

50/95

	25 Mar.	Pitt, John son of James, premium £1 Pitt, James, attorney, 6 yrs, tax paid 26 Mar.
	24 June	Bond, Elizabeth daughter of Thomas, premium £10 Merrick, Charles, gardener, 4 yrs, tax paid 26 July

50/141 **Samuel Worrall, Gloucestershire, brought 37 indentures, 18 Mar. 1743**

1741	23 Nov.	Hunt, George son of Edward, dec'd, premium £9 Heath, Samuel, joiner, 7 yrs from 29 Sept., tax paid 28 July 1742
1742	5 July	Price, John Beal, premium £30 Bond, Thomas, baker, 7 yrs from 2 Mar., tax paid 3 Aug.
	6 June	Bond, Capel son of William, premium £2 10s. Smith, Martin, organist, to do articles for 9 yrs from 6 June, tax paid 6 Aug.
	19 July	Webb, Samuel son of Arthur, premium £8 Weston, John, cordwainer, 7 yrs, tax paid 19 Aug.
	13 Aug.	Farren, William son of Abraham, premium £15 Moore, Winston, butcher, 7 yrs from 24 June, tax paid 19 Aug.

1742   19 July   Millard, William son of Nathaniel, premium £6 6s.
                    Workman, Hester, butcher, 7 yrs, tax paid 13 Sept.

        24 Aug.   Harris, Grace, of Churcham, premium £20
                    Newton, Mary & comp[any?], milliners, 7 yrs, tax paid 24 Sept.

        1 Nov.   Bower, William son of Thomas, premium £30
                    Taylor, Ellis, baker, 7 yrs from 22 Oct., tax paid 8 Nov.

        23 Oct.   Harris, Margaret, premium £12
                    Merrick, Sarah, mantuamaker, 7 yrs, tax paid 10 Dec.

1743   11 Feb.   Middleton, Richard son of James, premium £8
                    Jennings, John, whitesmith, 7 yrs from 2 Oct. 1742

50/161 **Samuel Worrall, Gloucestershire, brought 51 indentures, 26 July 1743**

1743   18 Feb.   Instock, William son of William, premium £10
                    Washbourne, George, clockmaker, 7 yrs, tax paid 15 Mar.

        22 Jan.   Stratford, Francis son of Walter, premium £126 (double duty)
                    Barrow, Charles, attorney, to do articles for 5 yrs, tax paid
                    18 Mar.

        18 Apr.   Cox, John son of Mary, premium £126 (double duty)
                    Punter, Joseph, mercer, 7 yrs, tax paid 14 May

        16 May   Jelliman, Thomas son of Daniel, premium £10 10s.
                    Smith, Abraham, cooper, 7 yrs from 16 May

        13 June   Smith, William son of Robert, premium £14
                    Cooke, James, baker, 7 yrs from 1 May

50/193 **Samuel Worrall, Gloucestershire, brought 53 indentures, 14 Feb. 1744**[1]

1743   13 Aug.   Tanner, John son of John, premium £105 (double duty)
                    Engley, Richard, goldsmith, 7 yrs, tax paid 22 Aug.

        20 July   Brewer, Christopher, son of Nathaniel, premium £70
                    Cheston, Joseph, apothecary, 7 yrs, tax paid 19 Sept.

        6 July   Brown, John, of Bristol, premium £2
                    Wyman, Ambrose, gingerbread baker, 3 yrs, tax paid 28 Sept.

50/194 1744   13 Jan.   Alexander, William son of William, premium £13
                    Robinson, Giles, cooper, 7 yrs

50/217 **Samuel Worrall, Gloucestershire, brought 117 indentures, 7 Aug. 1744**

1744   27 Jan.   Window, Robert son of William, premium £45
                    Cooke, George, grocer, 7 yrs from 27 Nov. 1743, tax paid
                    9 Feb.

---

[1] 23 Sept. 1743: To receive £4 of Mrs Sarah Browne's money: John Harding, Joseph Richards, Thomas Cooke, William Wells. To receive £5 of Mr William Holliday's money: James Badger, John Price, William Powell, Thomas Woolford, William Holder, Thomas Bromly, William Price. To leave Sir Thomas Rich's hospital and receive £10: Francis Wilson, Benjamin Hickman, Thomas Webley. GBR B3/10 f. 26.

	1744	16 Mar.	Bullock, Thomas son of John, premium £6 Ward, Thomas, cordwainer, 7 yrs,
			Jelliman, William son of Daniel, premium £6 6s. Cowcher, William, pinmaker, 7 yrs
		18 Apr.	Harrison, George, son of George, premium £1 Lombard, Jacob, weaver, 7 yrs from 1 Apr. 1738, tax paid 20 Apr.
	1742	25 June	Bayse, Joseph, son of Joseph, premium £12 Browne, Thomas, cordwainer, 7 yrs, tax paid 28 May 1744
	1744	1 May	Organ, John, son of John, premium £7 Weaver, Richard, blacksmith, 7 yrs, tax paid 28 May
	1743	18 Apr.	Lane, William, son of William, premium £10 Wintle, James, brushmaker, 7 yrs from 18 Apr. 1743, tax paid 1 June 1744
	1744	13 Apr.	Roberts, Samuel son of Samuel, premium £20 Wintle, James, brushmaker, 7 yrs from 20 Mar., tax paid 1 June
		1 June	Fletcher, Ralph son of William, premium £15 Gardner, Joseph, baker, 7 yrs
	1743	10 Oct.	Harrison, Winter son of Winter, premium £10 Buckel, Samuel, feltmaker, 7 yrs, tax paid 4 June 1744
50/218	1744	20 July	Gransmore, John Hilman, premium £13 Drew, Thomas, baker, 7 yrs from 25 June

50/259 **Samuel Worrall, Gloucestershire, brought 93 indentures, 28 Feb. 1745**[1]

	1744	13 Aug.	Smith, William son of Robert, no premium Fletcher, Thomas, baker, 7 yrs, tax paid 14 Aug.
		24 Aug.	Smith, Charles son of William, premium £4 Davis, John, pinmaker, 7 yrs from 1 June
		13 Aug.	Harding, William, premium £157 10s. (double duty) Jones, William, attorney, 5 yrs, tax paid 22 Sept.
		4 Oct.	Gazard, Jane, premium £5 Lewis, Richard, pinmaker, 8 yrs
		31 Aug.	Bond, Anthony son of Anthony, premium £11 Hooper, Charles, butcher, 7 yrs from 16 Jan., tax paid 15 Oct.
		14 Dec.	Mallett, James son of William, premium £30 Bonner, Thomas, grocer, 7 yrs from 20 Nov.

[1] 21 Aug. 1744: To receive £4 of Mrs Sarah Browne's money: John Dicks, William Elliott, John Soul. GBR B3/10 f. 40.

   20 Sept. 1744: To receive £5 of Mr William Holliday's money: Thomas Maverly, Thomas Jeffs, John Mason, John Wingate, Samuel Ricketts, John Hayford, John Bridger. To leave Sir Thomas Rich's hospital and receive £10: William Jeffs, Richard Webly, Joseph Williams, Anthony Motlow, William Bright, Samuel Harris, Charles Morris, Robert Arnold. GBR B3/10 f. 43.

50/280 **Samuel Worrall, Gloucestershire, brought 89 indentures, 6 Aug. 1745**[1]

1745	22 Feb.	Bright, Joseph son of William, premium £2
		Wood, William, cooper, 7 yrs from 14 Oct. 1744, tax paid 4 Mar.
	29 Apr.	Roberts, John son of Samuel, premium £5
		Nelme, Henry, cooper, 7 yrs from 1 Mar.
	3 May	Banks, Bryan son of Christopher, premium £6
		Hayes, John, cordwainer, 7 yrs

50/281

		Bond, Samuel son of Anthony, premium £15
		Weaver, Kirkham, harness man etc., 7 yrs from 25 Mar., tax paid 6 May
	29 Apr.	Bushell, William son of George, premium £10
		Weaver, William, saddler, 7 yrs from 25 Mar., tax paid 7 May
1742	21 June	Dix, Thomas son of Thomas, premium £80
		Ashmeade, John, mercer, 7 yrs from 25 Mar., tax paid 1 June 1745
1743	14 Feb.	Morton, Francis son of Thomas, premium £2
		Faucks, Thomas, butcher, 7 yrs, tax paid 1 June 1745
1745	10 June	Wood, Joseph son of William, premium £30
		Wadley, Thomas, baker, 7 yrs, tax paid 1 June
	28 June	Reeve, William son of John, premium £6
		Lane, John, farrier etc., 7 yrs from 20 Aug., tax paid 1 July

[1] 20 Sept. 1745: To receive £4 of Mrs Sarah Browne's money: William Wood, John Mumford. To receive £5 of Mr William Holliday's money: Thomas Dix, John Engly, John Rudge, John Jeffs, Nathaniel Bond, James Cole, Thomas Gaze. To leave Sir Thomas Rich's hospital and receive £10: Thomas Roberts, James Nott, John Richards, James Brotherton, Stephen Swayne, Charles Kemis, William Clark. GBR B3/10 f. 55.

2 Sept. 1746: To receive £4 of Mrs Sarah Browne's money: Charles Beard, Thomas Roberts, John Davis, Richard Butcher, Anthony Wilton, William Harding. To receive £5 of Mr William Holliday's money: Charles Tomlins, William Bloxom, Joseph Jeffs, Samuel Jeffs, James Townsend. To leave Sir Thomas Rich's hospital and receive £10: John Mutlow, Henry Stone, John Bower, John Brocke, Edward Stocke, Thomas Corr. GBR B3/10 f. 70.

11 Sept. 1747: To leave Sir Thomas Rich's hospital and receive £10: Thomas Lock, John Pace, James Ricketts, Samuel Groves, Ebenezer Lownes, Giles Horsington. GBR B3/10 f. 85v.

25 Sept. 1747: To receive £4 of Mrs Sarah Browne's money: Francis Strowd, William Dadd, Nathaniel Macocke, James Davis. To receive £5 of Mr William Holliday's money: William Hickman, Thomas Child, William Pace, Thomas Swayne, John Ward, Samuel Johnson, Richard Bicke. GBR B3/10 f. 86v.

14 Aug. 1748: To leave Sir Thomas Rich's hospital and receive £10: Edward Swayne, Nicholas Barnes, William Perry, John Smith, Giles Vyner Cooke, Richard Bakler. GBR B3/10 f. 105v

7 Sept. 1748: To receive £4 of Mrs Sarah Browne's money: James Lewis, William Linnell, William Lander, Samuel Watts. To receive £5 of Mr William Holliday's money: Henry Freeman, William Pace, William Merrett, Richard Overthrow, John Bullock. GBR B3/10 f. 108v.

6 Sept. 1749: To leave Sir Thomas Rich's hospital and receive £10. Daniel Freeman, Samuel Ricketts, Edward Smith, John Porter, Charles Gardiner, Francis Gregory. GBR B3/10 f. 127

22 Sept. 1749: To receive £4 of Mrs Sarah Browne's money: Charles Eldridge, John Roff, Thomas Hopley, William Maysey. To receive £5 of Mr William Holliday's money: Samuel Merrett, John Price, Richard Maverly, John Groves, James Bromley, John Weston, John Pyrton, Samuel Bower, John Glendall. GBR B3/10 f. 128v.

IR 1/51

51/4   **Peter Cocks, Gloucester, brought 59 indentures, 27 Oct. 1750**[1]

    1750   30 Apr.   Price, Richard son of Richard, premium £12
                           Fletcher, Thomas, baker, 7 yrs from 15 Jan., tax paid 21 May

             7 May   Warburton, Michael son of Thomas, premium £48
                           Cheston, Joseph, apothecary, 7 yrs from 26 Mar., tax paid
                              21 May

51/5   18 May   Goulder, John son of John, premium £10
                           Barrett, Thomas, baker, 7 yrs from 17 May, tax paid 1 June

                           Pew, Joseph son of Joseph, premium £17 18s.
                           Moore, Winstone, butcher, 7 yrs from 17 May, tax paid 1 June

         15 June Yarworth, Robert son of James, premium £30
                           Taylor, Richard, tanner, 7 yrs from 29 Sept., tax paid 23 June

         19 July   Farmer, Thomas son of Thomas, premium £10
                           Raikes, Robert, printer, 7 yrs from 3 Sept., tax paid 31 July

         20 July   Charlott, Stephen son of George, premium £10
                           Sexty, George, butcher, 7 yrs from 24 June, tax paid 3 Aug.

         23 July   Gale, Thomas son of Robert, premium £80 (double duty)
                           Wood, James, mercer, 7 yrs from 1 Jan., tax paid 10 Aug.

    1746   12 Nov. Roberts, Thomas son of Thomas, premium £6 6s.
                           Baker, John, joiner, 7 yrs from 13 Oct. [*year not given*],
                           tax paid 12 July 1750

    1748   29 Sept. Long, Thomas son of William, premium £14
                           Moye, Richard, currier, 7 yrs, tax paid 15 July 1750

    1745   9 Feb.   Glendall, John son of Sampson, premium £1
                           Daws, William, joiner, 7 yrs from 20 Jan. [—], tax paid
                           24 July 1750

51/48 **Peter Cocks, Gloucester, brought 47 indentures, 6 Apr. 1751**

    1750   12 Nov. Hayford, James Shatford, premium £11
                           Hales, Sampson, barber, 7 yrs, tax paid 6 Nov.

         20 Oct.   Middleton, James son of James, premium £6 10s.
                           Baylis, Benjamin, woolcomber, 7 yrs from 20 Nov.,
                           tax paid 5 Jan. 1751

51/49 1751   15 Mar. Webbley, William son of Joseph, premium £12 12s.
                           Weaver, William, saddler, 7 yrs from 1 Mar., tax paid 29 Mar.

---

[1] 4 Sept. 1750: To leave Sir Thomas Rich's hospital and receive £10: Amity Rodway, William Cullurne, Daniel Mayo, William Bright, Thomas Powell, Joseph Lewis. GBR B3/10 f. 141.

    28 Sept. 1750: To receive £5 of Mr William Holliday's money: Thomas Engley, John Wheeler, Robert Hyett, James Smith, Thomas Crump, Richard Child. To receive £4 of Mrs Sarah Browne's money: Caleb Wells, James Middleton, William Moore, William Caler. GBR B3/10 f. 142.

1751   29 Mar.   Spillman, James son of Joseph, premium £10
                          Blackwell, George, barber, 7 yrs from 25 Mar., tax paid
                          29 Mar.

51/99   **Peter Cocks, Gloucester, brought 59 indentures, 2 Nov. 1751**[1]

1751   22 Mar.   Nelme, John son of John, premium £15 15s.
                          Nelme, Henry, cooper, 7 yrs, tax paid 23 Mar.

           22 Apr.   Browning, Lyndon Charles, premium £10
                          Weaver, Matthew, baker, 7 yrs, tax paid 27 Apr.

51/100   5 July   Gyde, Thomas son of Thomas, premium £16 16s.
                          Sparrow, James, cooper, 7 yrs from 4 June, tax paid 15 July

           22 July   Cother, William son of William, premium £12
                          Cope, Richard, baker, 7 yrs from 14 May

           5 Aug.   Collins, Daniel son of Anne, premium £30
                          Wadley, Thomas, baker, 7 yrs from 1 Aug.

           13 Sept.   Wadley, Mary, premium £8 10s.
                          Bick, Elizabeth, mantuamaker, 3 yrs from 21 July, tax
                          paid 20 Sept.

1748   28 Mar.   Ascoe, George son of Joseph, premium £5 (double duty)
                          Mugg, Richard, carpenter, 7 yrs from 1 Apr., tax paid 11
                          May 1751

51/140   **Peter Cocks, Gloucester, brought 71 indentures, 5 May 1752**

1751   23 Sept.   Wells, Caleb, premium £4
                          Price, Thomas, whitesmith, 7 yrs from 1 July, tax paid 27 Sept.

           15 Oct.   Skinner, Thomas, premium £15
                          Buckle, Samuel, feltmaker, 7 yrs, tax paid 26 Oct.

           9 Nov.   Gardiner, Mary, premium £12
                          Twinning, John, shoemaker, 6 yrs from 25 Mar., tax paid
                          11 Nov.

51/141 1752   29 Jan.   Hale, James, premium £11
                          Cook, William, joiner, 7 yrs from 21 Jan., tax paid 31 Jan.

           21 Feb.   Green, Richard son of Richard, premium £20
                          James, Nathaniel Mallett, grocer, 7 yrs, tax paid 29 Feb.

           2 Mar.   Southall, John son of Morris, premium £20
                          Branch, Thomas, tinplate worker, 7 yrs from 2 Feb., tax
                          paid 7 Mar.

---

[1] 14 Aug. 1751: To leave Sir Thomas Rich's hospital and receive £10: John Watts, John Hoskins, John Dudley, William Bond, William Bradley, Henry Davis. GBR B3/10 f. 158v.

  26 Sept. 1751: To receive £5 of Mr William Holliday's money: John Clark, Nestor Nest, Jonas Bretherton, William Hall, Charles Merrett, Richard Bullock, James Reeve, Robert Jelfs. To receive £4 of Mrs Sarah Browne's money: John Machin, Samuel Hassele, Richard Toms, John Avery. GBR B3/10 f. 159v.

1745   1 June   Kirby, Dianah daughter of Jacob, premium £8 (double duty)
                  Gregory, Anne, mantuamaker, 7 yrs, tax paid 14 Dec. 1751

51/197   Peter Cocks, Gloucester, brought 57 indentures, 5 Nov. 1752[1]

1752   4 May   Wheeler, Samuel son of William, premium £10
                  Robinson, Giles, cooper, 7 yrs, tax paid 12 May

        26 May   Selwyn, James, premium £157 10s. (double duty)
                  Jones, William jr, attorney, 5 yrs, tax paid 5 June

        31 July   Dudley, John, premium £10 charity
                  Kurks, Henry, grocer, 7 yrs, tax paid 4 Aug.

        18 Sept. Watts, Thomas, premium £14
                  Webb, John, butcher, 7 yrs

        16 Oct.   Verinder, Thomas, premium £10
                  Parker, Thomas, barber surgeon, 7 yrs, tax paid 24 Oct.

        18 Apr.   Hayford, Mary, premium £14 (double duty)
                  Lugg, John, mantuamaker, 5 yrs, tax paid 25 Oct.

51/228   Peter Cocks, Gloucester, brought 52 indentures, 8 May 1753

1752   30 Oct.   Bennett, Joseph, premium £5
                  Weaver, Kirkham, collarmaker, 7 yrs, tax paid 5 Dec.

        17 Nov.   Wadely, Thomas, premium £10
                  Fowler, Giles, barber surgeon, 7 yrs from 6 inst., tax paid
                  5 Jan. 1753

        24 Nov.   Prosser, James, premium £3 (double duty)[2]
                  Yeates, Thomas, grocer, 7 yrs, tax paid 3 Feb. 1753

        10 Nov.   Moore, William, premium £6 (double duty)
                  Wintle, James, brushmaker, 7 yrs, tax paid 20 Apr. 1753

51/264   Peter Cocks, Gloucester, brought 64 indentures, 6 Nov. 1753[3]

1753   7 May   Powell, John, premium £10
                  Reading, Philip, cooper, 7 yrs, tax paid 16 May

        28 May   Watts, Francis, premium £10
                  Wadely, Ambrose, baker, 7 yrs, tax paid 5 June

[1] 29 Sept. 1752: To leave Sir Thomas Rich's hospital and receive £10: Daniel Bloxholme, James Garn, William Hathway, Solomon Bretherton, James Gun, Elias Jeffs. To receive £5 of Mr William Holliday's money: George Motlow, Richard Jeffs, Joseph Wingate, John Powell, Thomas Price, John Bishop, James Woolford. To receive £4: John Hinton, Thomas Ridler, Benjamin Wood, George Church. GBR B3/10 ff. 170–1.

[2] The tax was paid only a few days after the 2 month deadline and was originally charged at the normal rate. The clerk has marked a group of 6 late payers from around the county and doubled the duty.

[3] 14 Aug. 1753: To leave Sir Thomas Rich's hospital and receive £10: John Ricketts, John Holder, John Simpson, Henry Wilton, James Ady. GBR B3/10 f. 181.

   25 Sept. 1753: To receive £5 of Mr William Holliday's money: Abraham Smith, Joseph Pyrton, Edward Bloxholm, Thomas Sparkes, William Bower, Thomas Davies. To receive £4 of Mrs Sarah Browne's money: William Gibbs, John Bannister, Edward Benton, George Parrish. GBR B3/10 f. 182.

	1753	4 June	Hartfield, William, premium £10
			Webbley, Richard, perukemaker, 7 yrs, tax paid 16 June
		25 June	Drown, Thomas, premium £10
			Jones, William, baker, 7 yrs from 18 Apr., tax paid 7 July
		17 Aug.	Saunders, Thomas, premium £30
			Curtis, Henry, grocer, 7 yrs, tax paid 25 Aug.

51/285   Samuel Worrall, Bristol, brought 53 indentures, 19 Mar. 1754

	1753	11 Aug.	Cosham, William, premium £2 5s.
			Hulbert, William, weaver, 7 yrs, tax paid 18 Aug.
		30 July	Smith, Samuel, premium £10
			Crump, Charles & wife, turners, 7 yrs, tax paid 23 Aug.
		8 Sept.	Cosham, Sarah, premium £3
			Kingdon, Joseph, plasterer, 7 yrs, tax paid 8 Sept.
		24 July	Dawes, Godfrey, premium £4 4s. (double duty)
			Freath, John, brass founder, 7 yrs, tax paid 10 Nov.
		13 Oct.	Haynes, Sarah, premium £4
			Long, Mary, rugmaker, 7 yrs, tax paid 15 Nov.
	1754	4 Jan.	Packer, Frances, premium £12 12s.
			Packer, Thomas & wife, 7 yrs, tax paid 14 Jan.

51/291   Peter Cocks, Gloucester, brought 52 indentures, 27 Apr. 1754

| | 1754 | 14 Jan. | Lawrence, William, premium £63 (double duty) |
| | | | Timbrell, Robert, surgeon, 3 yrs from 15 inst., tax paid 26 Jan. |

IR 1/52

52/34   Peter Cocks, Gloucester, brought 50 indentures, 15 Oct. 1754[1]

	1754	6 May	Gardiner, Edward, premium £5
			Lumbard, Jacob, weaver, 7 yrs, tax paid 3 June 1754
52/35		27 May	Bamford, William, premium £10
			Cooke, Benjamin, staymaker, 7 yrs, tax paid 1 July 1754
		20 June	Keen, Rebecca, premium £30
			Randle, Elizabeth, milliner, 7 yrs, tax paid 27 July 1754
		26 Aug.	Smith, William, premium £10 10s.
			Spillman, Richard, baker, 7 yrs, tax paid 23 Sept. 1754

---

[1] 29 Aug. 1754: To leave Sir Thomas Rich's hospital and receive £10: Thomas Gann, James Randall, Charles Lindsay, William Holtham, William Watts, Samuel Jennings. GBR B3/10 f. 193.

26 Sept. 1754: To receive £5 of Mr William Holliday's money: Jeremiah Clark, William Bradley, the other petitioners being under the age of 14. To receive £4 of Mrs Sarah Browne's money: James Griggs, William Atkins, William Hinton, Thomas Goodenough. GBR B3/10 f. 194.

52/55   **Samuel Worrall, Bristol, brought 43 indentures, 8 Mar. 1755**

| 1754 | 8 Oct. | Stephens, Charles, premium £4 4s. |
| | | Mackarthy, Charles, blacksmith, 7 yrs, tax paid 14 Oct. |

52/66   **Peter Cocks, Gloucester, brought 64 indentures, 22 Apr. 1755**

1754 18 Oct. Mason, Joseph, premium £10 10s.
      Harper, Charles, butcher, 7 yrs from 5 Jan., tax paid 5 Nov.

    18 Nov. Lovegrove, Thomas, premium £12 12s.
      Robinson, Giles, cooper, 7 yrs, tax paid 4 Dec.

       Buckanan, William, premium £42
      Yates, Daniel, grocer etc., 7 yrs from 21 Oct., tax paid 7 Dec.

52/67   1755 17 Jan. Wintle, James, premium £10
      Ward, Thomas, pinmaker, 7 yrs, tax paid 27 Feb.

    20 Jan. Garner, Joseph, premium £31 10s.
      James, Nathaniel Mallett, grocer, 7 yrs, tax paid 28 Feb.

    31 Jan. Watts, William, premium £5 10s. charity
      Beard, Joseph, weaver, 7 yrs, tax paid 15 Mar.

    17 Feb. Bearpacker, George, premium £100
      Wood, Richard, mercer, 7 yrs, tax paid 26 Mar.

  1754 1 Apr. Ridler, Thomas, premium £1 1s. charity
      Price, William, cordwainer, 7 yrs from 17 Mar. 1754, tax
       paid 31 Mar. 1755

  1755 28 Feb. Truman, William, premium £15 15s.
      Niblett, Samuel, grocer etc., 6 yrs from 1 May last, tax
       paid 1 Apr.

    8 Mar. Cocks, Ann, premium £20
      Tavell, John & wife, milliners, 4 yrs from 1 Jan., tax paid 2 Apr.

52/102   **Samuel Worrall, Bristol, brought 70 indentures, 19 Sept. 1755**

1755 2 Apr. Haskins, Joseph, premium £4 4s.
      Pullen, Thomas, blacksmith, 7 yrs, tax paid 14 May

52/118   **Peter Cocks, Gloucester, brought 56 indentures, 1 Nov. 1755[1]**

1755 3 Apr. Wheeler, Ann, premium £15
      Cooke, Elizabeth, mantuamaker, 7 yrs from 1 Mar. last,
       tax paid 26 Apr.

---

[1] 26 Sept. 1755: To leave Sir Thomas Rich's hospital and receive £10: John Lane, John Cheeseman, Josiah Salcomb, Joseph Price, John Gardiner, Price Cleavley, William Stephens, Henry Holder. To receive £5 of Mr William Holliday's money: William Watts, Jeremiah Williams, Nathaniel Seyer, James Fords, Thomas Gregory. To receive £4 of Mrs Sarah Browne's money: Thomas Adey, William Floyd, George Goodyer, William Bonniwell. GBR B3/10 f. 203v.

 3 Nov. 1755: John Moulder to have the £4 voted to William Floyd who has since died without being placed apprentice or receiving £4. GBR B3/10 f. 208v.

1755   18 Apr.   Clarke, William, premium £22
                        Arnold, Robert, tinman, 7 yrs, tax paid 10 May

        18 Apr.   Brown, Thomas, premium £5
                        Pleydell, John, baker, 7 yrs from 18 Apr. 1754, tax paid 14 May

        1 May   Jelfe, Ann, premium £19 4s.
                        Longdon, Elizabeth, mantuamaker, 3 yrs, tax paid 20 May

52/151   **Peter Cocks, Gloucester, brought 50 indentures, 11 May 1756**

1756   5 Jan.   Fisher, Benjamin, premium £14 14s.
                        Radnige, Ralph, currier, 7 yrs from 1 Dec. 1755, tax paid 24 Jan.

        13 Feb.   Barton, Ira, premium £10 10s.
                        Coucher, William, pinmaker,7 yrs from 2 March, tax paid 22 Mar.

        20 Feb.   Driver, William, premium £12
                        Box, John, 7 yrs from 14 inst., tax paid 31 Mar.

        2 Apr.   Boughton, Edmund, premium £15
                        Richard, Moye, currier, 7 yrs from 25 Dec. last, tax paid 30 Apr.

52/190   **Peter Cocks, Gloucester, brought 52 indentures, 13 Nov. 1756[1]**

1756   29 Mar.   Partridge, Richard, premium £10
                        Cooke, Benjamin, staymaker, 7 yrs, tax paid 10 Apr.

        8 May   Barnes, Sarah, premium £20
                        Favell, Elizabeth, milliner, 7 yrs from 19 Jan., tax paid 12 June

        10 May   Hooper, Richard, premium £20
                        Cocks, Peter, surgeon etc., 7 yrs, tax paid 12 June

52/191   14 June   Ball, Joseph, premium £3 10s. 9d.
                        Weaver, Kirkham, collarmaker, 7 yrs, tax paid 10 July

        16 June   Benfield, Ann, premium £10
                        Twinning, Ann, mantuamaker, 7 yrs, tax paid 10 July

        19 July   Maverly, James, premium £21
                        Smith Martin, organist, 7 yrs, tax paid 20 Aug.

        23 Oct.   Baxter, Ann, premium £4
                        Lewis, Richard, pinmaker, 7 yrs, tax paid 28 Oct.

---

[1] 15 Sept. 1756: To leave Sir Thomas Rich's hospital and receive £10: George Stephens, John Window, Daniel Dix, Samuel Cripps, John Coleman, Thomas Cox. To receive £5 of Mr William Holliday's money: Samuel Harmitage, Thomas Jelf, Benjamin Freeman, John Drake To receive £4 of Mrs Sarah Browne's money: James Hulbert, John James, George Southern, John Powell Hall. GBR B3/10 f. 219v.

23 Sept. 1756: The £4 awarded to William Floyd deceased now awarded to William Drake. GBR B3/10 f. 222v.

8 Nov. 1756: To receive £5 of Mr William Holliday's money: John son of John Maverley and John son of Samuel Maverley. GBR B3/10 f. 226v.

IR 1/53

53/1   **Peter Cocks, Gloucester, brought 40 indentures, 5 May 1757**

1755   2 May   Long, Mary, premium £1 11s. 6d. (double duty)
                            Engley, Penelope, pastry cook, 7 yrs from 5 Apr., tax
                                paid 30 Oct. 1756

1756   15 Oct.   Longney, John, premium £10
                            Sparrow, James, cooper, 7 yrs, tax paid 8 Nov.

           13 Dec.   Burroughs, Benjamin, premium £60 (double duty)
                            Burroughs, Samuel, linendraper, 7 yrs, tax paid 8 Jan. 1757

           8 Nov.   Arch, John, premium £8 (double duty)
                            Bond, Thomas, baker, 7 yrs, tax paid 22 Apr. 1757

53/22   **Samuel Worrall, Bristol, brought 66 indentures, 20 Sept. 1757**

1757   16 May   Edwards, Thomas, premium £8
                            Jones, John, brightsmith, 7 yrs, tax paid 16 May

           13 July   Williams, Richard, premium £7
                            Bennett, Samuel, cabinetmaker, 7 yrs, tax paid 20 July

53/35   **Peter Cocks, Gloucester, brought 44 indentures, 7 Nov. 1757**[1]

1757   29 Apr.   Bridges, Edward, premium £18
                            Rodway, William, baker, 7 yrs, tax paid 28 June

           6 May   Braban, Newton, premium £10
                            Box, John, pinmaker, 7 yrs, tax paid 2 July

           31 May   Jones, John, premium £40
                            Wood, Richard, mercer, 5½ yrs from 24 June, tax paid 27 July

           6 June   Millington, Richard, premium £16 16s.
                            Wood, William, cooper, 7 yrs, tax paid 1 Aug.

           11 June   Chapman, George, premium £20
                            Bond, Richard, printer, 7 yrs, tax paid 4 Aug.

           13 June   Power, Thomas, premium £14
                            Wilton, Charles, pinmaker, 7 yrs, tax paid 9 Aug.

53/62   **Peter Cocks, Gloucester, brought 39 indentures, 13 May 1758**

1757   29 Apr.   Hill, Thomas, premium £15 (double duty)
                            Farren, William, butcher, 7 yrs, tax paid 6 Nov.

---

[1] 23 Sept. 1757: To leave Sir Thomas Rich's hospital and receive £10: James Ryder, Joseph Lewis, William Wheeler, John Drinkwater, Richard Price Kirby, William Ireland. GBR B3/10 f. 232.

30 Sept. 1757: To receive £5 of Mr William Holliday's money: George Phillipps, William Deane, George Bower, John Lewis. To receive £4 of Mrs Sarah Browne's money: Thomas Chapman, Daniel Pain, John Ingram, John Floyde. GBR B3/10 f. 234v.

53/63	1757	17 Nov.	Wells, John, premium £45 10s. Wells, John, wheelwright, 7 yrs, tax paid 6 Dec.
		5 Dec.	Vernon, Hawart, premium £2 Bonner, Benjamin, brazier, 7 yrs, tax paid 13 Dec.
		9 Dec.	Mayo, Francis, premium £31 Elton, Edward, grocer, 7 yrs, tax paid 16 Dec.
		10 Dec.	Jackson, Samuel, premium £10 Weare, Matthew, cordwainer, 7 yrs, tax paid 19 Dec.
	1758	1 Mar.	Cardwardiner, Edward, premium £15 Hornedge, William Gwinett, baker, 7 yrs, tax paid 1 Apr.
		24 Apr.	Adey, John, premium £12 Ward, Thomas, pinmaker, 7 yrs, tax paid 28 Apr.

53/89	**Peter Cocks, Gloucester, brought 43 indentures, 7 Nov. 1758**[1]		
	1758	29 Apr.	Jones, William, premium £10 Sadler, William, wheelwright, 7 yrs from 5 May, tax paid 29 May
		15 June	Marsh, John, premium £7 Wadely, Ambrose, baker, 7 yrs, tax paid 27 July
		15 Aug.	Jones, Samuel, premium £8 Wilton, Charles, pinmaker, 7 yrs, tax paid 15 Sept.
		10 Apr.	Grasing, Joshua, premium £12 12s. (double duty) Moore, Winston, butcher, 7 yrs, tax paid 25 Oct.

53/123	**Peter Cocks, Gloucester, brought 66 indentures, 5 May 1759**		
	1758	23 Oct.	George, William, premium £20 Wood, Joseph, baker, 7 yrs, tax paid 27 Nov.
		14 Nov.	Simpkins, Thomas, premium £8 Trinder, Richard, glover etc., 7 yrs, tax paid 22 Dec.
	1759	29 Jan.	Hale, William, premium £12 Hooper, Charles, butcher, tax paid 26 Feb.
		5 Feb.	Jones, Thomas, premium £8 8s. Hardwicke, John, tailor, tax paid 2 Mar.
53/124		2 Apr.	Spier, Thomas, premium £10 Ward, Thomas, pinmaker, tax paid 17 Apr.

---

[1] 18 Sept. 1758: To leave Sir Thomas Rich's hospital and receive £10: Henry Lye, William Stephens, Richard Fords, Joseph Cother, John Baker, Samuel Harris. GBR B3/10 f. 244.
    29 Sept. 1758: To receive £5 of Mr William Holliday's money: Thomas Matthews, Charles King, John Jones, John Mayor, John Savory. To receive £4 of Mrs Sarah Browne's money: Robert Morrison, John Jennings, Richard Hawker, John Grove. GBR B3/10 f. 247v.

53/142   **Samuel Worrall, Bristol, brought 42 indentures, 20 Sept. 1759**

    1758   23 Dec.   Bowles, Henry, premium £2 12s. 6d.
                               Tarr, David, cordwainer, 7 yrs, tax paid 8 Feb. 1759

    1759   30 Jan.   Hemmings, John, premium £5
                               Bryan, John, pig killer, 7 yrs, tax paid 19 Mar.

           15 Feb.   Martin, William, premium £10
                               Pearce, Richard, carpenter, 7 yrs, tax paid 26 Mar.

    1758   8 Nov.   Gaisford, James, premium £4 (double duty)
                               Hollaway, Thomas, barber & surgeon, 5 yrs, tax paid 7 Apr. 1759

    1759   24 Mar.   Burford, William, premium £5
                               England, Edward, stonemason & fisherman, 7 yrs, tax
                                 paid 2 June

53/156   **Peter Cocks, Gloucester, brought 60 indentures, 30 Sept. 1759**[1]

    1759   30 Apr.   Saunders, Thomas, premium £10
                               Hayward, William, grocer, 7 yrs, tax paid 30 May

53/157   16 July   Dunn, Thomas, premium £40
                               Bond, Richard, bookseller, 7 yrs, tax paid 14 Aug.

                    Sayes, Benjamin, premium £5
                               Way, Wadley, butcher, 7 yrs, tax paid 16 Aug.

           27 July   Stock, Thomas, premium £14
                               Swayne, Richard, butcher, 7 yrs, tax paid 23 Aug.

    1757   13 Sept.   Holland, John, premium £105 (double duty)
                               Wilson, Samuel, mercer, 7 yrs, tax paid 25 Aug. 1759

    1759   17 Aug.   Hill, William, premium £3
                               Comins, William, baker, 7 yrs, tax paid 28 Aug.

           15 Sept.   Joysey, James, premium £70 (double duty)
                               Ellis, Robert, ironmonger, 4 yrs, tax paid 10 Oct.

           19 Sept.   Thruppe, Elizabeth, premium £40
                               Wiltshire, Elizabeth, milliner, 4 yrs, tax paid 11 Oct.

           15 Oct.   Fletcher, Joseph, premium £12 12s.
                               Robinson, Giles, cooper, 7 yrs

53/189   **Peter Cocks, Gloucester, brought 58 indentures, 6 May 1760**

    1759   15 Sept.   Freeman, Ann, premium £25
                               Elms, William & Anne, milliners, 5 yrs from 25 July,
                               tax paid 25 Oct.

---

[1] 21 Sept. 1759: To leave Sir Thomas Rich's hospital and receive £10: John Phillipps, Thomas Guest, Samuel Hicks, Joseph Longden, George Crump, Thomas Cole. GBR B3/10 f. 259.

    27 Sept. 1759: To receive £5 of Mr William Holliday's money: Benjamin Elliott, Thomas Deane, Robert Phillipps, James Gardiner, William Grove, Stephen Reeves, Benjamin Price, William Hunman. To receive £4 of Mrs Sarah Browne's money: Charles King, Robert Bennett, William Jenkings, John Richards. GBR B3/10 f. 260v.

	1759	15 Oct.	Ursell, Francis, premium £14
			Powell, William, plumber etc., 7 yrs, tax paid 5 Nov.
		9 Nov.	Solloway, Robert, premium £20
			Cowcher, William, pinmaker, 7 yrs, tax paid 23 Nov.
		10 Nov.	Savage, Elizabeth, premium £15
			Lugg, Alice, mantuamaker, 7 yrs, tax paid 26 Nov.
53/190	1760	19 Feb.	Preston, John, premium £5
			Birt, Samuel, baker, 7 yrs, tax paid 17 Mar.
		17 Apr.	Darke, John, premium £52 10s. (double duty)
			Niblett, Samuel, grocer, 7 yrs, tax paid 23 Apr.

IR 1/54

54/19 **Peter Cocks, Gloucester, brought 44 indentures, 30 Oct. 1760**[1]

	1760	21 Apr.	Bonner, Richard, premium £5
			Read, Stephen, woolcomber, 7 yrs, tax paid 20 May
		2 June	Hartland, William, premium £30
			Jeffries, John, pinmaker, 7 yrs, tax paid 19 June
		7 July	Hale, Henry, premium £10
			Hooper, Charles, butcher, 7 yrs, tax paid 14 July
54/20		25 Aug.	Davis, Thomas, premium £30
			Curtis, Henry, grocer & tallowchandler, 7 yrs, tax paid 5 Sept.
		1 Sept.	Beavand, Richard, premium £12 12s.
			Ward, Thomas, pinmaker, 7 yrs, tax paid 15 Sept.
		15 Aug.	Dayvy, Margery, premium £15
			Grimes, Mary, mantuamaker, 7 yrs, tax paid 22 Sept.

54/47 **Peter Cocks, Gloucester, brought 60 indentures, 5 May 1761**

	1760	28 Apr.	Hyett, Samuel, premium £2 (double duty)
			Price, William, cordwainer, 7 yrs, tax paid 20 Oct.
54/48		15 Dec.	Price, John, premium £5
			Machen, William, cordwainer, 7 yrs, tax paid 19 Jan. 1761
		22 Dec.	Merry, John, premium £10
			Wintle, Henry, brushmaker, 7 yrs, tax paid 28 Jan. 1761
	1761	6 Feb.	Oakey, James, premium £8
			Davis, John, pinmaker, 7 yrs from 6 Jan., tax paid 20 Mar.
		10 Feb.	Dobbins, James, premium £6
			Carpenter, Joseph, carpenter, 7 yrs, tax paid 23 Mar.

[1] 5 Sept. 1760: To leave Sir Thomas Rich's hospital and receive £10: James Bingley, John Reeve, Robert Smith, James Clarke, William Swayne, Richard Houlton. GBR B3/10 f. 274v.

26 Sept. 1760: To receive £5 of Mr William Holliday's money: Christian Green, Thomas Grevile, William Mann, Dennis Hutchings, Charles Williams, John Stephens, Richard Bowers. To receive £4 of Mrs Sarah Browne's money: John Cooke, George Ruell, Charlemayne Dicks, James Smart. GBR B3/10 f. 276.

1761   12 Feb.   Dekins, Joseph, premium £6
                        Wadley, John, cordwainer, 7 yrs, tax paid 26 Mar.

        10 Apr.   Lawrence, John, premium £60 (double duty)
                        Webb, Richard, grocer etc., 7 yrs from 20 May 1760, tax
                            paid 20 Apr.

54/85   **Peter Cocks, Gloucester, brought 60 indentures, [Oct.] 1761**[1]

1761   27 Apr.   Cheesman, William, premium £6
                        Wintle, James, brushmaker, 7 yrs, tax paid 29 May

        25 May   Winney, William, premium £3 10s.
                        Darke, James, fisherman, 7 yrs, tax paid 6 July

                   Cole, James, premium £12 12s.
                        Branch, Thomas, tinplate worker, 7 yrs, tax paid 13 July

        11 June   Selwyn, Ann, premium £25
                        Elmes, William, milliner etc., 7 yrs, tax paid 30 July

        14 Oct.   Nuthall, Margaret, premium £20
                        Lugg, Alice, mantuamaker, 5 yrs, tax paid 15 Oct.

54/93   **Samuel Worrall, Bristol, brought 55 indentures, 17 Dec. 1761**

1756   29 Sept.   Gardner, John, premium 6d.
                        Mason, Thomas, tiler & plasterer, 7 yrs, tax paid 17 July 1761

54/119   **Samuel Worrall, Bristol, brought 40 indentures, 23 March 1762**

1761   8 Sept.   Fulk, Lawrence, premium £4
                        Frainder, Samuel, cordwainer, 7 yrs, tax paid 21 Sept.

54/123   **Peter Cocks, Gloucester, brought 49 indentures, 25 Apr. 1762**

1761   10 Oct.   Cowles, Thomas, premium £5
                        Bryan, Joseph and John his son, masons, 7 yrs, tax paid 26 Nov.

        30 Nov.   Bennett, Thomas, premium £15 15s.
                        Worrall, Mary, pinmaker, 7 yrs from 28 Oct., tax paid 10
                            Jan. 1762

1762   22 Jan.   Salcomb, William, premium £12
                        Jennings, Michael and Mary his wife, butcher, 7 yrs from
                            1 Jan., tax paid 2 Feb.

[1] 11 Sept. 1761: To leave Sir Thomas Rich's hospital and receive £10: Seth Haynes, Daniel Jackson, John Hook, John Ireland, Pettat Gardiner, James Lander. GBR B3/11 f. 10v.

25 Sept. 1761: To receive £5 of Mr William Holliday's money: Samuel Wilkes, Henry Bradley, Benjamin Matthews, Charles Jones, Thomas Smart, William Gunn, Richard Jones, Thomas Gardiner. To receive £4 of Mrs Sarah Browne's money: William Walker, Thomas Snow, John Beale, Henry Harris. GBR B3/11 f. 12.

1762   15 Mar.   Stephens, Merrott, premium £100 (double duty)
                  Wood, Richard & Elizabeth his wife, mercer, 7 yrs,
                     tax paid 22 Mar.

       22 Mar.   Burrows, John, premium £10 10s.
                  Viner, William & Deborah, grocer, 7 yrs, tax paid 25 Mar.

       26 Mar.   Wood, John, premium £10
                  Rogers, John & Mary his wife, baker, 7 yrs from 25 Jan.,
                     tax paid 30 Mar.

1758   17 July   Cole, Charles, premium £10 (double duty)
                  Sparrow, James and Elizabeth his wife, cooper, 7 yrs
                     from 17 July 1758, tax paid 10 Apr. 1762

54/162   **Peter Cocks, Gloucester, brought 57 indentures, 2 Nov. 1762**[1]

1762   3 May   Plaistead, Thomas, premium £12 12s.
                  Farren, William, butcher, 7 yrs, tax paid 28 May

       4 May   Breatherton, James, premium £15
                  Jenning, John, whitesmith, 7 yrs, tax paid 7 June

       5 July   Taylor, Charles, premium £8
                  Branch, Thomas, tinplate worker, 5 yrs, tax paid 5 Aug.

       19 July   Ladbrook, Mathew, premium £5
                  Maverley, James, barber, 7 yrs, tax paid 23 Aug.

       31 July   Smith, Richard, premium £8
                  Middleton, James, woolcomber, 7 yrs, tax paid 28 Aug.

54/204   **Peter Cocks, Gloucester, brought 47 indentures, 3 May 1763**

1762   23 Aug.   Wilse, John, premium £31 10s.
                  Cook, Barnard, grocer, 7 yrs, tax paid 20 Oct.

54/205 1763   26 Feb.   While, Daniel, premium £10
                  Roberts, Samuel, brushmaker, 7 yrs, tax paid 8 Mar.

       28 Feb.   Wetmore, Anne, premium £40
                  Willshire, Elizabeth, milliner, 4 yrs, tax paid 31 Mar.

1762   17 Oct.   Rayer, Moses, premium £30 (double duty)
                  Curtis, Henry, grocer, 7 yrs, tax paid 27 Apr. 1763

---

[1] 22 Sept. 1762: To receive £5 of Mr William Holliday's money: Isaac Kirby, James Ireland, John Bourn, William King. To receive £4 of Mrs Sarah Browne's money: Thomas Wood, Daniel Floyd, Richard Reade, John Paul. GBR B3/11 f. 25.
    30 Sept. 1762: To leave Sir Thomas Rich's hospital and receive £10: Thomas Wilkins, Richard Heath, Philip Bossley, John Latham, Charles Barrett, William Powell. GBR B3/11 f. 26v.

IR 1/55

55/11   **Peter Cocks, Gloucester, brought 60 indentures, 3 Nov. 1763**[1]

    1763   25 Mar.   Field, Thomas, premium £36 15s.
                       Smith, Martin, organist, 7 yrs, tax paid 30 Apr.

          10 June   Woore, John, premium £80 (double duty)
                       Wood, Richard, mercer, 7 yrs, tax paid 29 July

          1 July   Jones, John, premium £5
                       Wilton, Charles, pinmaker, 7 yrs, tax paid 13 Aug.

          23 July   Witts, George, premium £8
                       Cheslin, William, cordwainer, 7 yrs, tax paid 23 Aug.

55/12   29 Aug.   Bennett, Isaac, premium £8 8s
                       Bennett, Joseph, collarmaker, 7 yrs, tax paid 19 Sept.

          12 Sept. Fletcher, Charles, premium £2
                       Ward, William, pinmaker, 7 yrs, tax paid 28 Sept.

          17 Sept. Dobbes, Nicholas, premium £80 (double duty)
                       Rogers, William, apothecary, 5 yrs, tax paid 29 Sept.

          14 Oct.   Roberts, Edward, premium £10
                       Branch, Thomas, tinplate worker, 7 yrs, tax paid 27 Oct.

55/12   **Joshua Green, Worcester, brought 92 indentures, 17 Apr. 1764**

    1764   20 Mar.   Millward, John, premium £30
                       Crump, John, cabinetmaker, 7 yrs, tax paid 24 Jan.

55/44   **Peter Cocks, Gloucester, brought 48 indentures, 3 May 1764**

    1763   2 Dec.   Ricketts, John, premium £10 10s.
                       Lovett, James, barber, 7 yrs, tax paid 7 Jan. 1764

    1764   20 Jan.   Selwyn, John, premium £4
                       Washborne, Nathaniel, baker, 7 yrs, tax paid 3 Mar.

          6 Feb.   Mirrell, Charles premium £10
                       Hooper, Charles, butcher, 7 yrs, tax paid 22 Mar.

55/82   **Samuel Worrall, Bristol, brought 43 indentures, 9 Oct. 1764**

    1764   23 Apr.   Pittman, John, premium £4 4s
                       Motby, George, cordwainer, 7 yrs, tax paid 2 May

---

[1] 23 Sept. 1763: To leave Sir Thomas Rich's hospital and receive £10: Wintour Harris, Giles King, John Hutchings, John Stephens, John Lewis, Thomas Organ. GBR B3/11 f. 40.

   9 Sept. 1763: To receive £5 of Mr William Holliday's money: James Bower, Joseph Williams, William Gardiner, William Cooke, Charles Bradgate, William Jeynes, Edward Clark. To receive £4 of Mrs Sarah Browne's money: Edward Young, Nathaniel Tarling, Charles Maisey, John Selwyn. GBR B3/11 f. 41v.

1764   5 Mar.   Hannery, George, premium £10 (double duty)
                  Naish, John of Bell Inn, Gloucester, blacksmith, 7 yrs, tax
                     paid 17 May

        5 Apr.   Higheram, Jacob, premium £40
                  Higgs, Thomas, currier, 7 yrs, tax paid 30 May

55/85 **Peter Cocks, Gloucester, brought 71 indentures, 30 Oct. 1764**[1]

1764   1 May   White, Elizabeth, premium £20
                  Lugg, Alice, mantuamaker, 5 yrs, tax paid 20 June

        14 May   Caruthers, John, premium £63 (double duty)
                  Smith, Robert, mercer, 7 yrs, tax paid 22 June

        18 May   Derrett, John, premium £7 17s. 6d.
                  Watts, Thomas, butcher, 7 yrs, tax paid 2 July

        23 May   Rudge, Anne, premium £30
                  Viner, Sarah, milliner, 5 yrs, tax paid 10 July

        16 June   Sutton, John, premium £43
                  Poulson, James of St Mary's, Barton Street, baker, 7 yrs,
                     tax paid 28 July

        1 July   Wells, Hannah, premium £12
                  Twining, Anne, mantuamaker, 4 yrs, tax paid 22 Aug.

        10 July   Ricketts, Edward, premium £14
                  Bennett, Joseph, collarmaker, 7 yrs, tax paid 27 Aug.

55/86 20 July Woodly, Charles, premium £10
                  Cox, Richard, barber & perukemaker, 7 yrs, tax paid 4 Sept.

        30 July   Nuthall, Nathaniel, premium £30
                  South Hall, John, tinplate worker, 7 yrs, tax paid 12 Sept.

        19 Feb.   Bourrough, Thomas, premium £15
                  Fletcher, Ralph, baker, 7 yrs, tax paid 14 Sept.

                  Preston, John, premium £35
                  Birt, Samuel of Barton Street, baker, 7 yrs, tax paid 14 Sept.

        28 May   Hawkins, Joseph, premium £14 14s
                  Webb, John, butcher, 7 yrs, tax paid 15 Sept.

        20 Aug.   Addis, Philip, premium £12
                  Maddocks, Cartwright, baker, 7 yrs, tax paid 29 Sept.

55/117 **Peter Cocks, Gloucester, brought 55 indentures, 30 Apr. 1765**

1764   2 Nov.   Biddle, Nathaniel, premium £40
                  Viner, William, grocer, 7 yrs, tax paid 4 Dec.

[1] 21 Sept. 1764: To leave Sir Thomas Rich's hospital and receive £10: Edmund Pembruge, Thomas Webley, Samuel Daniel, William Draper, William Dean, Richard Collerick. GBR B3/11 f. 52v.

27 Sept. 1764: To receive £5 of Mr William Holliday's money: Samuel Heath, Thomas Stroud, James Wilks, John Hutchings, Thomas Leach. To receive £4 of Mrs Sarah Browne's money: Robert White, John Beadle, William Glover, Joseph Hodges Hawker. GBR B3/11 f. 54.

	1764	19 Nov.	Reeves, Joseph, premium £10 Wood, William, cooper, 7 yrs, tax paid 8 Dec.
	1765	24 Jan.	Young, Thomas, premium £10 Wheatstone, John, shoemaker, 7 yrs, tax paid 28 Feb.
		8 Feb.	Draper, Francis premium £10 Crump, Richard upholder, 7 yrs, tax paid 15 Mar.
		1 Mar.	Chamberlayne, Joseph, premium £12 Hickman, Benjamin, cordwainer, 8 yrs, tax paid 25 Mar.
		19 Mar.	Weaver, Thomas, premium £13 15s. Gray, John, attorney, 7 yrs, tax paid 8 Apr.
		29 Mar.	Gammond, William, premium £15 Horsman, Roger, baker, 7 yrs, tax paid 16 Apr.
55/118		24 May	Abell, Thomas, premium £30 Marcutt, William, joiner, 7 yrs, tax paid 3 June

55/161 **Peter Cocks, Gloucester, brought 52 indentures, 2 Nov. 1765**

	1760	28 Apr.	Brown, James, premium £10 10s. (double duty) Holder, Joseph, tailor, 7 yrs, tax paid 1 Aug. 1765
	1765	8 July	Hook, James, premium £16 Maddocks, Cartwright, baker, 7 yrs, tax paid 16 Aug.
		13 July	Waite, John, premium £35 Gunn, Thomas of St Margaret's, Gloucester, cordwainer, 7 yrs, tax paid 2 Sept.
			Hollings, William, premium £30 Curtis, Henry, grocer etc., 7 yrs, tax paid 3 Sept.
		15 July	Cox, John, premium £150 (double duty) Browne, Richard, surgeon etc., 4 yrs, tax paid 4 Sept.
		2 Aug.	Lawrence, Henry, premium £30 Taylor, Ellis, baker, 7 yrs, tax paid 21 Sept. [*see 4/1 above*]
	1762	30 Aug.	Carruthers, James, premium £6 (double duty) Barther, John of Barton Street, tailor, 7 yrs, tax paid 4 Nov. 1765

55/193 **Peter Cocks, Gloucester, brought 52 indentures, 30 Apr. 1766**

	1765	1 Nov.	Maverly, Charles, premium £16 Trickey, Edward, basketmaker, 7 yrs, tax paid 7 Nov.
		18 Nov.	Court, John, premium £10 Ireland, William, cooper, 7 yrs, tax paid 24 Dec.
	1756	20 Aug.	Mason, Samuel, premium £2 (double duty) Weaver, Richard, blacksmith, 7 yrs, tax paid 2 Jan. 1766
55/194	1766	1 Feb.	Harrison, Mary, premium £15 15s. Barton, Elizabeth, mantuamaker, 4 yrs, tax paid 20 Feb.
		7 Mar.	Millton, Samuel, premium £10 10s. Workman, Anthony, butcher, 7 yrs, tax paid 18 Mar.

NOTE

All index references are to the *page numbers of the MS* given in the first column of text, except for those in roman numerals, which are to pages in the Introduction.

INDEX OF PERSONS

Cullurne, Jas, **3**/646; John, **3**/646; Wm, **51**/4*n*

Curtis, Geo, **3**/718; **4**/28, 28*n*; Hen, **3**/733; **51**/264; **54**/20, 205; **55**/161; Ric, **3**/501, 733; Wm, **3**/501, 718

Dadd, Jas, **4**/6, 6*n*; Nat, **4**/7, Rob, **4**/2*n*, 31*n*; Wm, **4**/10*n*, 11, 35; **50**/280*n*

Dance, Thos, **4**/14

Dancey (Dancy), Anne, **3**/661, 711; John, **3**/533; Jos, **3**/711; Wm, **3**/533, 661, 700*n*, 711*

Dangerfield, Thos, **4**/28

Daniel (Daniell), Geo, **4**/32, 38; Jas, **4**/16, 16*n*, 38*n**; Sam, **55**/85*n*; Thos, **4**/18*n*, 37*n*; Wm, **4**/22*n*, 37*n*

Darby, Anne, **3**/661, 711; Jos, **3**/651; Sam, **3**/651, 661, 711

Dark (Darke), Edw, **4**/15; Hen, **4**/38*n**, Isaac, **3**/490; Jas, **4**/15, 15*n*, 34*n*, 36*; **54**/85; John, **3**/624*; **53**/190; Jos, **3**/661*n*, 670; Mary, **3**/484, 529, 587, 639; Ric **3**/484, 490, 529, 587, 628*n*, 639*; Wm, **3**/670; **4**/32, 32*n*

Davies (Davis, Devis), Anne, **4**/8, 20; Benj, **4**/27*n*; Chas, **4**/ 34*n*, 38*n**; Eliz, **3**/415, 735, 738; Hannah, **3**/602; Hen, **3**/417, 424, 500, 559*n*, 568*, 643, 653*, 656*, 743; **4**/8, 12, 14, 20; **51**/99*n*; Howell, **3**/530; Jas, **4**/14*n*; **50**/280*n*; Joan, **3**/550, 608; John, **3**/418, 444, 478*, 505, 517, 639, 643*n*, 653, 656, 735, 738, 747*; **4**/2, 6*n*, 23, 27, 33, 39*n**; **50**/259, 280*n*; **54**/48; Jon, **3**/415; Jos, **3**/454*n*, 475*; Marg, **3**/418, 444, 517; Mary, **3**/417, 424, 475, 500, 568, 643, 653, 656; Moses, **3**/523*n*, 530, 602; Ric, **3**/503*; **4**/29*n*, 30; Rob, **3**/505, 747; **4**/14*n*, 34*n*; Sam, **3**/402; Sarah, **3**/747; Thos, **3**/544*n*, 560*, 700*n*; **4**/22*n*, 23; **51**/264*n*; **54**/20; Wm **4**/1*n*, 9*n*, 18*n*; —, **4**/34*n*

Dawes (Daw, Dawe, Daws), Chas, **4**/39*n**; Eleazer, **3**/570, 628*n*, 637*; Godfrey, **51**/285; Wm, **3**/552*n*, 570; **51**/5

Day, Hen, **3**/712; Rob, **3**/712; Thos, **4**/29*n*

Dayvy, Margery, **54**/20

Deane, Chas, **3**/732*n*; Geo, **3**/635*n*, 649, 693*n*, 706; **4**/14*n*; Joanna, **4**/8; Thos, **3**/478, 649; **53**/156*n*; Wm, **3**/400*n*, 478, 508*, 706*; **4**/3, 8, 13*n*, 31*n*; **53**/35*n*; **55**/85*n*; *and see* A'Deane

Defoe, Dan, p. xi

Dekins, Jos, **54**/48

Denman, Chas, **4**/12

Derrett, John, **4**/13, 14, 16*n*; **55**/85

Devis *see* Davis

Dew, Dan, **3**/748; Thos, **3**/737*, 748

Dickes (Dicke, Dicks, Dike, Dix, Dykes), Benj, **4**/14n; Charlemagne, **54**/19*n*; Dan, **3**/446; **4**/4*n*; **52**/190*n*; Hen, **4**/38*n*; John, **4**/1*n*, 2, 18*n*, 37*n*; **50**/259*n*; Jos, **4**/28, 28*n*; Ric, **3**/621*n*, 630; **4**/25*n*; Thos, **3**/446, 654*n*, 661*; **4**/7*n*, 19, 37*n*; **50**/280*n*, 281*; Tim, **3**/738*n*; Wm, **3**/630, 745*n*, 751*; **4**/4*n*, 14*n*

Diddamus, Wm John, **4**/31

Dike *see* Dickes

Dimocke *see* Dymocke

Dix *see* Dickes

Dobbes, Nic, **55**/12; Wm, **4**/22

Dobbins, Geo, **4**/26*n*; Jas, **54**/48; John, **4**/36

Dobles, Jas, **4**/4

Dobson, Thos, **4**/5

Dodd, Jas, **4**/5*n*

Doggett, Jon, **3**/732*n*

Dole, Ric, **4**/12, 18

Dolloman (Doleman), Geo, **3**/458; Thos, **3**/458

Done *see* Dunn

Dorsett, Wm, p. xv; **4**/3

Dovey, Wm, **4**/37*n*

Dowding, Geo, **3**/437; John, **3**/437

Dowdy, Eleanor, **3**/542, 563; Geo, **3**/542, 563, 637, 679; Rebecca, **3**/637

Dowell *see* Dowle

Dower, Ric, **3**/512*

Dowlas, Thos, **3**/590; Wm, **3**/590

Dowle (Dowell), Anne, **3**/430; Jas, **4**/14*n*; Job, **3**/430, 586; John, **3**/426*, 586; Wm, **4**/10*n*, 11

Drake, Hen, **3**/632*, 638; John, **52**/190*n*; Wm, **3**/638; **52**/190*n*

Draper, Anne, **3**/461, 538; Francis, **55**/117; Grace, **3**/571, 590, 620, 634, 638, 668, 700, 739, 750; Hen, **3**/461, 538; Mary, **3**/749; Ric, **3**/455, 571, 590, 620, 634, 638, 668*, 700, 739, 750; **4**/29; Thos, **3**/455, 461*; **4**/7, 12; Wm, **3**/661*n*, 668, 749; **4**/1; **55**/85*n*

Draysey, Geo, **4**/ 38*n**

Drew, Hannah, **3**/406, 455, 506, 512, 548, 567; John, **3**/523; Sarah, **3**/707, 737; Thos,

Faucks (Fauckes, Faukes), Eliz, **4**/3; Mary, **4**/9, 13; Rob, **4**/9; Thos, **3**/618; **50**/281; Wm, **3**/618

Faville, John, **4**/31*n*, 37*n*; Wm, **4**/30*n*

Feilder *see* Fielder

Felton (Phelton), Jos, **3**/581*; Ric, **3**/732; Wm, **3**/726*n*, 732

Fereby (Ferreby), Dan, **3**/709*n*, 713; Eliz, **3**/713; John, **3**/496*, 713*; Sarah, **3**/496

Fewster, John, **4**/34

Fewterell (Fewtrell, Phewterell), Geo, **3**/602; Hen, **3**/595*n*, 602; Ric, **3**/436*

Fido, Jas, **3**/483; Ric, **3**/483

Field, Anne, **3**/715; John, **3**/701*; John Print, **4**/27; Jos, **4**/20; Sam, **3**/452*, 715; Thos, **3**/738; **4**/32; **55**/11; Wm, **3**/732*n*, 738; **4**/39*n**

Fielder (Feilder, Filder), Benj, **3**/415; Geo, **3**/415*, 513, 524; Sarah, **3**/415, 513, 524

Fifield, Cornelius, p. xxv; **3**/704; Edw, **4**/3; Wm, p. xxv; **3**/704

Filder *see* Fielder

Finch, Ric, **3**/516

Fisher, Benj, **52**/151; Chris, **4**/33*n*, 34; Clement, **3**/612*; Jas, **3**/448; **4**/34*n*; John, **3**/448; Ric, **3**/479; Thos, **3**/479; **4**/28*n*

Fitche, Jas, **3**/732*n*

Fitchew, Eleanor, **3**/659, 714; Jas, **3**/741; Josiah, **3**/407, 659, 709*n*, 714*, 741; Thos, **3**/407, 714

Fleming, John Reece, **4**/27*n*, 28

Fletcher, Adam, **3**/654*n*, 662; Chas, **3**/727; **4**/1*n*; **55**/12; Edw, **3**/489, 557, 616; Eliz, **3**/452; Hannah, **3**/604; Jas, **4**/31*n*; John, **3**/611, 662*, 709*n*, 717*, 727; **4**/12; Jos, **3**/716; **53**/157; Lewis, **4**/12; Mary, **3**/ 611, 662, 685, 723; Ralph, **4**/5*, 11; **50**/217; **55**/86; Ralph, mayor, **4**/36, 39; Ric, **3**/604; Rob, **3**/489; Sarah, **3**/421, 493, 557, 616; **4**/11; Thos, **3**/421, 493, 604*, 685, 723; **50**/259; **51**/4; Wm, **3**/452, 700*; **4**/6, 22*n*; **50**/217

Flower, Wm, **4**/37*n*

Floyd (Floyde), Dan, **54**/162*n*; John, **53**/35*n*; Wm, **4**/10, 25*n*; **52**/118*n**, 190*n*

Fluck, Giles, **3**/596; Wm, **3**/596

Ford (Fords), Anne, **3**/423, 746; Hen, **4**/1*n*, 2; Jas, **52**/118*n*; John, **3**/599, 742*n*, 746; Ric, **53**/123*n*; Thos, **3**/423*; Wm **3**/599, 746*; **4**/2, 16

Forster, Thos, **4**/11

Fowle, Jos, **3**/542; Sam, **3**/542

Fowler, Giles, **3**/715; **51**/228; Sarah, **3**/401; Thos, **4**/6; Wm, **3**/401

Fowles, Jos, **3**/572*

Fownes, Gabriel, **3**/664; Godfrey, **3**/664*; Mary, **3**/664; Jos, **3**/656, 700, 742*n*, 749*; Sarah, **3**/656; Susannah, **3**/700

Fox, Edw, **3**/690*

Frainder, Sam, **54**/119

Fream (Freame), Eliz, **3**/548, 562, 606; Hannah, **3**/745; Jas, **4**/16, 16*n*; John, **3**/548*, 562, 745*; **4**/15, 15*n*; Jos, **4**/25*n*; Thos, **4**/12*n*, 13; Wm, **3**/502*n*, 606, 737*n*, 745; **4**/36*n*

Freath, John, **51**/285

Freeman (Freaman), Anne, **53**/189; Benj, **3**/658, 706; **4**/11*n*, 17; **52**/190*n*; Dan, **4**/16*n*, 17; **50**/280*n*; Frances, **3**/406, 452, 515, 550, 606, 649, 662; Hen, **50**/280*n*; Jas, **3**/502*n*, 514; John, **4**/28*n*; Jos, **3**/502*n*; **4**/31*n*; Penelope, **3**/687; Rob, **3**/406, 452, 515, 550, 602*n*, 606*, 649, 662, 687; Thos, **3**/425, 735*; **4**/20*n*; Tobias, **3**/514; Wm, **4**/5

Friend, Edw, **4**/7; Thos, p. xv; **4**/1

Fryer, John, **3**/453*; **4**/13*n*; Matt, **4**/13; Thos, **3**/607*n*, 613; Wm, **3**/613

Fulk, Lawr, **54**/119

Fuller, Hen, **3**/599; **4**/16*n*; John **3**/580, 599; Thos, **3**/580

Furley, Clement, **3**/645, 664; Hen, **3**/645, 664

Furney, Jas, **3**/518, 572*; Jas, mayor, **3**/544, 587, 595; Sarah, **3**/518, 572; Wm, **3**/572

Gaisford, Jas, **53**/142

Gale, Rob, **51**/5; Thos, **4**/3, 22; **51**/5

Gamblin, John, **4**/34

Gammond, John, **3**/403, 497; Sarah, **3**/403, 497; Wm, **55**/117

Gann, Thos, **52**/34*n*

Gardener, (Gardiner, Gardner), Adam, **4**/17, 29*n*; Andrew, **3**/581*, 686, 733*, 750; Ant, **3**/531, 564, 615, 729, 733; Chas, **4**/25*n*; **50**/280*n*; Cornelius, **3**/729; **50**/93; Edm, **4**/20*n*; Edw, **4**/29*n*; **52**/34; Edw Timothy Wilshire, **4**/38; Eliz, **3**/726; **4**/10, 12, 18, 31; Geo, **4**/32*n*; Hannah, **3**/410, 733; Jas, **3**/726*n*, 733; **4**/19*n*, 37*n*; **53**/156*n*; John, **3**/726, 729, 750; **4**/2*n*, 21*n*, 23, 25*n*, 28*n*, 31, 38; **52**/118*n*; **54**/93; Jos,

4/14*n*; Sarah, 3/511; Wm, 3/440; —, 3/669*n*

Grimes, Mary, 54/20

Grimmett (Grymett), Eliz, 3/670, 709, 735; John, 3/595, 670, 709, 735; Thos, 3/595

Grindall, John, 3/471*; —, 3/454*n*

Groutage, Jos, 4/21

Grove (Groves), Hannah, 3/583; John, 3/636; 50/280*n*; 53/89*n*; Sam, 3/583, 636*; 50/280*n*; Wm, 53/156*n*

Grymett *see* Grimmett

Guest, Jacob, 3/705, 751; Jane, 3/751; John, 3/705; Thos, 53/156*n*

Guilding, Wm, 4/20

Guise, Sir Berkeley John, mayor, 4/31; Sir John, mayor, 4/15; Sir Wm, mayor, 4/38

Gulliford, Geo, 3/544; Thos, 3/544

Gulliver, John, 3/714*n*

Gun *see* Gunn

Gundimore, Anne, 3/435; Jos; 3/435; Tobias, 3/435; Walt, 3/435

Gunn (Gun), Arthur, 3/413; Benj, 4/17*n*; Jas, p. xxii; 3/413, 506*, 643*n*, 652*, 667*; 4/10*n*, 17*n*; 51/197*n*; Jos, 4/13*n*, 20–1; Marg, 3/652; Sam, 3/652; Thos, 4/11*n*, 24, 28, 32, 38; 55/161; Wm, 4/14*n*; 54/85*n*

Gunter, Jas, 3/506*

Gurner, Jas, 3/733; John, 3/733

Gurney, Benj, 4/15*n*; John, 4/16*n*, 36; Wm, 4/18*n*

Gustavus, Howell, 4/36

Gutheridge *see* Gotheridge

Gwilliam (Gwillim), John, 3/406; Steph, 4/19*n*, 21

Gwinet (Gwynett), Geo, 3/405*, 683*

Gyde, Thos, 51/100*

Gyles *see* Giles

Gythens (Gyttens), Chas, 3/577; Geo, 3/577, 584; Ric, 3/584

Hague, Hester, 3/427; Jas, 3/427

Haines *see* Haynes

Hale (Hales, Hayle), Abraham, 3/487*n*, 497; Anne, 3/555, 594, 689; 4/15; Eliz, 3/520, 554; Ephraim, 4/5; Hen, 54/19; Jas, 4/13*n*; 51/141; Jesse, 3/657; 4/1*n*; John, 3/497, 516, 555, 594, 642, 689*; Jos, 3/454*n*, 531*, 533, 570, 613, 709, 737*; Marg, 3/613, 709, 737; Mary, 3/601, 615, 657, 660, 725; Ric, 3/651, 743; 4/20; Rob,

3/651; Sampson, 3/689; 51/48; Sam, 3/749*n*; Sarah, 3/642; Thos, 3/532*n*, 533, 601, 615, 660, 693*n*, 709*; Wm, 3/454*n*, 478*, 520, 554, 589*, 725, 732*n*, 737; 4/13*n*, 31; 53/123

Halford, Benj, 3/742*n*, Edw, 3/422*; John, 3/422, 478, 548; Marg, 3/478, 548; Phil, 3/660; Thos, 3/693*n*

Hall, Geo, 3/705; John, 3/412, 454, 553, 616; 4/20*n*, 21; John Powell, 52/190*n*; Ric, 3/454; 4/34*n*; Sam, 3/622; Sarah, 3/553; Steph, 4/2, 9, 15; Thos, 3/614*n*, 622; 4/4*n*; Wm, 3/705; 51/99*n*

Halliday *see* Holliday

Halling, John, 3/514*n*, 522; Walt, 3/522; Wm, 3/504*

Ham, Giles, 3/532*n*; Wm, 3/411*n*, 429*

Hambling (Hamblin, Hamlin), Chas, 4/16*n*; Francis, 3/621*; Wm 4/14*n*; Wm Andrew, 4/13*n*

Hamlett, Malachiah, 3/717; Thos, 3/717

Hamlin *see* Hambling

Hammond, Rob, 3/728; Thos, 3/728; 4/2*n*

Hampton, John, 3/543, 595, 622; Peter, 3/595; Thos, 3/532*n*, 543; Wm, 3/614*n*, 622

Hanckes, Wm, 3/595*n*

Hankins, John, 3/563; Wm, 3/563

Hanman, Ansel, 4/6*n*; Jas, 4/2*n*, 3; John, 4/28; Thos, 4/32

Hannery, Geo, 55/82

Hannis, Anne, 3/424; Chas, 3/559*n*, 568*; Honour, 3/679; Thos, 3/424, 679*

Harbert *see* Herbert

Harding, John, 3/446, 500; 50/193*n*; Marg, 3/689; Ric, 3/607*, 689, 726*n*; Rob, 3/446; Thos, 3/487*n*, 500; Wm, 50/259, 280*n*

Hardwicke (Hardwick), Chas, 53/123; Esther, 3/484; John, 3/675; Nat, 3/484; Thos, 3/436*; Walt, (*alias* Mason), 3/545; Wm, 4/18; —, 3/675

Hare, Benj, 3/732*n*, 738; 4/6*n*; Edw, 3/452; John, 3/681, 738; 4/6*n*; Rob, 4/9*n*, 10*n*; Roger, 3/452; Wm, 3/669*n*, 681

Harmer, John, 3/656; Ric, 3/656

Harmitage *see* Armitage,

Harper, Chas, 52/66; Jas, 4/1*n*, 2, 11*n*; John, 4/11

Harris, Anne, 3/630; Benj, 3/593; David, 3/453; Edw, 3/484; Edwin, 4/37*n*; Eliz,

3/438, 495, 590, 715, 740; Frederick,
4/39; Gabriel, mayor, 3/614, 700; Grace,
50/141; Hannah, 3/558, 650; Hen, 3/621*n*,
630*, 651, 654*n*; 4/35*n*; 54/85*n*; Hester,
3/422, 472, 542, 546; Jas, 3/540;
Jeremiah, 3/583; John, 3/495, 590, 597,
599*, 608, 651, 667, 749*; 4/13*n*, 17,
31*n*, 32, 37*n*; Jos 3/411*n*, 438*, 472, 540;
Kath, 3/453; Marg, 50/141; Mary, 55/194;
Nat, 3/558, 583*, 650; 4/4, 4*n*; Ric, p. xix;
3/422, 472, 503, 542, 546, 667, 737; Sam,
3/599, 682, 715, 730, 740; 4/18*n*, 37*n*;
50/259*n*; 53/123*n*; Sarah, 3/651; Thos,
3/472, 730, 732*n*, 737; 4/4*n*, 5, 20, 38*n*;
Walt, 3/484; Wm, 3/503, 593, 597; 4/7*n*,
11*n*, 15, 37*n*; Wm Hen, 3/630; Wintour,
3/651; 4/16*n*; 50/217*; 55/11*n*
Harrison, Geo, 50/217*; Eliz, 3/491;
  Martha, 3/670; Thos, 3/491, 605*, 670
Hart, David, 4/20*n*
Hartfield, Wm, 51/264
Hartland, Benj, 4/32*n*; Chas, 4/17, 21; Jas,
  4/4, 4*n*, 27*n*, 28; John, 3/411*n*, 457, 744;
  4/3*n*, 15*n*, 24*n*, 25; Mary, 3/428; Thos,
  3/428*, 744, 749*n*; 4/4, 7*n*; Wm, 3/411*n*,
  428, 457; 4/11n; 54/19; Wm (*alias* Jones),
  3/608
Haskins, John, 4/2; Jos, 52/102
Hassele, Sam, 51/99*n*
Hathaway (Hathway), John, 3/661*n*, 673,
  680*; 4/14; Ric, 3/454*n*, 673; 4/3; Thos,
  3/421; Wm, 3/401*, 421; 51/197*n*
Hatton, John, 3/667; Wm, p. xvii*; 3/661*n*,
  667; 4/1*n*, 2*, 15, 24
Havard, John, 3/603; Wm, 3/603
Haviland, Ric, 4/8; Wm, 4/13
Hawker, Edw, 3/493; Jos Hodges, 55/85*n*;
  Ric, 53/89*n*; Sam, 3/493
Hawkes, Jas, 4/4*n*; John, 3/411*n*; Jos,
  3/745*; Rob, 4/1, 23*n*
Hawkins, Chas, 4/3; Jas, 3/444*; Jeremiah,
  3/546, 619, 668; John, 3/574, 635, 742*n*,
  746*; Jos, 55/86; Mary, 3/635; Sam,
  3/574, 603; Thos, 3/546, 603
Hayes, Alice, 3/501, 514; Chris, 3/424*n*,
  439*, 519; Eliz, 3/521, 523, 669; Hen,
  3/501, 514; John, 3/411, 521, 607*n*, 614;
  50/259; Josiah, 3/523, 614, 669*; Marg,
  3/439, 519; Sarah, 3/504, 512, 613, 686,
  690, 703; Wm, 3/411, 504, 512, 613,
  661*n*, 669, 686, 690, 703

Hayford, Jas Shatford, 51/48; John, 3/561*;
  50/259*n*; Mary, 51/197
Hayle *see* Hale
Hayling (Haylings), Thos, 4/34*n*; Wm,
  4/20*n*, 21
Haynes (Haines, Hayns), Chas, 4/31, 31*n*;
  Christian, 3/721, 722; Edw, 3/516, 520,
  552*n*, 560*, 568*n*, 576; Frances, 3/614;
  Geo, 4/33; Hen, 3/549, 624*; Jas, 4/22,
  37*n*; John, 3/414, 576, 654*n*, 671, 721–2;
  Jos, 3/535; Mary, 3/516, 520, 556; Nat,
  3/535; Peter, 3/528, 558, 623*; Phoebe,
  3/550; Sam, 3/535*; Sarah, 3/740, 751;
  51/285; Seth, 54/85*n*; Susannah, 3/528,
  558, 623; Thos, 3/414, 556, 671; 4/29*,
  35*n*; Wm, 3/442*, 549–50, 614, 643*n*,
  740, 751; 4/29; 50/93
Hayward, Anne, 3/437, 620; Apphia, 3/552;
  Clement, 3/560; Edw, 3/424*n*, 437*, 509,
  552*, 647; Eliz, 3/580; Hannah, 3/492,
  546, 598; Jeremiah, 3/580*; John, 3/427,
  514*n*, 590; John, mayor, 3/714; Sam,
  3/427, 492, 546, 560, 598; Sam, mayor,
  3/538; Sarah, 3/744; Thos, 3/532*n*, 552,
  552*n*, 590, 620; Thos, mayor, 3/749; Wm,
  3/580, 647, 744; 53/156
Hazzell, Rob, 4/1*n*
Head, Sam, 3/737*
Healing, Wm Chadborn, 4/37*n*
Heane *see* Heene
Heard, Humph, 3/435, 512; Jane, 3/435, 512
Heath, Edw, 4/7*n*, 32, 34, 37*n*; John, 4/24,
  38*n**; John Ambrose, p. xxiii; John
  Hanbury, 4/13*n*; Mary, 3/620, 663, 736,
  750; Ric, 4/18, 20, 23, 27*; 54/162n; Rob,
  4/6*n*; Sam, 3/487*, 620, 663, 736, 750;
  50/141; 55/85*n*; Thos, 3/419*
Heaven, Deborah, 3/446, 481, 542, 544, 579,
  620, 646, 688; John, 3/446, 481, 542, 544,
  579, 620, 646, 688; Sam, 4/34; Thos, 4/4
Heene (Heane), Hen, 3/598; Jas, 3/598; Wm,
  4/18*n*
Hellyard, John, 3/468*
Heming, Anne, 3/402; Mary, 3/448; Ric,
  3/448; Wm, 3/402
Hemmings, John, 53/142
Hendy, Sam, 3/479, 615; Sarah, 3/479, 615
Herbert (Harbert), Hen, 4/36*n*; Jas, 3/627;
  4/3, 12, 15*; John, 3/577*n*, 627; Jos, 4/19;
  Ric, 3/735; Thos, 3/661*n*, 667*, 735; 4/12,
  17, 19, 24–5, 30; Wm, 4/6, 14, 22, 32, 37*n*

Herring, John, **3**/463, 565; Ric, **3**/565; Wm, **3**/463

Hervey, Octavius, **4**/25

Hewett, John, **3**/746; Peter, **3**/618; Phil, **3**/714*n*; Sarah, **3**/724, 746; Thos, **3**/618; Wm, **3**/724, 746*

Hewlett, John, **4**/19, 27*, 28, 30*, 31, 33*, 34, 37*; Phil, **3**/720; Thos, **3**/720; Wm, **4**/34; *and see* Howlett, Ulett

Hickes *see* Hicks

Hickman, Benj, **4**/1, 7*n*; **50**/193*n*; **55**/117; Eliz, **3**/653; John, **3**/454*n*, 488*, 616, 635, 653, 700*n*; **4**/17*n*; Wm, **4**/10*n*, 17, 19, 23, 30*n*; **50**/280*n*

Hicks (Hickes), Jas, **3**/659; Rob, **4**/14*n*; Sam, **3**/643*, 659, 677; **4**/15*n*; **53**/156*n*; Thos, **4**/18*n*; Wm, **3**/677; **4**/6*n*, 15*n*, 21, 25, 25*n*, 30–3, 35, 38*n*

Higgins, Anne, **3**/442, 458, 473, 478; Ephraim, **3**/442, 458, 473, 478, 621*n*, 632*, 739

Higgs, Thos, **55**/82

Higheram, Jacob, **55**/82

Hill, Geo, **3**/482; Jas, **4**/2; John, **3**/482, 693*n*, 694, 701*; **4**/22, 32; Ric, **3**/657; **4**/9; Rob, **3**/420; Sam, **3**/602*n*; Thos, **3**/420, 425, 546, 603, 657, 699; **53**/62; Thos, mayor, **3**/732; Wm, **3**/425, 694; **53**/157

Hillier, Wm, **4**/36

Hincksman, Jas, **4**/8; Wm, **4**/8

Hinton, Ant, **4**/20*n*; Hen, **4**/38*n*; John, **4**/6*n*, 7; **51**/197*n*; Ric, **4**/12; Thos, **4**/18*n*; Wm, **4**/13, 13*n*; **52**/34*n*

Hippisley (Hipsley), Frances, **3**/714; John, **3**/616*, 714

Hoare, Eliz, **3**/450; Thos, **3**/450

Hobbs, Ric, **3**/491; Thos, **3**/491, 499*

Hobson, John, **3**/602*n*, 609; Jos, **3**/411*n*, 609

Hockley, Jos, **3**/669*n*, 678*

Hoddinott, Wm, **4**/8

Hodskis, Thos, **3**/720*

Holbert *see* Hulbert

Holbrow, Nat, **4**/29

Holder (Houlder), Adam, **4**/20*n*, 21; Chas, **4**/16*n*; Edw, **3**/434; **4**/2, 14, 22; Geoffrey, **4**/24; Geo, **4**/10; Hen, **3**/709*n*, 714; **52**/118*n*; John, p. xviii; **3**/444, 477, 520, 543, 548, 595*n*, 601*, 625, 636*, 652, 694, 714*, 744–5; **4**/14*n*; **51**/264*n*; Jos, **3**/434, 469, 520*, 628*n*, 636; **55**/161;

Josiah, **3**/543, 567; Mary, **3**/469; Sarah, **3**/444, 477, 520, 543, 548, 572, 601, 636, 652, 694, 714, 744–5; Thos, **4**/11*n*; Wm, **3**/567; **4**/7, 14*n*, 37*n*; **50**/193*n*

Holford, Benj, **3**/750; Edm, **3**/543; Elisha, **4**/32; John, **3**/507, 621*n*, 631*, 664, 721; Jos, **3**/702, 721, 750; Luke, **4**/14*n*; Marg, **3**/507, 631; Thos, **3**/702, 750

Holiday *see* Holliday

Holister, Job, **4**/38*n**

Holland, John, **53**/157

Hollaway, Thos, **53**/142

Holliday (Halliday, Holiday), Hen, **3**/584*; Ric, **4**/26; Wm, alderman, p. xxi–xxiii

Hollings, Wm, **55**/161

Holt, Gabriel, **4**/4; John, **4**/3, 6; Wm, **4**/12, 24, 28

Holtham, Geo, **4**/28; Wm, **52**/34*n*

Holton (Houlton), Eliz, **3**/425, 507; Ric, **3**/425, 487*n*, 507*; **54**/19*n*; Wm, **4**/1*n*

Homan, Rob, **4**/31*n*; Sam, **4**/29*n*

Hone, John, **3**/459, 466, 478

Hook (Hooke), Jas, **4**/1; **55**/161; John, **54**/85*n*; Jon, **3**/491, 621, 651*, 678*n*, 741; Luke, **3**/635*n*, 651; Rebecca, **3**/491, 621, 651, 741; Wm, **4**/20*n*

Hooper, Chas, **50**/259; **53**/123; **54**/19; **55**/44; John, **3**/500; **4**/19; Ric, **52**/190; Wm, **3**/632*; **4**/2

Hope, Holman, **3**/615; Wm, **3**/615

Hopkins, Edw, **3**/465; Jas, **4**/36*n*; John, **3**/465, 533*; Ric, **4**/1*; Susannah, **3**/441, 505; Theophilus, **3**/441, 505; Wm, **4**/13*n*

Hopley, Thos, **3**/490; **50**/280*n*; Titus, **3**/490

Hopton, Dan, **4**/37*n*; Jas, **4**/36*n*

Hornage (Hornedge, Hornidge), Anne, **3**/434, 499; Eliz, **3**/467; Jas, **3**/425, 439*n*, 517, 521*, 576*; John, **3**/454*n*, 467*, 502*n*, 521, 610; Jos, **3**/559*n*, 576; Mary, **3**/425, 517, 521, 682, 695; Thos, **3**/414, 544*n*, 562, 610, 682, 695; Wm, **3**/414, 434, 487*n*, 499*, 562; Wm Gwinett, **53**/63

Horniel (Horniell), John, **3**/429; Wm, **3**/429

Hornsby, Jas, **4**/14; Sam, **3**/714*n*, 721*; Thos, **4**/10

Horrold, Jane, **3**/427; Wm, **3**/427

Horsington (Horsenton, Hossington), Giles, **50**/280*n*; Sam, **3**/502*n*, 516*, 554; Thos, **3**/544*n*, 554

Horsman, John, **3**/719; Roger, **3**/709*n*, 719; **55**/117

Rob, **3**/731; Wm, **3**/731; **4**/27; **53**/156*n*

Jennings, Abigail, **3**/436, 650; Anne, **3**/404, 497, 508; Benj, **4**/14*n*; Edw, **3**/502; Eliz, **3**/580; Harry, **3**/741; Hen, **3**/420*; Jeremiah, **3**/404, 497, 508, 579, 580, 582; John, **3**/693*n*, 705*; **4**/4*n*, 28*n*; **50**/141; **53**/89*n*; **54**/162; Marg, **3**/485; Mary, **3**/698, 720, 745; **54**/123; Michael, **3**/436, 650, 698, 720, 745; **4**/27, 28*; **54**/123; Rob, **3**/741; Sam, **4**/23*n*; **52**/34*n*; Thos, **3**/502; **4**/6*n*, 38*n**; Wm, **4**/18*n*, 34*n*, 39, 39*n**

Jew, Eliz, **3**/693; Jas, **4**/10*n*; Jos, **4**/25; Sam, **3**/693; Wm, **4**/26*n*, 28

Jewell, John, **4**/1, 1*n*

Jewsberry (Jewsbury), Wm, **4**/25*n*, 26

Jeynes (Jaines, Jeanes, Jeans, Jeenes, Jeens, Joynes), Edwin, p. xx; **4**/1, 8, 14, 16; Edwin, mayor, **4**/14, 25; Eliz, **4**/8, 14, 16; John, **4**/11*n*; Jos, p. xv; Martha, **3**/426, 527, 580, 626; Matt, **3**/716; Nat, **4**/10*n*; Ric, **4**/4*n*; Thos, **3**/426, 527, 580, 626*; **4**/13*n*; Wm, **3**/716; **55**/11*n*

Jobbins, Thos, **3**/577*n*

Jocham, Jas, **3**/717*

Johnson (Johnsons), Dorothy, **3**/427; Fred **4**/37*n*; Jas, **3**/613; **4**/19; Sam, **3**/427, 607*n*, 613; **50**/280*n*; Wm, **4**/3

Jollyman (Jelliman, Jolliman), Dan, **50**/161, 217; Thos **50**/161; Wm, **4**/36; **50**/217

Jones, Alice, **3**/498; Anne, **3**/447, 512, 522, 578, 617, 629, 662, 690; Chas, **3**/400*n*, 447, 512*, 522; **4**/13*n*, 32, 35*n*; **54**/85*n*; Denis, **3**/439*n*, 456; Edw, **3**/728; **4**/26, 30; Edw Gardiner, **4**/25*n*; Eliz, **3**/550, 569, 728; Frances, **3**/411, 455; Geo, **3**/607*n*, 614; **4**/15*n*; Geo Thos, **4**/20*n*, 21; Giles, **3**/415; Hen, **3**/600*, 632; **4**/13*n*; Hopeful **4**/13; Jas **4**/13*n*, 14*n*, 39*n**; Jas Steph, **4**/38; Jane, **3**/454, 456, 477; John, **3**/404*, 463, 502*n*, 512, 632, 728; **4**/1, 26, 37; **52**/190*n*; **53**/22, 35, 89*n*; **55**/11; Jos, **3**/411, 455, 559*n*, 569; Marg, **3**/547; Mary, **4**/19*n*; Nat, **3**/461, 498, 694; Phil, **3**/528; Ric, **3**/532*n*; **4**/21*n*; **54**/85*n*; Ric Dillar, **4**/37*n*; Sam, **4**/12, 16*n*, 17, 20, 24, 28, 33; **53**/89; Sam, mayor, **4**/37; Shadrach Hezekiah, **4**/37*n*; Thos, **3**/439*n*, 454, 454*n*, 456*, 473*, 477, 482, 528, 547, 550, 569*, 574*, 614*, 629, 693*n*, 702*, 711; **4**/1, 1*n*, 20; Walt, **3**/461; Wm,

3/482, 687*n*, 694, 711, 728; **4**/4*n*, 5, 7*n*, 13*n*, 17, 22*n*, 39*n**; **50**/259; **51**/197, 264; **53**/89, 123; Wm (*alias* Hartland), **3**/608

Jordan, Eliz, **3**/496; Josiah Jenner, **4**/9, 19; Thos, **3**/518*; Wm, **3**/496

Joseph, Marg, **3**/419; Thos, **3**/419

Joy, John, **4**/33; Wm, **4**/31*n*

Joynes *see* Jeynes

Joysey, Jas, **53**/157

Kaise *see* Keyse

Kane *see* Cane

Kearsy (Keersey, Kesey), Jas, **4**/7; Thos, **3**/720*; Wm, **3**/427*

Keeble *see* Kibble

Keele, Jas, p. xxiii; **4**/1; Thos, **4**/1*n*

Keen, Jas, **4**/19; Rebecca, **52**/35

Keersey *see* Kearsy

Kemble, John, **3**/594; Wm **3**/594

Kemis (Kemmis, Kemys), Chas, **50**/280*n*; Joan **3**/646; John, **3**/501*, 732*n*, 740*; Sam, **3**/414*, 573, 646

Kent, Hannah, **3**/429*; Jane, **3**/416, 495; John, **4**/36*n*; Jos, **3**/617; Sam, **3**/416, 495, 617; Wm, **4**/39

Kesey *see* Kearsy

Keveren, Edw, **4**/35*n*, 36

Key, Wm, **4**/34

Keylock, Dinah, **3**/679; Jasper, **3**/507, 679*; Thos, **3**/507, 679; Wm, **4**/32*n*

Keyse (Caise, Kaise, Keys), Eliz, **3**/691, 710, 746; Jas, **3**/691; **4**/2*n*; John, **3**/628, 691, 710, 746; **4**/4*n*; Patrick, **3**/445, 475; Ric, **3**/628; Thos, **3**/621*n*; 628; Wm, **3**/445, 475, 628, 691

Kibble (Keeble), Benj, **4**/15, 15*n*; Geo, **4**/4*n*; Jon, **3**/678*n*; Thos, **4**/16*n*

Kilmaster, Chas, **4**/15

Kimber, Nat, **4**/36

King, Adam, **4**/23*n*; Andrew, **3**/602*n*; Chas, **4**/1*n*, 14*n*; **53**/89*n*, 156*n*; Edw, **4**/11*n*; Eliz, **3**/408, 670; Francis, **4**/3*n*; Geo, **4**/12*n*; Giles, **3**/476, 502, 661*n*, 670; **55**/11*n*; Jas, **3**/687*, 689, 714*n*, 722; **4**/1*n*; John, **3**/447, 502, 539, 605, 661*n*, 670*, 676, 687*n*, 695; John, mayor, **3**/607, 669; Sam, **3**/476, 665*, 676, 687*n*, 689, 695, 722; **4**/17; Susannah, **3**/539, 605; Wm, **3**/408, 424*n*, 447, 614*n*; **4**/32*n*, 33; **54**/162*n*; —, p. xxii

Kingdon, Jos, **51**/285

Kingman, Anne, **3**/487, 568; Eliz, **3**/720,

Wm, **3**/409, 436, 538, 574, 633, 749;

Lombard *see* Lumbard

Long, Andrew, **3**/402, 436; Benj, **3**/669*n*, 703; Edw, **3**/436, 720*n*; Geo, **3**/402, 568; **4**/31; Giles, **3**/563; Jas, **3**/678*n*; **4**/2, 23; John, **3**/467, 564; **4**/37; **54**/119; Mary, **3**/521, 537, 622, 678; **51**/285; **53**/1; Newton, **3**/687*n*, 703; Rob, **3**/467; Thos, **3**/563, 614*n*, 622; **4**/4, 12*n*; **51**/5; Wm, **3**/521, 537, 622*, 669*n*, 678*; **51**/5

Longden (Longdon), Anne, **3**/439; Capel, **3**/609, 630; Eliz, **3**/630; **52**/118; Jos, **53**/156*n*; Lucy? **3**/603; Mary, **3**/588, 609; Rob, **3**/602*n*, 603; Thos, **3**/409*, 508, 588, 609

Longford, John, **4**/22; Ric, **4**/11

Longney, John, **4**/17*n*, 18; **53**/1

Lord, John, **3**/406; Thos, **3**/406

Lovegrove, Thos, **52**/66

Lovell, John, **3**/444; Jos, **3**/444; Wm, **4**/7

Lovett (Lovet), Jas, **3**/410, 559, 574, 657; **4**/4; **55**/44; John, **3**/410; **4**/9, 37; Martha, **3**/559, 574, 657;

Lownes, Ebenezer, **50**/280*n*

Lucas, Eliz, **3**/420, 487, 506; Sam, **3**/420, 487, 506; Thos, **3**/602*n*

Ludlow, Thos, mayor, **3**/568, 613, 654

Lugg, Alice, **53**/189; **54**/85; **55**/85; Jasper, **3**/562*; John, **3**/409, 726*n*; **51**/197; Mary, **3**/562; Peter, **3**/714*n*; Rupert, **3**/607*n*; Thos, **3**/409, 552*n*, 562

Lumbard, Isaac, **3**/425; Jacob, 454*n*, 588, 611, 628, 661, 685–6, 705; **50**/217; **52**/34; Jas, **3**/411*n*, 425, 517, 570; Mary; **3**/517, 570; Sarah; **3**/611, 628, 661, 685–6

Luter, Eliz, **3**/529, 625, 716; John, **3**/529, 565*, 574, 625; Sam, **3**/574

Lye, Eliz, **3**/611; Francis, **3**/470*n*, 489, 710; **4**/17*n*; Hen, **3**/489, 700*n*, 710; **53**/123*n*; Sam, mayor, **3**/401, 470; Thos, **3**/611

Lynsey *see* Lindsey

Machin (Machen), Edw, mayor, **3**/742; John, **51**/99*n*; Wm, **3**/750*; **54**/48

Mackarthy, Chas, **52**/55

Macock, Benj, **3**/639; Ebenezer, **3**/665; John, **3**/639, 665; Nat, **50**/280*n*

Maddocks (Madocks, Maddock, Maddocke, Maddox), Cartwright, **4**/1, 6, 13*, 22*, 23, 34; **55**/86, 161; Thos, **3**/417; Wm, **4**/22*, 34*

Maisey (Maysey), Chas, **55**/11*n*; Hen, **4**/35*n*; Jas, **4**/19; John, **4**/14, 30*n*; Wm,

4/9*n*, 10, 32*n*; **50**/280*n*; Wm Giles, **4**/31, 31*n*

Makepeace, John, **3**/559; Sam, **3**/559

Mallett, Jas, **50**/259; Wm, **50**/259

Mamby, John, **3**/402*, 518; Thos, **3**/518

Man (Mann, Manns), Edw, **3**/412*, 700*n*, 708; Hester, **3**/708; Jas, **3**/461*, 509, 572, 678*n*, 689; **4**/2*n*, 3*n*; John, **3**/434, 461, 500, 568*n*, 577, 689, 708*; **4**/12*n*, 24*n*, 37*n*; Jos, **4**/20*n*, 25*n*, 35; Mary, **3**/461, 500, 509; Ric, **3**/434, 577; Thos, **4**/25*n*, 26–7, 29*n*; Wm, **3**/572; **4**/1*n*, 25*n*, 27–8, 35; **54**/19*n*

Mansell, John, **4**/34; Thos, **4**/30

Mantle, Abraham, **4**/26*n*; Thos, **3**/743; Wm, **3**/743

Marchant, John, **3**/706*; Jos, **4**/10

Marcott (Marcutt, Murcutt), Wm, **4**/5, 11; **55**/118

Marsh, Jas, **4**/25*n*; John, **4**/26, 35, 37, 38*, 39; **53**/89; Wm, **4**/31*n*

Marshall (Martshall), Chas, **4**/15; Job **3**/600*; John, **4**/12, 17; Thos, **3**/443; Wm, **3**/443

Marshfield (Mashfield), Geo, **3**/532*n*; Jas, **3**/426, 511, 697; Thos, **3**/511, 697; —, **3**/502*n*

Martin, David, **3**/495; Geo, **4**/3, 13; Jas, **4**/4; John, **3**/495; Jon, **4**/28; Wm, **53**/142

Martshall *see* Marshall

Mashfield *see* Marshfield

Mason, Adam, **3**/416*; Anne, **3**/742; Dan, **3**/439*n*, 458; Eliz, **3**/488, 545; John, **3**/470*n*, 488*, 575, 742*; **50**/259*n*; Jos, **52**/66; Mary, **3**/575, 593, 637, 690, 724; Peter, **3**/424*n*; Ric, **3**/458, 488; Sam, **55**/193; Thos, **54**/93; Walt, **3**/643*n*; Walt, (*alias* Hardwicke), **3**/545; Wm, **3**/488*, 553, 575*, 593, 637, 690, 724, 738*n*, 742

Mathews (Matthews), Anne, **3**/406, 518; Ben, **54**/85*n*; Dorcas, **3**/426; Edw, **3**/555; Eliz, **3**/710; Hen, **4**/18*n*; Hester, **3**/544; Humph Scutt, **3**/673; John, **3**/406, 418*, 426, 454, 518, 710; **4**/5, 6*n*, 21*n*, 27, 34; Marg, **3**/441; Ric, **3**/454, 544, 709*n*, 712; **4**/6*n*; Rob, **3**/635*n*, 643; Sam, **3**/700*n*, 710*; **4**/2*n*; Thos, **3**/424*n*, 441*, 488, 555, 673; **4**/22*n*; **53**/89*n*; Wm, **3**/712; —, 643

Maude, John, **3**/443; Mary, **3**/443

Maul, Lawr, **3**/530; Ric, **3**/530

Maverly (Maverley), Anne, **3**/744; Chas, **4**/1*n*; **55**/193; Edwin, **4**/35*n*; Jas, **3**/424*n*,

Mugg, Ric, **51**/100
Mumford, John, **50**/280*n*
Murcutt *see* Marcott
Murrell, Wm, **4**/37
Muskett, Hen, **3**/641; Thos, **3**/641
Musto, Wm Window, **4**/15*n*
Mutley *see* Motley
Mutlow (Mutloe, Motloe, Motlow, Mowtlow), Ant, **3**/411, 456, 502*n*, 514, 518*, 539; **50**/259*n*; Chas, **4**/19*n*; Elinor, **3**/411; Eliz, **3**/589, 623, 663; Frances, **3**/456, 514, 518; Geo, **51**/197*n*; Hen, **4**/4*n*; Jas, **3**/476, 593, 749*n*; John, **3**/510*, 589, 623; **50**/280*n*; Marg, **3**/476, 593; Martha, **3**/523, 570; Miles, **3**/523*, 532*n*, 539, 570*; Paul, **4**/9*n*, 16, 22–3, 25; Rob, **3**/559*n*, 570, 663; Sam, **4**/11*n*; Thos, **4**/3; Wm, **3**/720*n*; **4**/6*n*, 8
Myles *see* Miles,
Mynett, Thos, **3**/644*
Myon *see* Meighen

Naish *see* Nash
Nanfan, Bridges, **3**/422; John, **3**/422
Nash (Naish), Benj, **3**/638*; Jesse, **3**/418, 678*n*, 689*; John, **55**/82; Jos, **3**/749*n*; Walt, p. xiv; **3**/548*
Nayler, Ric, mayor, **4**/29, 34
Neale, Geo Wm, **4**/38
Neen, Wm, **4**/14*n*
Nelme (Nelmes), Edm, **3**/445; Ellis, **3**/445; Hen, **3**/690; **50**/280; **51**/99; John, **3**/654*n*; **51**/99*; Thos, **3**/690; Wm, **3**/700*n*
Nesele, Francis, **4**/25*n*
Nest, Barbara, **3**/404, 414, 423, 429, 499, 508, 513; Edwin, **4**/39; Jas, **4**/16*n*, 17, 26*n*, 27; John, **3**/404, 414, 423*, 429, 499, 508, 513*; **4**/25; Mary, **3**/419, 717; Nestor, **51**/99*n*; Ric, **3**/423; Thos, **3**/502*n*, 513; **4**/1*n*, 21, 27; Wm, **3**/419, 491*, 503, 508, 559*n*, 717; **4**/37*n*
Netherwood, Ric, **4**/4*n*
Newcombe, Wm, **3**/707*
Newman, John, **3**/426; Ric, **3**/426
Newton, Mary, **50**/141; Thos, **3**/471*
Niblett, Dan, **3**/462, 680; Deborah, **3**/462; Edwin; **4**/37; John, **4**/2–3; Sam, p. xix; **3**/680; **4**/2–3; **50**/93; **52**/67; **53**/190
Niccolls (Nicholl, Nicholls), Eliz, **3**/414, 435, 448, 507; Gregory, **3**/654*n*, 672; Hen, **3**/440*, 499; Hester, **3**/440, 499; Jas,

4/14, 38*n**; John, **3**/499*; Mary, **3**/534, 564; Rob, **4**/38; Thos, **3**/414, 435, 435*n*, 440, 507, 522, 534, 564, 672, 735*; Thos, mayor, **3**/577; Wm, **3**/448*; Wm, mayor, **3**/738
Nokes, John, **3**/556; Ric, **3**/556
Norman (Normand), Edw, **3**/595*n*, 601*, 667; Eliz, **3**/667
Nott (Knott), Edw, **3**/635*n*; Geo, **3**/404, 419; 596, 720; Jas, **3**/635*n*, 646; **50**/280*n*; Lawr, **3**/404, 646; Mary, **3**/596, 720; Nat, **3**/454*n*, 508*, 587; Nic, **3**/400*n*, 419
Nurse, John, **3**/482, 484*, 566*; Mary, **3**/482; Ric, **3**/732
Nuthall, Marg, **54**/85; Nat, **55**/86

Oakey (Okey), Benj, **3**/511; Chas, **4**/37*n*; Edwin, **4**/38*n*; Hen, **4**/31*n*; Jas, **4**/18; **54**/48; John, **3**/511, 696; **4**/39*n**; Sam, **3**/751; Thos, **4**/2, 38*n**; Wm, **3**/696, 751; 13*n*, 27*n*
Oatley, Francis, **3**/407*, 510; Isaac, **3**/407; John, **3**/407; Sarah, **3**/407*, 510, 560, 564, 605, 612
Offlett, Thos, **3**/549*
Okey *see* Oakey
Oldaker, Jas, **3**/617*
Oldham, Augustine, **3**/577*n*
Olliver, Jas, **4**/3
Olney, John, **4**/6
Onyon, John, **3**/542*
Organ, John, **50**/217*; Jos, **4**/29*n*, 30; Thos, **55**/11*n*
Orpin, Edw, **4**/22*n*, 23*n*, 24; John, 22*n*; Thos, **4**/21*n*, 22*n*
Osborn (Osborne), John, **4**/8, 16
Overbury, Thos, **4**/14
Overthrow, Ric, **3**/532*n*, 535, 542; **50**/280*n*; Sam, **4**/37*n*; Thos, **3**/682; Wm, **3**/535, 542, 682
Owen, Francis, **3**/506*
Owner, Jos, **4**/24*n*, 25

Pace, Anne, **3**/452, 458, 483, 509, 714*n*, 733; Chas, **4**/15; Francis, **3**/400, 421, 494; Hester, **3**/587, 592; Jane, **3**/551; John, **3**/452, 457–8, 483, 509, 577*n*, 587, 714*n*; **50**/280*n*; Mary, **3**/628, 638, 666; Ric, **3**/652; Rob, **3**/637, 652; Solomon, **3**/637; Susannah, **3**/400, 421, 494; Thos, **3**/551, 577, 614*n*, 661*n*, 676*, 726*n*, 733*; Wm,

Rock, Henry, **4**/37*n*; Jas, **4**/27*n*; Sam, **4**/34*n*

Rodway, Amity, 51/4*n*; Edith, **3**/437; Giles, **3**/416; Giles, mayor, **3**/514; Hester, **3**/546; John, mayor, **3**/628; Thos **3**/437, 546*, 734; **4**/1, 14–5, 17, 21, 23–4, 26, 29; Wm, **3**/734; **4**/2; **53**/35; —, alderman, **3**/454, 587

Roff (Roffe), John, **3**/709*n*; **50**/280*n*; Thos, **4**/27

Rogers, Eliz, **3**/400; Hester, **3**/590; Jas, **3**/526, 654, 722; Jane, **3**/442, 524, 549; John, **3**/400, 442, 524, 526, 544, 549; **54**/123; Mary, **3**/413, 718; **54**/123; Ric, **3**/538*n*, 544; Sam, **3**/596; Sarah, **3**/745; Susannah, **3**/654, 722; Thos, **3**/519, 590; **4**/11; Wm, **3**/413, 596, 677, 718, 745, 748; **4**/8; **55**/12

Rolfe, Jasper, **3**/424*; John, **3**/443, 497*; Thos, **3**/424*n*, 443

Rooke, Alice, **3**/597; Thos, **3**/470, 597; Wm, **3**/470

Rooksby, Edw, **4**/38

Rope, Michael, **4**/30

Rose, Chas, **4**/29; Thos, **4**/25*n*

Rosse, Geo, **3**/751; Jasper, **3**/715; John, **3**/715*, 726*n* , 751*; Marg, **3**/715, 751

Roston, Jas, **4**/2

Rowles, Eliz, **3**/497; Mary, **3**/410, 517; Rob, **3**/497; Thos, **4**/18*n*; Tim, **3**/410, 517

Rowley, Francis, **3**/610; John, **3**/610

Ruck, Jas, **4**/2

Rudge (Ridge), Anne, **55**/85; Hen, **3**/617; **4**/34*n*; Jas, **4**/23*n*, 24, 38*n**; John, **3**/617, 727*; **4**/1, 3*n*; **50**/280*n*; Rob, **4**/38*n**; Thos, **3**/581, 637, 737; **4**/10*n*, 11*n*; Wm, **3**/581, 637, 732*n*, 737

Rudhall, Abraham, **3**/420, 455, 617; Eleanor, **3**/420, 617; Wm **3**/455

Ruell, Geo, **54**/19*n*

Rush, Cath, **3**/466; John, **3**/466

Russell, Joan, **3**/499; John, **4**/37*n*; Rob, **3**/473; Thos, **3**/473, 499

Ryder *see* Rider

Sadler, Elisha, **4**/15; Elisha Farmer, p. xx; **4**/2, 17, 19, 24*; Jas, **3**/736; **4**/15; Jas, mayor, **4**/11–2, 16, 26; John, **3**/736; Wm, **53**/89

Salcomb (Salcombe), Anne, **3**/747; Hannah, **3**/702; Jas, **3**/524; Josiah, **52**/118*n*; Sam, **3**/742*n*, 747; **4**/14*n*; Wm, **3**/524, 693*n*,

702*, 747*; **4**/4*n*; **54**/123

Saunders (Sanders), Abraham, mayor, **4**/6, 12–3; David, mayor, **4**/30, 37; Eliz, **4**/15; Jas, **4**/13; John, **3**/628; John Michael, **4**/28; Ric, **3**/643*n*, 653; Thos, **3**/411*n*, 426*, 628, 653; **4**/3, 6, 10, 14, 25*n*, 37, 39; —, **3**/621*n*; **51**/264; **53**/156

Savage, Eliz, **53**/189

Savory (Savery), Eliz, **3**/615; John, **53**/89*n*; Mary, **3**/416, 468, 481, 535; Rob, **3**/416, 468, 481, 535, 615, 714*n*, 722; Wm, **3**/722

Sayer (Seyer), Cath, **3**/460; Dan, **3**/471, 568*n*, 634; Jas, **3**/445, 460; Jarvis, **3**/711; Jos, **3**/711; Marg, **3**/445; Mary, **3**/471; Nat, **52**/118*n*; Sam, **3**/621*n*, 634

Sayes, Benj, **53**/157

Scott, Hen, **4**/39; Thos, **3**/523; Wm, **3**/523

Scudamore, Capel, **3**/678*n*, 688*; Rowles, **3**/714*n*

Seaverne *see* Severne

Segrey, Hen, **4**/38

Selby, Jas, **4**/34*n*

Selwyn, Anne, **3**/611, 630; **54**/85; Chas, **3**/620; **4**/12*n*; Chas, mayor, **3**/726; Geo Augustus, mayor, **4**/1; Jas, **51**/197; Jas, mayor, **3**/661; Jasper, **4**/1*n*; John, **3**/620; **55**/11*n*, 44; John, mayor, **3**/709; Mary, **3**/451; Ric **4**/9; Thos **3**/451, 611; Thos (*alias* Blainsh), **3**/630; Wm, **4**/4

Serjeant, Jas, **3**/439; John, **3**/439

Sermon *see* Surman

Sessions, Jas, **4**/23, 38*n**

Severne (Seaverne), Luke, **3**/595*n*, 601; Sam, **3**/601

Sexty, Geo, **3**/744; **51**/5; Wm, **3**/744

Seyer *see* Sayer

Sharp, John, **3**/469*; **4**/4*n*; Jos, **4**/2*n*

Shatford, Dan, **3**/677; Jas, **3**/453; John, **3**/441, 561, 567, 617, 662, 673, 724, 737; Mary, **3**/561, 567, 617, 662, 673, 724, 737; Thos, **3**/441, 453, 477; Wm, **3**/477, 677, 730*

Shaw, Sam Collins, **4**/38

Shearman, Jacob, **4**/34*n*

Sheppard, Geo, **3**/609; John, **3**/568*n*, 575*; **4**/35; Joshua, **3**/609; Sam, **3**/604; Wm, **3**/604

Sherry, Thos, **4**/22

Sherwood, Wm, **4**/27

Shingler, Eliz, **3**/653; John, **3**/458, 566, 582, 586*n*, 591*, 625, 629, 653, 688, 702;

Sarah, **3**/458, 566, 582, 591, 625, 629, 688

Shipton, Cowcher, **3**/429, 464, 486, 549, 605, 689; John, **3**/532*n*; Martha, **3**/464, 486, 549, 605, 749; Thos, **3**/614*n*, 749*

Shurmer, Ric, **3**/705; Wm, **3**/705

Silvester, Chas Hookham, **4**/34

Silvey, Jas, **4**/35

Simmonds (Simons) *see* Symonds

Simpkins, Thos, **53**/123

Simpson, Chas, **4**/13*n*, 18, 33*n*, 37*n*; John, **4**/35*n*; **51**/264*n*; Rob, **3**/588, 722, 737; Sarah, **3**/722, 737; Thos, **4**/3, 14*n*; 31*n*, 32; Wm, **3**/588; **4**/12*n*, 25, 32, 34*n*

Sims, Ric, **3**/720*n*; Sam, **4**/16

Singleton, John, **3**/486; Sarah, **3**/486

Sinnocks, Thos, **3**/400*n*

Sizemore (Sysemore), John, **4**/9; Wm, **3**/475

Skey, Ric, **3**/463; Thos, **3**/493; Wm, **3**/463, 493

Skillerne, Anne, **3**/494; Isaac, **3**/584; Jos, **3**/584; Wm, **3**/494

Skinner (Skynner), John, **3**/585; Luke, **3**/585; Mary, **3**/404, 444; Sarah, **3**/482; Steph, **3**/484; Thos, **3**/482; **51**/140; Wm, **3**/404, 444, 484

Small, John, **3**/557; John, mayor, **3**/687; Jos, **3**/557

Smart, Chas, **4**/38*n**; Edw, **3**/720*n*, 727*; Giles, **3**/513*, 522, 742; **4**/20*n*; Jas, **3**/737*n*, 743; **4**/16*n*, 17, 23*, 25*n*, 34; **54**/19*n*; John, **4**/6*n*, 32*n*; Mary, **3**/622; Ric, **3**/742–4; Thos, **54**/85*n*; Wm **3**/522, 622, 743, 744; **4**/3*n*, 4, 8, 12*n*, 24*n*, 30*n*

Smith, Aaron, **3**/549*; Abraham, **3**/442, 549, 600, 641, 705, 715; **50**/161; **51**/264*n*; Anne, **3**/705, 715, 743; Chas, **3**/494*, 595*n*, 605, 687*n*, 697*; **4**/37*n*; **50**/259; Dan, **4**/3, 11, 37; Edw, **3**/657, 697; **50**/280*n*; Eliz, **3**/642, 693, 713, 718; Frances, **3**/426; Francis, **3**/697; Giles, **3**/559*n*; Hen, **3**/417*; **4**/36; Humph, **3**/602*n*, 611, 642, 693, 713, 718; Isaac, **4**/25, 28*n*; Jas, **3**/442, 454, 515, 585, 634; **4**/5, 32, 37*n*; **51**/4*n*; Jarrett, **3**/538*n*, 544; John, **3**/426, 449, 544, 568*n*, 576*, 582, 587, 605, 611, 691, 709*n*, 718*, 732; **4**/6, 16, 36; **50**/280*n*; John Stafford, p. xxi*n*; Jos, **3**/551, 592, 607*n*, 615, 644, 657, 667, 702, 743; Martin, p. xxi; **50**/141; **52**/191; **55**/11; Mary, **3**/582; Rebecca, **3**/551, 592,

644, 667, 702; Ric, **3**/736; **54**/162; Rob, **4**/3; **50**/161, 259; **54**/19*n*; **55**/85; Sam, **4**/10; **51**/285; Sarah, **3**/515, 585, 634; Susannah, **3**/549, 600, 641; Thos, **3**/442, 449, 615, 691, 720, 736; **4**/15, 18; Walt, **3**/577*n*; Wm, **3**/587*, 720; **4**/6*n*, 11*n*; **50**/161, 259*; **52**/35

Snow, John, **4**/16; Thos, **54**/85*n*

Sollis, Ben, **4**/13*n*

Solloway, Anne, **4**/8; Rob, **4**/8, 11–2, 14; **53**/189

Soul *see* Sowle

South, Benj, **4**/7*n*, 9; John, **3**/723; **4**/7*n*; Jos, **4**/4*n*, 5; Wm, **3**/723

Southall, John, **4**/10; **51**/141; **55**/86; Morris, **51**/141

Southern, Geo, **4**/13*n*; **52**/190*n*

Sowle (Soul), Israel May, **4**/34; John, **50**/259*n*

Sparks (Sparkes), Ellen, **3**/467; Fream Window, **4**/18*n*; Hester, **3**/601, 616, 637; John, **3**/450*; Ric, **3**/467, 520; Thos, **3**/643*n*, 660*; **4**/35*n*; **51**/264*n*; Wm, **3**/520, 601, 616, 637

Sparrow, Eliz, **54**/123; Jas, **3**/740; **51**/100; **53**/1; **54**/123; Noah, **3**/740; Thos, **3**/476; Wm, **3**/476

Sparrowhawk (Sparrowhawke), Hannah, **3**/574, 619; Wm, **3**/480, 515, 553, 574, 619

Sparry, Marg, **3**/415, 541; Sam, **3**/415, 541

Spencer, Beata, **3**/446, 489, 526, 577; Benj, **3**/634; Chas, **4**/16, 29, 31, 33, 37; Dan, **4**/17, 20, 25, 29; Geo Augustus, **4**/17; Grace, **3**/607, 642, 699; Lewis, **3**/634; Sam, **3**/514*n*, 526, 607, 642, 699; Thos, **3**/446, 489, 526*, 568*n*, 577*

Spicer, Thos, **4**/15*n*

Spier, Geo, **4**/38*n*; Hen, **4**/37*n*; Jas, **4**/38*n*; John, **4**/35*n*; Thos, **53**/124

Spiller, Jas, **3**/489; John, **3**/470*n*, 489, 746; Jos, **3**/711; Sam, **3**/742*n*, 746

Spillman, Benj, **3**/641; Edm, **4**/34*n*; Hen, **4**/32*n*; Jas **51**/49; John, **3**/411*n*, 428*, 519; **4**/5, 6, 10, 12; Jos, **4**/13*n*; **51**/49; Joyce, **3**/692, 736; Ric, **3**/612, 692, 736; **52**/35; Thos **3**/519, 612, 641

Spire, John, **4**/18

Stait (Staight, Stayte), Grey, **3**/404, 572; Ric, **3**/404; Wm, **3**/669*n*

Stanley, Thos, **4**/38

Starling, Jas, **4**/1*n*

Stayte *see* Stait

Steel, Francis, **3**/501; Sarah, **3**/717; Thos, **3**/642, 717

Stephens (Stephen), Anne, **3**/622; Chas **52**/55; Eliz, **3**/474, 487, 503, 545, 561, 588; Francis, **3**/624; Geo, **52**/190*n*; Hannah, **3**/602, 620, 669, 710, 721; John, **3**/532*n*, 543, 622, 721; **4**/11, 18*n*, 23, 25*n*, 37*n*; **54**/19*n*; **55**/11*n*; Marg, **3**/581, 626, 655; Mary, **3**/576, 591, 621; **4**/36; Merrott, p. xix; **4**/4, 11, 13, 15; **54**/123; Paul, **3**/614*n*, 624; Ric, **3**/683; **50**/93; Rob, **3**/439*n*, 471, 543, 635*n*; Thos, **3**/400*n*, 410*, 418, 474, 487, 503, 545, 561, 588, 683, 696, 700*n*, 710*; **4**/17*n*, 34; Warren, **4**/14*n*; Wm, **3**/418, 576–7, 591, 595*n*, 602*, 620–1, 669, 696, 710, 721*; **4**/1, 5, 15*n*, 16*n*, 19*n*, 35, 36*, 37, 39; **52**/118*n*; **53**/123*n*; Zachariah, **3**/454*n*, 471, 581, 626, 655, 709*n*

Stiles, Ric, **4**/15

Still, Edw, **3**/423, 678; Francis, **3**/423, 678; Mary, **3**/678; Wm, **3**/423, 678

Stirt, Thos, **3**/454*

Stock (Stocke), Benj, **3**/714; Edm, **4**/9, 14, 16, 25–6, 29; Edw, **50**/280*n*; Hannah, **3**/536, 608, 665; John, **3**/422, 543, 611, 667, 714, 726*n*; Sam, **3**/422, 536*, 608, 665; Susannah, **3**/543, 611, 667; Thos, **4**/2; **53**/157; Thos Ric, **4**/3; Wm, **4**/19, 37*n*

Stone, Hen, **50**/280*n*; Hester, **3**/447; Jas, **4**/34, 34*n*; Thos, **3**/447

Stoner, Antioch, **3**/734; John, **3**/734

Stratford, Francis, **50**/161; John, **3**/419*, 645; Joshua, **3**/715; Valentine, **3**/645; Walt, **3**/723*; **50**/161; Wm, **3**/715

Street, Chas, **3**/519; John, **3**/519

Stroud (Strowd), Francis, **50**/280*n*; Geo, **4**/10*n*; Septimus, **4**/4*n*; Steph, **4**/7, 17; Thos, **3**/749*n*; **4**/21*n*; **55**/85*n*

Summers, Eliz, **3**/464; Thos, **3**/464

Surman (Sermon), John, **4**/3, 5; Jos, **3**/460; Sam, **3**/460, 536; Thos, **3**/536*

Sutton, John, **55**/85

Swaine (Swain, Swainer, Swayn, Swayne, Sweyn), Blanche, **3**/525, 561; Edw, **3**/592, 606*, 659; **50**/280*n*; Eliz, **3**/747; Jas, **3**/573, 712, 747; John, **3**/552*n*, 561; Jon, **3**/525, 561; Kath, **3**/506; Marg, **3**/712; Rejoice, **3**/474, 492, 504, 630; Ric,

3/487*n*, 506*, 573, 625*, 652; **4**/3, 9*; **53**/157; Steph, **50**/280*n*; Thos, **3**/457, 474, 492, 504, 561, 614*n*, 621*, 630, 636, 652, 659; **50**/280*n*; Wm, **3**/586*n*, 592, 628*n*, 636; **4**/14*n*, 15*n*; **54**/19*n*

Sweetland, Chas, **4**/25*n*

Swett, Bridget, **3**/552; Wm, **3**/552

Swettman, Geo, **3**/730; John, **3**/730

Sweyn *see* Swaine

Symon, David, **3**/423; Eliz, **3**/536; Thos, **3**/400*n*, 423, 536

Symonds (Simmonds, Simons), Benj, **3**/668; Jas, **4**/30*n*; Sam, **3**/668; Thos, **3**/466*, 614*n*, 619, 622*; Wm, **3**/619

Synocks, Thos, **3**/408*

Sysemore *see* Sizemore

Talbott, Sam, **3**/634; Thos, **3**/634

Tanner, John, **50**/193*; Sam, **4**/33*n*; Thos, **4**/29

Tarling, Rob, **4**/34*n*, 35; Nat, **55**/11*n*; Thos, **4**/29*n*; Wm, **4**/11*n*

Tarr, David, **53**/142

Tavell, Eliz, **52**/190; John, **52**/67

Taylor (Tayler), Alice, **3**/670, 722; Anne, **3**/608; Chas, **4**/7; **54**/162; Cornelius, **4**/37*n*; Dorothy, **3**/428; Ellis, **3**/602*n*, 608, 670, 722; **4**/1, 6, 15*n*; **50**/141; **55**/161; Francis, **3**/617; **4**/32; Giles, **4**/38*n**; Hester, **3**/655, 659, 717; Hugh, **4**/35; Jas, **3**/626; **4**/32, 34, 34*n*; Jasper, **3**/626; John, **3**/586*n*, 592, 604*, 725*; **4**/28, 31, 35*, 37*, 38; Jos, **4**/33; Mary, **4**/6; Ric, **3**/585*, 655, 659, 717; **4**/1*n*, 18*n*, 19; **51**/5; Sam, **4**/5, 24; Thos, **3**/544*n*, 551*, 592, 617; **4**/32, 37; Wm, **3**/428, 608*; **4**/32*n*; Wm Edwin, **4**/37

Taynton, Wm, **3**/614*n*

Tench, Hester, **3**/467; Steph, **3**/467*

Terrett, Chas, **4**/31, 31*n*; Jos, **3**/712; Wm, **3**/712

Thackwell, Paul, **4**/22; Rob, **4**/30

Theach, Thos, **4**/33

Thomas, Abraham, **3**/622; Dan, **4**/26; John, **4**/6*n*, 7; Jonah, **4**/37*n*; Wm, **4**/29

Thompson (Tompson, Tomson), Spencer, **4**/10*n*, 11; Wm, **4**/1, 1*n*

Thruppe, Eliz, **53**/157

Thurstone, Jos, **3**/412; Nat, **3**/412

Till, Mary, **3**/409; Ric, **3**/409, 425

Timbrell, Rob, **51**/291; Wm, **3**/700*n*

Tippetts (Tipetts), John, **4**/32; Josiah, **4**/14,

INDEX OF PLACES

INDEX OF TRADES, OCCUPATIONS, AND RANKS

INDEX OF SELECTED SUBJECTS